TO LOVE AND LET GO

SUZANNE ARMS

To Love and Let Go

Alfred A. Knopf   New York

1 9 8 8

THIS IS A BORZOI BOOK
PUBLISHED BY ALFRED A. KNOPF, INC.

Library of Congress Cataloging in Publication Data
Arms, Suzanne.
To love and let go.
1. Adoption—United States—Case studies. I. Title.
HV875.64.A75   1983   362.7′34′0973   83–47938
ISBN 0–394–50319–8

Manufactured in the United States of America

Published November 30, 1983
Reprinted Once
Third Printing, July 1988

AUTHOR'S NOTE

The names of some of the main characters in this book have
been changed to protect their privacy.

To every woman who has given up
a child she gave birth to, who did so out of
love, and who then suffered the grief
in silence and alone

CONTENTS

Contents

Contents

PROLOGUE

The young woman standing quietly off to one side of the auditorium waiting to ask a question hardly looks old enough to be expecting a baby, yet she is obviously about to become someone's mother. Her name is Martha and she has come quite a distance to hear this talk about birth. With watery eyes she tells a bit of her story, how she is a fire spotter for the forest service, how her boyfriend lives at college and they only see each other on weekends, how they hadn't meant to create this baby. When the young man declared himself unready and unwilling to be a parent Martha saw no way she could be a mother alone and give her baby all she felt it deserved. She intends to give this baby up but she wants a very special beginning for her child and parents whom she feels she can trust to raise and love it as she would.

I introduced Martha to a close friend of mine, a midwife who I knew would help her. Martha found a friend in Marianne and spent the last weeks of her pregnancy living at Marianne's home, helping care for her kids and finally laboring there in Marianne's arms before going off to a small community hospital for her birthing. She had the gentle, natural birth she'd wished for and through her midwife had met the couple who would become the parents of her baby and make the exchange a tender and sensitive one. Martha's child entered her new home within hours of her birth. Martha hung around town for a few weeks, living at Marianne's home, before she disappeared back into her own life. She let go reluctantly, as any caring person might, but she did let go, taking with her the name and address of the couple who were now the baby's parents. An attorney in the community handled all the legal work; the state sent its representative to see the new parents and give official approval. No other agency was involved at all. The whole process—Martha's secure last month of pregnancy, finding the kind of parents she wanted for her baby, the exchange, her letting go, the beginning of her grieving with the compassionate support of another woman to help her, her being able to grow up first, before taking on the responsibility of being a mother—all of this struck a chord in me.

Until I met Martha adoption had always seemed a bit unsavory to me, and the parents who gave their children up for adoption were not quite real parents. Apart from one experience during college, I knew nothing of the reality and the pressures people face who choose adoption. In the 1940s and '50s, when I grew up, adoption wasn't talked about any more than divorce was. Parents were permanent fixtures in children's lives and being adopted was tantamount to not being wanted. When kids felt like outsiders in their families they would question whether they were perhaps adopted and wonder if that was the reason they felt so different. This was certainly true for my own sister. Our mother had kept a full baby book for our older brother, from day one. She still managed to jot notes in my pink album and to collect hair clippings and smiling black-and-white snapshots. But there were no baby pictures, no baby hair souvenirs for my sister. By the time she arrived enthusiasm and leisure for such record keeping had been swept away in the day-to-day business of being a mother of three young ones. Confronted by this lack of clear proof that she was one of us and her lack of resemblance to our immediate family, my sister concluded that she must be adopted. I always associated adoption with my sister's sense of alienation.

In the early 1960s, when I was in college, adoption was almost as unacceptable a solution to unplanned pregnancy as abortion. But many women needed these solutions. As I was stumbling into adulthood and sexuality and becoming a woman, my friend Rosalie (who lived in my dorm) always struck me as being from another era, another culture: all modesty, circumspection and gentleness. I was shocked when she whispered to me one day with her head bowed that she was three months pregnant. She asked me to help her get an abortion. The young man involved was a foreign student on campus, and he'd unceremoniously given Rosalie the boot as soon as she told him the news. It had been her very first sexual encounter. Her father was a Presbyterian minister and she was sure he'd kill her if he ever found out. Abortion was still illegal in New York State in 1963 and I hadn't the vaguest idea how to find someone, let alone someone competent, who would perform one for my friend. So one weekend Rosalie faced the unthinkable, took the bus to her home and confessed to her parents. She wasn't killed but she was beaten up by her father, called a slut by her mother and thrown out of the house. I think she felt she deserved as much.

Rosalie dropped out of school and moved off campus to a converted studio apartment in an old home at the other side of the city. I used to visit her there each week. When she wasn't working at the menial job she'd taken to cover her expenses she would read or walk or cook for herself; but she was always alone. It must have been a joyless pregnancy. A month before the baby was due she gave up the apartment, left town and checked herself into a home for unwed mothers in a rough part of a city fifty miles away. I think I was her only visitor. She looked whipped whenever I saw her, wearing a shapeless housedress and loafers, but she never complained about her treatment at the home. The food wasn't very good, she admitted, but the place was clean, cleaned by herself and the other women who lived there as part of the bargain of getting room and board; and she did have some time to herself to read. I could see that Rosalie was a prisoner and the home smelled like a prison. They "let" me take her for a walk around the block once, but I never did get permission to see her room. For Rosalie this was just part of the punishment she accepted for having done a terrible wrong, becoming pregnant at the wrong time and with the wrong person.

I don't know whether Rosalie ever saw her baby before she gave it up forever. She returned to school the next semester and we never talked about what had happened. I still wonder what her experience did to Rosalie and to her baby.

This book is the stories of some of the women, men and children I have known since Rosalie and Martha who have been involved in adoption. Most of the adoptions described are private, independent adoptions. But I feel that they all have something to teach anyone interested in the adoption process. The stories are all true, and to the best of my ability, and with much help from the people themselves, I have told them as honestly as possible. We enter each account somewhere in the middle and we leave it before it is over, because giving or getting or being a child of adoption never really ends, any more than growing up ends. Here are some of those you will meet:

MARIA, a mother whose two pregnancies and deliveries occurred under very different circumstances a dozen years apart, but who has not seen or heard of her first child since she left him at the hospital where she gave birth. Today Maria still wrestles with feelings of shame at her own passivity throughout the process; but she was hardly more than a child, a very naïve one, in the complex world of adoption.

JUDY, a single woman in her thirties who was adopted as an infant in a standard, closed-file, agency adoption, and is only now beginning to make sense of her life, and feels her adoption is at the root of her struggle. Her search has brought her many things: frustration, pain, surprises and satisfaction.

PAT, a teenager growing into adulthood during the six years we follow her, who gives up her baby for adoption in a most unusual way. With Pat's story is woven that of the couple named Vicki and Paul who are now parents to Pat's baby: two people ready for the challenge and the risk of acquiring a baby in a legal but decidedly unconventional manner, and facing up to the lifelong issues of being adoptive parents.

KATHERINE, a young woman who defies the expectations of friends and family by choosing first to go through with her unexpected pregnancy and then to give the baby up for adoption. She sets about designing a kind of adoption she's never heard of to make the whole experience a celebration. That the adoption doesn't live up to her vision is partly due to the rigid attitudes of the adoptive parents she chose, who have memories that haunt them, and partly to Katherine's own failure to predict the depth of the grief she would suffer.

Within Katherine's story is the story of Claire, a woman of similar age and circumstances, who when faced with the same dilemma made a different choice and now must live with another kind of pain mixed with the satisfaction of motherhood.

DIANE, single like Pat and Katherine, yet feeling ready to be a single mother, who is then stunned by the discovery that she is carrying not one but two babies and is forced to make a most difficult decision. Within Diane's story is the story of Evelyn and Arnie, a couple able to deal comfortably with a new kind of adoption that has almost no rules and leaves everything open and possible.

Friends who read these stories as they were being written tell me they are more than stories of adoption, they are stories of what it is like to let go of someone we love. I had never realized how inescapable grief is for all of us who risk loving, especially when the one we love is our child and when true loving means letting go. I had never understood how having the information and power freely to make personal choices doesn't necessarily make the work of living less hard or painful. Rather it makes the pain more sharply focused and more bearable. That which we have chosen seems so much more easily understood and finally accepted.

I have been told these are women's stories. To be sure, they are about mothering; but I use that word in the genderless sense of protecting, nourishing, nurturing life, the work of the mother. Giving a child up out of love and respect for its needs is one form of mothering. Raising a child as an act of resignation or in defiance of those considered to be authorities is also among the forms mothering can take, but neither is what we like to think of as "good" mothering. The women in these stories who chose adoption for their babies have reaffirmed my belief that mothering ought not to be an endurance contest or a battle waged to prove something. And they have taught me that there is more than one way to be a good mother. The children in these stories remind me that we really haven't the right to expect something in exchange for all we give a child. No child should have to barter for love and attention and the right to be well-enough cared for until it can do that for itself.

This book is a tribute to women who for various and personal reasons admit they cannot do justice to their children or to themselves by raising them. I chose to focus on women who give up their children at birth because they are a large voiceless group and a misunderstood one. But I recall one mother, in particular, whom I met at a childbirth conference. When she heard that I was writing a book on women who give up a child for adoption, she told me how—after being pressured into going through with an unplanned pregnancy and trying desperately to raise her baby alone—she found herself two and a half years later on the verge of either committing suicide or going crazy. And so she had made the terrible decision to give her child up then, and the giving up and letting go was all the more painful for the time she'd spent trying to be that good enough mother to the child she loved and seeing herself fail her own expectations. This woman is the product of a society that considers itself enlightened yet still tells women what to do with their sexuality and their reproductive system. This makes it all the more difficult for a thoughtful woman of any age or circumstance to choose either abortion or adoption. It is a myth in our society that in raising our children we have even the partial support of our community. Parenting done in isolation, without financial or emotional resources, can only be felt as a burden and seldom brings the joy that should be associated with the process.

It continues to amaze me that women like Maria, Pat, Katherine and Diane show so much raw strength because they are all young and, except for Diane, have little around them to draw strength and inspiration from. Their capacity is exceptional. Even in the most difficult circumstances (where, for example, the young woman is barely a teenager herself and has no skills to earn a living and no support to help her raise a child) most women today who become pregnant and continue with the pregnancy then go on to raise the baby. They hardly ever consider adoption. It is simply not thought of as an expression of caring for a child to give it up for adoption, though there are many who would seek to adopt a child and can find none. The social pressures of our culture have had much to do with this, as do the naïve yearnings of many women to prove their womanhood by being mothers against all odds. Part of the reason must also lie in the form adoption has taken, a system that for the most part locks out the birth mother, takes away her sense of power and treats her as an obstacle standing in the way of her baby and the "good" parents who will adopt it.

The women in this book do not consider themselves extraordinary or deserving of special praise for giving up their children for adoption. But they *are* exceptional in their honesty and willingness to admit that they were unready and unwilling to be mothers in their present circumstances. That takes a very special kind of courage. By taking the path they did, with all its risks and pain, they have shown us some of what it is to love and let go. And in the future perhaps others will find the road easier because of them. And we who observe and care will be better able to offer support and love because of them.

Parenting ought to be more than a form of punishment for having sexual relations. Children deserve to be able to depend upon the adult world, and to ask much of their parents without feeling guilty for existing. Children are not ours in the sense of being possessions. Neither are they capable of supplying our missing parts. If children deserve to be treated as individuals with needs and rights, their mothers, and their fathers too, who face very difficult personal decisions, deserve our compassion and our support for the choices they make.

Adoption must be considered a feminist issue in all its many facets. Women bring a unique perspective to adoption and to all that is involved in giving birth and caring for children, an understanding that arises from the fundamental fact of inhabiting a female body.

I hope these stories will expand our sense of what is possible and set us all dreaming, envisioning, and working toward a less violent and better world where everyone feels valued as a part of life, and where our human frailties need not always lead to guilt and punishment.

TO LOVE AND LET GO

Maria, and her daughter at 18 months

Somewhere a Woman
Is Mourning

Maria is thirty-two, a mother watching her toddler at play. "Sometimes," she says, "I lose track of where the mother in me ends and I begin. My 'should' sense of what a good mother is seems so strong, I find myself giving and giving till there is nothing left. Maybe some of it is just overcompensation."

Fourteen years ago, when she was eighteen, Maria gave birth to a baby she gave up for adoption. A bright young woman entering her second year at college with all the benefits of a middle-class upbringing, she was as ignorant of her choices and as isolated as a fourteen-year-old girl bound by poverty. Largely because of the attitudes of her culture—Midwestern America of the mid-1960s—Maria's reserve of self-esteem was quickly eroded during the months she waited for the birth of a baby she could only raise with shame or relinquish with guilt. When I met Maria the adoption was well behind her, yet she was still carrying around the pain and the guilt of it.

She had lived at home during the summer after her first year at college. She'd been dating a man five years older than she was and felt she was madly in love. They always used contraceptives when they made love—except for one time. Maria thinks she may have been secretly hoping she would become pregnant so she could keep Bill's love; their relationship hadn't been very good the last months. But when she realized she might actually be pregnant, she reacted with shame and fear, and despair. Her situation was complicated by her ignorance and her isolation.

She started back to college the next month certain she was pregnant, not yet showing, and hoping for a miracle. "I called Bill to see about catching a ride back to school with him and told him then I might be pregnant. He was very, very silent. I guess he refused to believe it." Maria had really known pregnancy was not the answer from the beginning, but the illusion of a future with Bill had kept her going. Unlike Bill, she now had nowhere to retreat. If she was pregnant it was happening to her body, an inescapable part of her. She finally made an appointment with an obstetrician near campus to find out the truth and asked Bill to drive her there. Well aware of his own responsibility, he agreed, but he waited outside in his car while she went through the humiliation of the examination alone. The diagnosis was rapid: Maria was three months pregnant. She went out to break the news to Bill.

"It was very cold that day and we didn't drive straight back to campus but parked by the woods for a while. I can hardly remember our conversation, it was all so unbelievable, but we must have talked about what to do. My fantasy was to stay in town, to get a job and a place of my own, and to be close to him." Abortion was out of the question for Maria. It was still illegal then in Michigan and she wouldn't have known where to begin if she had wanted to obtain an abortion outside the law.

Maria found that she no longer fit in on the campus; her anxiety about the pregnancy was incompatible with the life of a student. She drew inward and retreated from her friends and classmates. She was alone, despite her boyfriend's offer to help. She didn't feel he was there for her. Instead she turned to the one person she felt she could trust, her older brother, Jay.

"He was working on his doctorate at another university and his wife was supporting them by teaching. They have a little boy who was then eighteen months old. I sat down and wrote Jay a long, intellectual-sounding letter telling him everything. He must have heard a cry for help because he called me as soon as he got it and told me he was coming right down to get me. He drove all 600 miles in one night." During the drive to his home they talked. "Jay said he'd stand behind me whatever I decided about the pregnancy. He said that Mom and Dad didn't have to know anything, and that he thought it would be good for me to live at his place. I could see what it was like to have a toddler and maybe I could make a better decision about keeping the baby or not. If I decided to keep the baby, Jay said he'd be a surrogate father, and I could go on living with them."

Maria had dreams about an education and a career, even though she didn't then know what she wanted to do. She was grateful for her brother's nonjudgmental support but she felt like someone who had been exiled from her people for a misdeed, never able to return. Following her instinct to go where she would find support had meant leaving behind the man she loved, the father of this baby. As a result of her leaving college, her path and Bill's split permanently.

She and Jay arrived at his apartment on a Saturday and that very night their father telephoned. The school had immediately noticed her absence and called her parents' home to find out if she was planning to return. He asked Kate, Jay's wife, if they knew where Maria was. Kate said she knew nothing about it, but she didn't make a very convincing liar. When she got off the phone they talked about what to do. Finally Jay called his parents back and admitted that Maria was with them and that she was pregnant.

"My parents were outraged. They told him they wanted to have nothing more to do with me." It was something Maria would hold against them years later but she didn't blame them at the time. She felt she'd brought it on herself.

By the following Monday Maria had pulled herself together sufficiently to go looking for a job. She found one as a clerk-typist at the university, giving a false name and the story that she was married to a man named Jay Ferris (her brother's name), who was getting a graduate degree. At her pre-employment physical the pregnancy was discovered by a perceptive nurse. Maria feigned shock and surprise. She then assured her supervisor that she would go to a doctor to make sure she was in good enough health to take the job and promised to keep working right up until the birth and to return to work soon after. She got the job, her first. The pay was minimum wage.

People at work sometimes asked Maria about her husband and the baby and her response was always the same. "I was the happy mother-to-be. I did a lot of sewing at my brother's and would come in every morning wearing something pretty. I would be told how talented or how pretty I was. All day long I kept a smile on my face. I went home exhausted and closed myself off in my room and cried, out of anger that I didn't get to tell the truth at work, and frustration that I couldn't express my feelings at home either. Crying helped a bit. Then I'd come out of my room and help take care of Jay's baby or make dinner."

Maria was withdrawing for self-protection, but the price was high. It meant more loneliness and self-pity at the very time when her thoughts ought to have been directed at taking care of herself and the growing life inside her. She had no energy left for positive feelings toward her own baby.

She was reluctant to see a doctor for prenatal care, but under pressure from Jay and Kate she made an appointment with someone recommended by a friend of theirs. On the first visit she couldn't bring herself to tell him that she was not married, but the next time she blurted out everything. Fortunately she had found a sensitive physician. Her appointment was the last of the afternoon and he stayed for several hours talking with her. He asked if she was considering adoption—an idea Maria had already rejected without ever looking at it.

"I told him I wanted to keep the baby. He looked hard at me and said something which was a turning point in my life. He said, 'Maria, what would be easier for you? To keep the baby? Or to give it up for adoption?' I answered that it would be easier to keep the baby. He looked me straight in the eyes and said, 'Well, what do you think would be easier for your baby? To be raised by you alone, without a father, when you have no means of supporting the two of you? What will you be doing for this baby?' "

The mere thought of giving her baby up hurt too much for Maria to answer him. But that night at her brother's, she was so full of emotion she couldn't keep it to herself any more. For the first time she and Jay and Kate really talked, or rather Maria talked and they listened. Talking was a great relief. She saw that she needed help to face all the choices. Soon afterward Maria found the courage to take off early from work one day and go to see a social worker at the Children's Aid Society, an agency her doctor had told her about. She began to see the woman each week and continued right up until the birth. By making Maria feel that she cared and by helping her see all sides without judgment, the social worker helped Maria start thinking realistically about her future and her baby's.

Meanwhile Maria began to make friends with several couples who lived in her brother's apartment building and to babysit for their children too on her evenings and weekends. Becoming more involved with other people's children made her want this baby even more, yet she couldn't forget the doctor's question about what would be best for the baby. "I'd wonder, 'What am I doing to you, kid? What will life be like for you with me away at work all day, and just the two of us when I am home?' "

Somewhere along the way, she doesn't really know when or how, she began seriously thinking about giving the baby up. Part of it was seeing the difficulties Jay and Kate had with their son, whose birth Maria knew had been unplanned. The parents were both gone all day, Kate working and Jay at school, and Jared was with a sitter from breakfast right up until dinner five days a week. "I would watch him cry as they left the house in the morning and I'd watch Kate come home from work each day exhausted and unable to give him much of anything in the evening except dinner. I wanted more than that for my child." And given her lack of resources Maria did not have much hope that her life with her baby would be even that good.

It didn't occur to Maria to turn to the baby's father for help in deciding what to do. Bill had withdrawn from her life when Maria left college, and her response was to take all responsibility upon herself. "It was *my* body. It was *my* trip." Maria made no emotional demands on Bill and was unaware of any anger she might have toward him, but she did find that her love and even her memory of him faded as the pregnancy went on. "It's funny, when I refer to him now, it's as 'the father of my son,' not 'an old boyfriend of mine' or 'my lover.' "

All Bill was asked to contribute was money, which he had volunteered. Maria resisted and resented her brother's insistence that the biological father should accept a greater share of responsibility for his child. "I had pressure from Jay to go after Bill legally and to make sure he would pay. I finally did, but I didn't want to. A paternity suit was brought against Bill and he never tried to deny it. I think I went along with it so my brother wouldn't reject me as our parents had. I was a guest living in his house and I needed his love. But I felt very guilty. I trusted Bill and

I wished I'd followed my feelings and let him do just what he felt comfortable with doing, whether he sent money or not." In the end Bill did pay all the medical bills and even the cost of foster care until the child was placed for adoption. But because the paternity suit forced the issue it was never clear whether he would have made even this contribution had he not been pressured into doing so. He was 600 miles away when his child was born, and apparently never even knew when Maria made the decision to relinquish the baby for adoption. Maria thinks he heard about the birth from a mutual friend who came down to see the baby at the hospital just afterward, but she never again initiated contact with Bill and has not seen him since.

In the United States in the '60s giving birth was something people didn't talk much about. A woman just went into a hospital and came out five days later with a baby. Maria, like most women of her generation, was unprepared for giving birth, medicated heavily for labor, and left alone. With so much on her mind about herself and her baby's future, she had thought it would be a welcome relief to put herself totally in a fatherly physician's hands. Unfortunately, the loss of a major part of the experience to drugs and the suffering that came with laboring unprepared and alone left her with regret and longing she would carry all the way into her next birthing twelve years later.

"Friday, April twenty-third, the baby was due and I was still working full-time. Saturday I had a show of mucus and a few light contractions. I thought I was going into labor. Sunday nothing much happened. I didn't go to work Monday and I had a doctor's appointment on Tuesday. I'd been having light contractions but nothing much. He said my labor was beginning and told me to go to the hospital when the contractions were coming every five minutes. I took a taxi from his office and by the time I arrived home contractions were five minutes apart."

Nervousness in the face of the unknowns of labor often causes a woman's body to create frequent contractions even though the birth may be many hours away. With the doctor having given her no real sense of what to expect in early labor, Maria began to panic.

"No one was home. I went to the neighbor's and nobody was home there either. I had visions of calling another taxi and having the driver refuse to take me because he didn't want to have a baby born in his taxi." Finally, Maria thought of calling a friend of their neighbor's whom she had met a few times. She was babysitting for five children but drove right over in her station wagon, children and all, and took Maria with her packed bag to the hospital. Maria seemed calm. "I felt I was ready. There were too many other things in my mind for me to be frightened of the birth."

Once in the hospital she was dressed in a hospital gown, placed in bed, had her pubic hair shaved, was given an enema, tagged with an identification band and left alone in the room. Her confidence quickly crumbled.

"I knew I was strong and I thought I'd be all right. But I was so uncomfortable lying on my back I sat up in the bed. I could hear a woman in another room screaming and screaming and I thought to myself, 'Why can't she control herself!' I also thought, 'Who am I to make any noise?' I didn't want to be in anyone's way."

So she labored alone, kept herself quiet and remained sitting up in bed. "Every couple of hours, a nurse would come into the room and tell me I had to lie down. As soon as the nurse left I would sit back up. It was the only way I could take the contractions. Finally, it hurt so much I just got out of bed and sat in a chair. Then I paced around the room. I was *so* lonely."

Later that evening Maria's sister-in-law came to the hospital room. She brought along Maria's mother, whom Maria hadn't seen or heard from for seven months. Their awkward reunion did little to comfort Maria or help her labor. "I guess my brother thought she should be there with me and I was happy to see her, but the contractions hurt so much I had to ask them to leave after a few minutes."

They left. Maria had been unable to ask for the support and presence she so needed. She continued to labor in silent pain throughout that night. "Every few hours another nurse would come in, do an anal exam, then a vaginal exam, check the baby's heart, and walk out. I began to allow myself to moan quietly during contractions and that made me feel better. I could still hear screams from the other rooms and there were men's and women's voices out in the hall; but whenever I pressed the button for help, a nurse would come in, do another anal exam, another vaginal exam, listen to the baby and leave. Once, when she came in after I just had pressed the button for help, I asked her couldn't she please stay. She just stood around. I didn't know what to say to her, nor she to me. Finally, she left."

By then it was almost dawn, although Maria could not see the sky because the room was windowless. There was only a clock. The contractions were very strong and close together and Maria was afraid she couldn't go on this way. A different nurse came in and checked her and announced that she was ready to deliver.

In the delivery room Maria faced a different ordeal. There were people with her now, but strapped to a metal table with her legs spread apart, she was suddenly the object of a lot of orders. "I was threatened a lot, told I had to push or that they would break the membranes. I didn't know what they meant. I didn't have any feeling to push. But I pushed anyway, as hard as I could. They told me I had to push harder, that otherwise I'd be in labor the rest of the day! A man about my age came in. He put his fingers into my vagina and suddenly water was spurting right in his face. Then the nurse gave me a shot and they all told me to push again. Another man walked into the delivery room, my doctor—not the same nice doctor I'd seen in pregnancy. He didn't say one word to me and nobody bothered to introduce us. My legs were up in stirrups and I was draped all over with sheets. I couldn't see the mirror to watch because there was a screen in front of my face. I didn't ask any questions. I couldn't feel anything. Finally, somewhere in the room, I heard a baby cry. I couldn't see where it was. My doctor had told me in his office that I shouldn't look when the baby was born. I must have fallen asleep while they stitched me up because the next thing I knew I was being wheeled down a hall. The day after the birth someone came into my room to ask me what I wanted put on the baby's birth certificate. I asked what sex the baby was and how much it weighed." Maria named her son William James, after her boyfriend and her brother.

Maria's childbirth experience did nothing but add weight to her already hefty bundle of guilt. Like many women who have had lonely, demoralizing births, Maria saw the experience as somehow merited. Childbirth, like pregnancy, was a punishment and there was no possibility of atonement or forgiveness.

"The baby was in the nursery and I was a nobody. I'd done this terrible thing and I had no rights. I couldn't stand lying on my stomach in the bed because I wanted the feeling of the baby still being there."

The next day Maria's mother came again to the hospital to visit. Maria told her of her decision to give the baby up for adoption and that the social worker said her mother would have to sign the papers before Maria or the baby left the hospital because she was underage. Her mother might have intended to comfort her daughter, but once there she could speak only of herself. Maria thinks she was trying to cover her own guilt, which she felt for not living up to something she expected of herself, that she should take and raise this grandchild.

"She'd already told me, when she came in to see me in labor, that she wouldn't raise my child for me. But when I told her I was giving the baby up she didn't want to sign the paper. She said she didn't want me to hold it against her that I was giving the baby up. She didn't want to see the social worker either. She didn't know what I'd said to this stranger about her, and she said she didn't want to be judged by her."

The social worker was Maria's one comfort during that hospital stay. She visited several times, and always made Maria feel, as she had from the beginning, that she cared about her and wasn't judging her. Unlike Maria's mother, she had no emotional involvement in Maria's decision to have the baby adopted. She could offer nonjudgmental support more easily than Maria's family because whatever Maria did was of no emotional threat to her own sense of security, as it so often is among family members.

Despite her refusal, Maria's mother did return the next day to sign the papers, and she came again five days later with Jay to take Maria home. Maria was still unable to assert herself but before she walked out of the hospital she did one independent act: she stopped at the nursery window and asked to see her baby. "He was lying in a plastic cart way in the back of the room, behind a post, as if they knew I might want to look at him and had hidden him from me." When the nurse wheeled his cart past the window, Maria was surprised to feel no joy, no flutter of recognition at the sight of her son, only her own worthlessness.

"It was like going to a funeral home and looking at a dead person, just standing, looking and turning away. I'd wanted so much to see some similarity to me and to Bill. I wanted him to be beautiful. I wanted to hold him. But I wasn't entitled to. He wasn't mine any more."

Other women, feeling that same sense of having no rights once they have placed a baby up for adoption, might go home to repeat the experience with another pregnancy and then insist on keeping that baby, out of defiance and to fill the bitter hole the first baby left. But Maria decided that she would never have another child.

"Obviously, since I had given a child up, I could never be a good mother." For the next ten years she carried the memory, only confiding about his existence to people she felt would give her support for what she'd done. She was finally able to say goodbye to her son after twelve years, when, pregnant for the second time, she began to work with a therapist. Still, despite the pain it brought her, Maria feels certain she did the right thing at the time for her baby and for herself.

"I guess it would have been possible for me to live on welfare with my child or to continue living at my brother's; but the baby's well-being was so much more important to me than my feelings. I feel a lot of sadness that I did give up such an important piece of myself, but I think under the same circumstances, I would do it again. I wanted my child to be a person in his own right. But I couldn't give him a sense of worth when I had none myself."

For Maria some sadness is still there, for the pain she endured and the loss. The guilt is gone at last, as she has at last been able to grieve and move beyond grief. But there is still the feeling of shame at how helpless she was throughout her pregnancy, her baby's birth and the adoption.

Ten years after she gave up her son, Maria married and, ready to start a family, became pregnant again. She lost the baby through a spontaneous abortion. At first she could not help feeling that the heavens must be punishing her for her past sins. But she did not let it deter her from becoming pregnant again. This time she did not miscarry and she was able to use what she had learned through pain so many years before to make sure that this pregnancy and birth would be joyful. It was during this pregnancy that she felt compelled to write to the agency that had handled her son's adoption twelve years earlier.

"I had to know if he had gone to a loving and stable home, how long it had been after he was born before he had been given parents. Secretly, I felt any bad news I heard would justify the last of the guilt I still carried. I still imagined terrible things." The woman who wrote her back said Maria's son was fine and well, that he had been adopted when he was three months old. He had made "a good adjustment" in his new home and "has been raised with the knowledge that he was adopted and that his biological mother's decision had been made for his best interests." That is all she learned. Of his current life and well-being Maria heard nothing.

Even a small bit of news helps when someone is searching. "It hurts to know that my son had to wait three months before he was adopted, but at least I know he found a family who wanted him. I went to an adopt-search group meeting last year and heard a woman talk about finding and finally meeting her biological mother. She saw firsthand the way this woman lived, could see the kind of person she was and imagine what her life might have been with this woman as her mother. She said she felt she wanted to thank her for having given her up. I think my son would thank me too. But I am still waiting for that knock on the door when he will come looking for me."

It was during the final weeks of her recent pregnancy that Maria met a young woman named Pat. She was at a gathering of pregnant women and their mates to learn more about her options for childbirth because she was still searching for pieces missing from her first birth experience.

"Someone mentioned to me that there was a woman at the meeting who was planning to give her baby up for adoption and the adoptive parents-to-be were there too. When Pat introduced herself as we went around the circle, I felt a really strong connection to her. And a lot of envy too, like 'Gee, I wish I could have done it all differently.' "

In Pat, Maria thought she saw all the strength she felt she had lacked and the support she wished she'd had. Direct, private adoption had never even been mentioned to Maria as a choice, yet she'd always wished her son could have been given a home and loving parents immediately. Pat's decisions to meet the parents who would raise her baby, to bring her baby into the world without drugs, to hold her baby and to be able to part with her baby consciously, all of this left Maria in awe.

"It's impossible to look back on the past and say for certain I would or would not have done this the same way, knowing all I do now. I think I'd probably still have given the baby up, although I might have thought seriously about abortion, now that that is possible. Most of all I would like to have taken more care to do what would nourish the child while I was carrying him in pregnancy. I wish I could have been glad to carry a life inside me and been happy in pregnancy. Today if I were to choose adoption for my baby, I would make sure the birth was a gentle birth, not a birthing like mine. And I would want some choice in the kind of people who would take the baby, to make sure I felt they would be able to give him the love and care he needed."

Judy and her adoptive mother, Meg, outside Judy's cottage

Somewhere a Child
Is Still Searching

Stories about adopted children who grow up and start on a search for their biological parents were rare just a decade ago, but the evolution in adoption practices, which has been hastened by a demanding, vocal and growing minority of adopted adults, is bringing out the natural desire of most people to know their roots. Judy is one of many adoptees searching for their hereditary past.

Judy has always known she was adopted, just as she has always known the love of two parents, her adoptive ones. She considers her childhood to have been a happy one and her family to be close, yet she feels she suffered from lack of knowledge about her roots and the void that lack of knowledge created in her sense of who she was.

"I was raised knowing I was a 'chosen' child, that there was something special about that, and that I was supposed to feel good about it. I remember lying awake at night thinking, "Why did you choose me from all those babies?" There was something uncertain about being chosen. If you were chosen you could be 'unchosen.' And I found out later it was not even true. As adoptive parents you can't choose a baby. You take what you get." Her "story" comforted her no longer.

"In my family there never was much room for negative feelings or for emotion. Whenever I wanted to say, 'I feel bad because I'm adopted,' which I did at times, and whenever I felt rejected or unconnected, which I did especially during my teenage years, I knew that to say so would seem ungrateful. Once, just before I went away to boarding school, my mom and I had an awful fight. I was shouting, 'You keep talking about me being chosen, but I sure never had a choice! And when I go out in the world, I'm going to choose someone I want, and it's not going to be you!' My mother, who always tried so hard never to let herself get angry at me, stopped me short with just two sentences. 'I do love you, Judy, and I wouldn't have adopted you if I didn't want to! But you know, Judy, you can kill love; and you're doing a damn good job!' With that she turned and walked out."

That argument ended a long period of Judy testing her mother's love, but she didn't find the connection she was searching for until she met her other parents fifteen years later.

Judy had been told nothing about her birth parents. As her curiosity grew over the years, Judy satisfied her need for a past with a story she created from her imagination. She clung to this story because it was an answer to her question, "Where did I come from?"—and it also satisfied the curiosity of those who knew she was adopted and asked about her background. But it wasn't accurate.

"Two or three years ago Mom and I were talking late one night about my adoption and I dropped something about my mother having been a 'red-haired floozie.'

"Mom said, 'Where'd you ever get such an idea?'

"I was floored. I really thought that was my story. For years I'd believed my natural mother was a red-haired floozie and a dancer. And that my father was probably killed in the war. I thought I knew what kind of a woman would give a baby up for adoption—a floozie, a prostitute, a whore. Well, Mom told me my mother was a beautiful, well-educated woman who was interested in music and dance, my grand-father was a superintendent of schools somewhere in the South, and they always thought my father must have been killed in the war.

"After that incident I needed to know the truth badly. I knew Mom had gotten me from a large agency in Texas and that it was called Hope Cottage. My adoptive father used to tell me a story while I was growing up about how he was the one who carried me out of Hope Cottage and, as he was leaving, he turned to ask the woman who showed them out, 'Is that all?' She said, 'Well, just one thing—you haven't paid for her yet.' He was shocked and embarrassed that he'd forgotten that and asked, 'Well, how much do I owe you?' 'That'll be one dollar,' the woman said, smiling. And my father, telling me the story, would always finish with, 'And I would've paid a million!' "

When Judy was sixteen she and her mother happened to pass through the city in Texas where Hope Cottage was located, and Judy decided on the spur of the moment she wanted to see it. Her mother didn't think it was a good idea. She warned Judy that the place was very institutional.

"We went, and boy was she right. I knew it was in a city, but my fantasy was still grass and trees all around. It was nothing like a cottage. Just a big, ugly, bare brick building. We walked up the stairs and inside and I told the woman at the desk, 'I was adopted from Hope Cottage.' Well, she practically jumped up and down, she was so friendly.

" 'Oh, you're a Hope Cottage baby! Well, come with me!' She took us into a large, empty gray room with lots of steel equipment, and said, 'This is where the babies lived when you were here, Judy; at that time this room was filled with bassinets. And here was where you were bathed!' She pointed to one of the steel sinks along the wall. I felt stone cold and sick to my stomach. Then she took us into another room. That room was sunny, and warm; and there were half a dozen kids playing at one end of it. All of them were disabled.

" 'These children haven't found homes yet, Judy. You were lucky.'

" 'Oh, my God!' I thought. 'I could have been one of them.' Then we went out into the hallway and there, on the walls, were hundreds of pictures of babies. She said that I must send them a picture of myself.

"I said to myself, 'Never. I don't belong here. I don't want to be connected with this place in any way.' "

Judy and her mother left quickly without so much as asking to see Judy's records. In spite of her mother's warning, the reality left her shaken to the core. It was years before she dared take the next step in her search.

Judy put her misgivings in terms of fear of her adoptive parents' rejection. "I didn't want to hurt my parents. What if I was betraying them by my search and they rejected me? Then I would have nothing! It was when I had a job teaching nursery school after I was married and we'd started thinking about having kids of our own that I began to think about searching. I joined a therapy group with my husband. The leader of the group, a man named Roy, turned out to have been married once before and had two kids from the first marriage. He told us all about it, how his son was now living with him, but how he and his new wife had felt it was too much for them to keep the little girl as well, so they'd left her with the mother. We heard that the mother, who lived in another part of the state, had a boyfriend who beat up the little girl. There was a lot of discussion in the group about what Roy should do.

"One session, Roy dropped the news that one of the couples in our group would be leaving the group because they were going to adopt his daughter and it would be too complicated for them to remain in the group. The couple, Michelle and George, were there that night and they all talked about their concerns. How was the little girl going to feel as she grew up, knowing her father and stepmother had chosen to keep her brother and to give her up?

"Everyone got into the discussion. Everyone, that is, but me. I sat speechless as everyone around me gave their opinions. I didn't realize that I felt myself as that little girl. All I could think about was that poor little child. I hurt like I'd never hurt before. In another instant the whole room turned red for me. We'd been sitting around in the large circle and suddenly I felt myself jump up and lunge at Roy. I threw my hands round his neck and I heard myself screaming, 'I hate you! I hate you! I hate you!' Then, everyone was pulling me off him and I ran out to the car. I couldn't breathe for a long time. That was the first time I realized how much anger and hurt about my adoption I was carrying. That was a turning point in my life. I knew I had to work those feelings out; but I was terrified of flying out of control ever again." Judy knew she would have to search.

The subject of Judy's biological parents had been assiduously avoided among family and friends during her childhood, but the '70s and her adulthood brought a new frankness into family discussions about such subjects as sexuality, birth, aging, death and adoption. During a visit from her father when she was thirty he told her that he'd seen a program on TV about adoption and that he wondered how she felt about being adopted. "He'd actually never asked me before. I told him about the anger and the resentment I sometimes felt and that I was trying to think of my birth mother in a more positive light now that I knew she was not a red-haired floozie. I said I realized she must have gone through hell having me, coming as she had from the Deep South and being unmarried at the time.

"My father listened to everything I said and then came back with, 'What do you mean 'unmarried'? Where'd you get that idea?'

"My insides felt like jelly. Once again I was about to find out I was not who I'd thought I was. Every small detail made a difference. Well, goddammit, what excuse did my mother have for giving me up if she was married? My father told me he figured I must not have been her husband's child. So my mother had chosen her husband over me! The thought of that hurt tremendously."

A few months after this conversation, in the course of a routine physical, Judy found out that she has a rare inherited disease. Her condition is not serious yet, but it might become so. She was asked whether other relatives had ever been known to have symptoms of the disease. Of course, this was just one of the many pieces of Judy's puzzle that were missing—her genetic background.

The question was a spur to Judy to begin her search in earnest. "I had to find out who these birth parents of mine were. I believe you just can't have a baby and walk away thinking you have no more responsibility to it than giving birth."

She asked her doctor to write to Hope Cottage. Her adoptive father also contacted the home. A couple of months went by with no news. Then one day, Judy's doctor called. She had heard from Hope Cottage. Did Judy want to know what she had found out?

"In the letter she read me over the phone it said my mother was twenty years old when she had me. It gave her height, her weight, and said she'd had three years of college, was interested in music, and her father was, in fact, a superintendent of schools in some small town in the South. It also said my father was twenty-six years old at the time of my birth. The letter gave his height and weight too, but that was all. By law, the agency was not permitted to hand out actual names because birth parents could then come back and sue them for invasion of privacy. The agency also told my father I was wrong to try and contact my parents, that they were a prominent family in town, and that the maternal grandparents did not know their daughter had even been pregnant with me."

That information gave Judy material for many fantasies. Her husband and parents heard every detail of what she'd discovered and lived with the emotional turbulence that the news created in her. She remembered the home movies she had seen and what her mother had told her of the day they brought her home from Hope Cottage. She was six months old, but so weak that she could not even hold her head up. It was a mild form of what is called "failure to thrive" in pediatric literature, a condition that results from emotional neglect. Babies need more than food and a clean environment. They need nurturing, something most easily given through a loving touch, carrying and breast-feeding, but also through eye contact and the spoken word. Judy's first months seem, objectively, no more traumatic than those that thousands of children have experienced. But some essential nurturing was apparently missing, and she associates this start in life with some of the pain she always felt about having been given up by her biological parents.

Judy joined an adopt-search group in her town, which offered support and the opportunity to share some experiences. There she heard of a woman in another state who, through the use of a computer terminal in her home, was successfully matching up people with their birth relatives and finding their biological roots. It was through her that Judy first heard about a judge in Texas who had, on occasion, been known to open closed adoption files to adoptees. Judy got the number of the courthouse from Information, and was astonished when the judge himself answered the phone. She was shocked when, after hearing her story, he said that he would contact the Bureau of Vital Statistics and have the information—her original birth certificate, with no names deleted—sent directly to her.

"Two weeks later my sealed adoption file arrived in the mail. The cover letter said, 'These are all the records that are contained in the sealed adoption file.' I flipped over the letter, and there staring out at me was my original birth certificate. Suddenly, I was looking at my own mother's name—rather her four names, because it gave her maiden and her married name too. My birth father was listed as her husband. The space for my name was blank. I couldn't believe how painful that was. But there was a name for me on my Notice of Adoption—Joyce Marie."

That very night, Judy phoned Information in the city where the birth certificate listed her father's address. She had slim hope he would, thirty-one years later, still be living in the same town; but there was a listing for a man of that very name.

"I had to find out if it was the same man and if his wife, my mother, and he were still together."

Judy made the call the next day from her friend Maryann's house with Maryann standing by her for support. "A woman with a Southern accent answered the phone. I asked, 'Is Francie there?' That was my mother's name according to my records. The voice answered straight out, 'Just a minute, I'll get her.' I froze on the spot. Maryann ran over and slammed down the receiver for me, just in time. I wanted to call her right back and say, 'Hello, I am your daughter.' But for her sake I wanted to give her some space to get adjusted before I got in touch with her myself. I knew it was going to be a real shock." After talking it over with her friend, Judy decided it might be better if she went through a third party. Maryann offered to be intermediary and make the next call. Judy would listen on an extension phone.

"Maryann dialed the number. A woman with a thick Southern accent answered. Yes, she said, she was Francie. Maryann very carefully began speaking. 'I am acting as an intermediary for a woman who believes she is your daughter,' she said first. Pause. 'She very much wants to make contact with you and she does not want to put you in an awkward situation.' There were several minutes of silence.

" 'Well. This *has* come out of the blue! You know, this *is* quite a shock. I'm going to have to think about this and discuss it with my husband. I've got other people to consider here. I've got three children and three grandchildren.' She paused. I could hardly breathe. She asked for more information about me.

"Maryann read directly from my birth certificate. More silence.

" 'I'll have to get back to you.' She spoke slowly after the long silence. 'And it might be a few weeks.' "

Maryann gave her name and phone number, instead of Judy's, since they had decided that Judy would that way be protected from threatening phone calls in the middle of the night telling her to lay off her search. "I was so excited I could have died. I decided to give her three weeks to call back; but more than that I would not wait. I would call them myself if I had to. That first call was on Saturday. The following Wednesday a man with a Southern accent called Maryann; and it was obvious he was just scared to death. 'We want *nobody* in this family contacted! Do you understand? NOBODY.'

"Maryann just managed to get in a few words, that I had an inherited disease and that I needed and wanted to know my roots, and that I wanted to meet my mother.

" 'Well.' He paused a minute. 'She can certainly get a medical history. I can understand her wanting that.' Then, 'But what does she think she's going to get by a meeting? Let me speak to her! You give me her number and her name!'

"Maryann said she wasn't at liberty to give him that information without checking with me first." So they arranged that he would call Maryann back two weeks later to the day at the same time.

Judy went to Maryann's before the appointed time, and so did all her close friends. They all waited with their eyes on the telephone but he didn't call—one hour, two hours, three hours passed. Finally, they all gave up and went home. The next morning Maryann's phone rang. It was he, and his voice was angry and hostile. He was defensive about not having called the night before, saying they'd had people over for dinner without notice. There was no apology. He wanted Judy's name and her telephone number and he didn't want any phone calls from her. Maryann attempted to set another time for the following Thursday evening for him to call to speak with Judy at her house. He kept on arguing. Judy remembers what Maryann told her of the conversation, word for word.

" 'I want to call her when it's all right with *me* to call!' That's what he said. He was fighting for control and I could relate to that; but he wasn't going to get it! Maryann had a list of times when it was good for me and she'd read them to him. She says he turned his mouth away from the phone and spoke to someone, asking whether they'd be home on Thursday. It was Francie and she must have been standing there by the phone the whole time. So it was set. Next Thursday, eight p.m., their time."

Judy was compelled to press on, despite the resistance she had found. She was fortunate to have the friends around her who would be there as she took each anxious step. They were all with her at Maryann's, waiting once again.

Five p.m. West Coast time came and went and he didn't call. After another hour Judy couldn't wait any more so she called him. He answered, and their conversation began with a tussle about his failure to call at the appointed time. It turned out there was only two hours' time difference between the two states, not three. "There we were, battling across a couple thousand miles, and I was thinking, 'This is crazy!' Finally, I suggested we get on with the reason I'd called.

" 'Well, who's *this*? Is this the daughter?'

" 'Yes. This is the daughter. Me. Judy.'

" 'Judy? Judy who?'

"We danced some more. It was a regular battle of wills. I gave him my full name and all the information I had about him and my mother. I also told him it was his name listed on my original birth certificate as the birth father, not someone else's. He wouldn't say anything. When I began to tell him more about my disease, though, he listened really intently and began to ask me questions. I was more impressed with him than I thought I'd be.

" 'I *can* tell you this, Judy,' he began. 'You come from very good stock. On *both* sides!'

"I asked him if he knew my birth father.

" 'Oh, yes. I know him quite well; and I know he doesn't have any such disease, I can tell you that.'

"I said, well, he couldn't be certain of that because I didn't know I had it till recently myself. I explained all about the disease, how his wife could have it, their children, and it might not show up for years."

He assured Judy that she would have her medical history but he added that any further contact, like Judy's getting to know her siblings, was out of the question. Judy's birth had been a secret in the family for thirty years and there were now other children to protect.

"I found out they have a twenty-nine-year-old daughter and two sons aged twenty-six and twenty-four. Two of them were married and the youngest son still lived at home. Francie had just been in the hospital for three months and she was still convalescing.

" 'Well,' I asked, 'where *is* Francie? I thought I was going to get to talk with her.'

" 'She's vacationing with one of her daughters.'

" '*One* of her daughters!' I was shocked. 'I thought there was only one!'

" 'Well,' he said, 'apparently she has two daughters!'

"That was his first acknowledgment of me. I could tell he wanted me to promise I would never get in touch with my sister and brothers, and to say that all I wanted from them was the medical history, that when I got it they would never hear from me again. But I'm not a good liar, so I told him, 'My first goal is to meet my mother. Later we can discuss my meeting my sister and brothers and my father too.'

"He flipped out again when I mentioned that and said if I made any attempt to contact any of them I would lose *all* communication.

" 'Look,' I told him. 'I'm not looking for parents, I've already got wonderful ones; everything's worked out for the best for me.' I wanted him to know that. He talked a bit about the decision to give me up and said my mother had even considered abortion because there was so much embarrassment for a woman pregnant out of wedlock back then. There had been curiosity about how I was, he said, but 'it's something you try to bury and put out of your mind.'

"I asked him straight out what my chances were of meeting my mother.

" 'Well, I can tell you this, Judy,' he began. 'You've got a greater chance of meeting your birth father than you do of meeting your birth mother.'

"Suddenly I just had to tell him, 'Richard, I think *you're* my birth father and I just wish you would tell me.' " The voice on the other end of the phone chuckled and refused to answer the question directly; but he promised to call her again soon, after talking to his wife. Before they hung up, he told Judy that Hope Cottage had already written them and suggested they hire a lawyer to protect themselves from her in case she found them. The director of the agency had actually told him she thought it was terrible, Judy's trying to locate them, and dangerous too. Under no circumstances, the director told him, should they ever tell their other children about Judy.

Judy put the puzzle pieces together and told herself Richard must be her father and that he and her mother must have married after she became pregnant, but that they couldn't go back to their home town with a baby born so soon.

In that first conversation, Judy found an opportunity to share some of her beliefs about adoption with the man she believed to be her father.

She talked about the damage she feels ignorance, repression and lies have done to everyone in the "adoption triangle." When the conversation ended she was left with a great deal more information than she'd started with and a lot of hope as well.

Judy's search must have had a profound effect on the two strangers who lived thousands of miles from her. A few weeks later, after Richard had had time to chew over the shock of Judy's arrival in their lives, there was a brief and very hostile call from him.

It was after this call that Judy had her first bleeding episode from her disease, which, though minor, caused her a lot of fear. She sat down and wrote Francie a letter and included in it a medical questionnaire she asked her to fill out. She felt the need for communication of any kind. Another five weeks went by. Finally, beside herself with the need to hear, she phoned. Francie answered. She showed great reluctance to go any further in her relationship with Judy, but she was willing to talk, and they spoke for quite a while. One of the things she volunteered was that her own parents did know of her pregnancy with Judy, but they had been told the baby died at birth.

Judy laid all her hopes on the table when she asked Francie, "Do you want to meet me?" She was really saying, "Do you care?" Francie answered, "Oh, Judy, I don't know. I think so." Her voice was soft and she added, "But I've had to start a whole new life." Judy could hear her crying. "You have to let me do this my way," Francie said. Judy thought she understood what she must be going through. "But only once in our whole conversation did she reach out to me at all. She asked at one point, out of the blue, 'Judy, are you musical?' She said none of her other children are musical and I guess that is a very important thing for her. I wished I could tell her I am a concert pianist, anything so she'd be proud of me and want to know me."

Judy feels that all her life she has been missing a sense of being glad to be alive—partly because of her knowledge that she grew in the womb of a woman who didn't want her. Her own mother was never happy that she'd been born. She had to begin to accept that she and her biological mother are two separate human beings and to realize that she does not now need that mother's love in order to love herself.

Soon after this conversation with Francie depression hit. "I found myself one day in bed in the fetal position. For three hours I couldn't move at all. I felt so utterly rejected. I've always felt powerless about having been adopted. Growing up, I felt my cousins weren't *really* my cousins, my grandparents weren't *really* my grandparents, my brother not *really* my brother."

Judy's search also awakened many feelings and memories for Meg, her adoptive mother, feelings that had lain buried for years under the weight of social custom. Today she can readily admit to feeling she had missed a piece of the process by not knowing the parents who gave Judy up. This lack of information always seemed significant to her and to her raising of Judy.

"While Judy and I were talking recently about her adoption, I realized that even in the thrilling excitement of getting her, I had felt there was something that could have made it more fulfilling. I remember wishing, even then, there could be a way to meet her parents, at least her mother. What harm would there have been if we'd met, in some neutral zone, perhaps without knowing each other's names? I felt a void when raising Judy, that I couldn't tell her more about her past. I think I would have been far more at ease if, when the 'terrible teens' had started at our house, I could have been able to say, 'Let me tell you some more about your birth mother. I know because I met her.'"

Some adoptive parents claim their bias in favor of keeping adoption files closed results from a desire to protect their children from the pain of knowledge. Meg feels her daughter's pain, yet she has no desire to protect Judy from living her own life. "Every parent who loves her child wants to see her settled and secure; but who is these days? I also had traumatic feelings when Judy first separated from her husband. But I understand Judy's feelings about her need to search."

Six months after I interviewed Meg, Judy finally met her birth parents; but it was not until her adoptive father, Sam, had stepped in on her behalf and had written a blunt letter telling them that not knowing Judy would be their loss. In a way her search had become their search too. Judy continued to assure them that she was not rejecting them as her parents, and they never felt threatened by her searching. When the birth parents flew out to California, Meg and Sam were there with Judy to greet them in the lobby of a downtown hotel. Sam went out onto the street to watch for Francie and Richard. Judy and her mother, waiting nervously inside, could not take their eyes from the revolving door.

Then, suddenly, there they were, walking toward her, and Judy found herself standing among four of the most important people in her life.

She felt like a child once more. No one spoke directly to her as the two sets of parents grabbed onto small talk to fill the space. The five of them sat down to lunch together. At first no one seemed able to swallow a bite, then everyone began stuffing the food down as they continued to talk about the weather, vacations, where each of them had lived. From her place at the table Judy watched it all. She noticed immediately that Francie would not make eye contact with her, but that Richard periodically turned to give her a hard stare that felt like he was trying to peer inside her.

After lunch Francie invited everyone up to their hotel room. There she cast her shoes off and curled up on the double bed, which took up most of the space in the small room. Judy sat on the foot of the bed near Francie. Her father sat behind her and her mother leaned against a bureau, facing them. Into this circle Richard thrust a chair. "Well," he started, "*someone* needs to lead this discussion and it might as well be me." He stared hard at Judy as he spoke, with the same combination of aggression and curiosity she had felt from him in their phone conversations. "Now that you've got us here, what is it you want? I want to hear it all!"

Judy had a hard time finding words to begin, but she stated her goals in a straightforward way. First, she said, she wanted to know her medical history. In addition to that, she wanted to meet her brothers and sister. And besides that, she wanted to know who her birth father was.

The discussion quickly turned into argument and it went on for five straight hours. Voices rose to angry shouts, and everyone wept. At the heart of the drama was the conflict over whether Judy had the right to do what she was doing, opening up her closed adoption. Francie, still tightly curled up on the bed, did everything she could to force her position on the others. She said Judy might be her daughter but she still had no right to do this thing. It was allowing her no sleep, making her sick, and she would not tolerate her making contact with anyone else in the family. For her part, this meeting was to be both the beginning and the end of it. Judy's parents supported Judy's position on her right to search, first attempting to persuade, then trying to soothe the hurts.

Suddenly Richard turned to Judy and with tears in his eyes blurted, "Judy, I have to tell you. I *am* your father!"

There was momentary silence. Then Richard began to talk. He described their family and the children who were all her full siblings. Judy's pictures of her life swam before her. She could not take in all of this new information. The hotel room meeting wound to an end with everyone thoroughly exhausted and shaken.

Three days later Francie and Richard pulled up in a rented automobile out in front of a small shop that sold imported gifts and clothing. Judy had arranged everything carefully; her parents had had to return home, but her friends were there in her shop posing as browsing customers. Her birth parents were on *her* home territory now and she felt the stronger for it. Francie and Richard stayed a few minutes and then drove with her the mile to where she lived at the edge of the university campus in a small well-kept cottage. She invited them into her living room. In contrast to the other, this meeting was very subdued. Judy was surprised and touched when Francie brought out photo albums she had carried with her on the plane, giving her a full accounting of her heritage, introducing her to the various aunts, uncles, showing her pictures of her sister's wedding, of her brother's children, whom Judy was never supposed to meet. At one point Judy had to ask them to close the book— she could not take so much in all at one sitting. She wanted to take a picture of them but Francie would not permit her to. But Richard asked for a picture of Judy. *"No!"* his wife shouted. "You can't do that! What will you tell people when they see it?" He answered that he would say it was a young woman they met in San Francisco during their vacation— "After all," he added, "there are lots of young women who like me."

They ate, and then while Francie sat on the couch in the living room and Richard wandered around the house looking at everything, Judy went to see if she could find a picture of herself to give him. She couldn't find anything but a proof of an ancient baby picture, of her at nine months sitting at a photographer's studio. "That's nice, Judy," was all her mother would say when she looked at it, "but we can't take it. We would have no place to put it." The double message might have been unintended, but it was all too clear. Meanwhile, Richard made a thorough search of the cottage, opening Judy's closed bedroom door, reading everything posted on her refrigerator, asking who the man was in the photographs in her room. (It was Judy's adoptive brother.) Then he came across a list of questions Judy had written down after the last meeting, brought it into the living room and said, "Well, Judy, you better ask all these questions now." But there were no satisfactory answers. Francie would give no details about her pregnancy or Judy's birth. When Judy asked why they chose the name they did for her, Francie insisted that there had been no name—she had neither seen nor named Judy after the birth. Judy held back from asking a number of questions she'd hoped to find answers to.

She was relieved when they finally left her home and drove off for a weekend on the coast—and thoroughly surprised when Richard called her later the same night. "Why aren't you at the conference?" he demanded. What conference? "The one posted on your refrigerator." She told him she had decided not to go after their visit. She wanted to rest and assimilate everything that had gone on. Why was he calling? "I've never been so upset in my life," he told her. "I can't sleep. I don't know what to do!" Judy recalled that Meg had told her that when she called Richard to cancel a second meeting of all five of them, he had said he'd felt like putting his arms around Judy when they said goodbye, but he didn't feel he had the right. Judy acknowledged that the whole experience since their arrival had been very upsetting to her too, and that was why she chose not to go to her workshop. "If I'd only known that," Richard said, "I'd have invited you to go up to the country with us today." That was the very last thing Judy could have handled then. Their parting had been emotional enough, watching them leave in their rented car, seeing them both turn around to look at her one last time, with tears running down their faces. Richard told her he couldn't stand driving back through her town without stopping to call her. He couldn't bear thinking of her standing alone on the curb, a lonely little girl. Judy quickly assured him that she was in fact neither a little girl nor lonely. She was happy, she said, and next time he visited she would introduce him to her life and friends. There would be a next time; he had assured her of that at their last meeting. But now, standing in a phone booth somewhere in the center of town, the man who was her biological father could only repeat how this was the most upsetting thing he'd ever been through. He seemed incapable of breaking the phone connection, unable to shut Judy out of his life, he who had for more than a year refused to admit he was even her father.

Winter passed. The meeting in the fall had been so rich, though exhausting, that Judy found no need to contact Richard and Francie afterward. But in the summer, when she had still had no word about when they might come to see her again, she decided it was time to make contact with her siblings directly. Through Information she found a phone number and address for Tim, the one who was going through a divorce, and she wrote him a letter. A few days later he telephoned her. Unlike their parents he was not in the least ambivalent in his feelings. He was surprised and shocked, he said, but he was also delighted and curious.

Over the next few months Judy established a good relationship with Tim by phone. When Tim asked Richard about Judy, Richard tried at first to deny her existence and then refused to speak about her. Tim took it on himself to tell the other children about Judy, and since then Judy has spoken once to each of them on the phone, without sensing any great warmth on their part. Her sister sounded less interested in Judy than in the details of her search, as though this might give her some clues about what it would be like one day with the daughter she herself had recently adopted. She did open up to Judy a bit about that.

But the full welcome Judy had once hoped for from her birth family has not been there. Richard has strictly forbidden the children to mention Judy to their mother, or to have any further communication with her. He feels that his wife's health is too fragile. Judy's birth mother is convinced that her life has already been ruined not once but twice by Judy, since her relationship with her three children will never be the same now that they know of Judy's existence. Judy, she feels, came back into her life just to torture her. Judy's father's loyalty is clear: it lies with his wife, and with his belief that the truth brings too much pain.

And Judy, now? The woman who conceived and bore her considers her an unwelcome, unwanted burden, a shame and a pain she only wants to forget. Judy cannot pretend this isn't so or that it doesn't hurt. But she is not sorry that she searched for and found her parents. She knows that although the majority of adoptee searches result in happy reunions, there was always the chance hers would not. And she was searching for the truth, for knowledge to fill the void inside her, not for simple happiness. Her overriding feeling today about her search is that it has given her life new meaning. It was always the process, the doing of it, not the end result that motivated her. Nor is the process complete. Judy is still young. Her parents' attitude may still change; if not, she has at least gained a brother. She and Tim are making plans to meet. No longer does she say, "My life began when I was adopted. And I have never felt connected to anyone or anywhere." Who would deny her this search?

Phil Adams in his law office

Times Change

When he talks, Phil Adams seems to be playing to a crowd, though he works in a private office and seldom sees more than two people at a time. With his arching bushy gray eyebrows, twinkling eyes, and the large, unlit cigar in his broad mouth, he looks the rakish old gentleman. This man may know as much about adoption law as anyone in the United States. At seventy-seven, he's been arranging direct adoptions for almost forty years, is the author of the standard text on adoption in the State of California, and is regularly quoted on the subject. To date, he has personally shepherded about 3,000 petitions for adoptions, and has never had one denied.

When Phil Adams became an attorney in 1938, adoption was a minor phenomenon in America. In the State of California, for example, there were fewer than 1,000 adoptions per year prior to World War II, of which half were direct placements (California has always had a larger proportion of direct adoptions than most other states). At that time, there were only two adoption agencies in his state, and they were small.

Phil recalls the strict social restraints before World War II, the strongly disapproving attitudes with which society viewed premarital sex and in particular the young woman who made the mistake of becoming pregnant outside of marriage. The personal tragedies borne by unfortunate young women and felt by a few guilt-ridden young men are still, for the most part, well-kept family secrets. All a young woman could hope for was to hide the truth as long as possible, then skip town with a story about acute appendicitis or some other illness and bear the child out of everyone's sight. She would give the resulting baby up for adoption and then quietly return, acting as if nothing had happened. There were few social agencies to help a woman through her grieving for the lost child and the pain of the experience she had been through alone. But society's ignorance didn't prevent individual trauma.

Then World War II began. With wartime priorities, families were broken up, and young girls were no longer so carefully protected. Their fathers were in the war and their mothers were thrust into the work force, often putting in a six-day work week for the war effort, leaving babies in the nation's first day-care centers and older children home alone after school. Young women dreamed of serving their country too, and as soon as they graduated from high school, many went off in search of the current romantic dream—to serve their country in some faraway battleground. First came the Bataan nurses, then the Corregidor nurses, then the WACs, the WAVEs, the Women Marines, and the young women who joined the Red Cross and the USO. Phil Adams remembers the innocence of those years and also the noncombat casualties of war—the many unmarried young women who became pregnant.

"It was unthinkable for the family doctor to take those sweet young things aside and warn them what it would be like to be on, say, Saipan —with just a handful of other gals and 12,000 lonely guys. Unheard of to give them a quick course in sex education and offer to fit them all with diaphragms. All of a sudden, here in San Francisco, they were delivering thirty to forty girls a month at the local military hospital! They were just nice girls in uniform who'd gone across the ocean to take care of our boys, that's all. But they weren't married, they hadn't the vaguest idea of how to prevent pregnancy, they couldn't get abortions and, though they came home to deliver them, they weren't keeping the babies. There was no way they could."

Abortion was illegal in those days, and though there were doctors who would perform the operation their services were too expensive and too hard to find for most women. Adoption suddenly acquired a new importance.

"Take my wife's good friend, Sally, who stood up for us at our wedding. Sally asked if she could ride along with me one weekend when I was driving to Los Angeles on business. Said she was going to visit a cousin there. I dropped her off at a house and expected we'd hear from her when she returned. But we didn't hear a thing from her for the next couple of months. Next time I drove down to Los Angeles, I tried to find Sally, but she had disappeared and left no trace. I told my wife, and for some reason we thought we should both go down and check all the maternity homes. We finally found Sally at a place called St. Anne's. The interesting thing was that she'd had this baby five or six weeks earlier, but she was still there because in those days at these homes a mother usually had to agree to remain at least six weeks after the birth in order to nurse her baby."

It is likely that strong bonds formed between Sally and her baby by the end of the period of nursing, making it that much more difficult for her to give her baby up. But the practice at least assured the child of the benefits of close, one-to-one human contact through its first month of life. Perhaps for Sally the benefit of knowing she was giving her baby something precious, that only she could give, outweighed the pain of becoming attached to someone she knew she would leave behind. In those days there was scant choice in the matter of infant feeding. The rejection of breast-feeding in favor of artificial formulas couldn't occur until the formulas themselves had been made safe and convenient. Today, with baby formulas the popular way to freedom in mothering and no obligations placed on a mother planning to give up her baby, it has become not only possible but usual for women choosing adoption to carry their babies for nine months, give birth under sedation and anesthesia with no participation or consciousness, and then be separated forever from their offspring without so much as a glimpse.

Phil's story of Sally shows how much adoption practices have changed since the '40s. "We found Sally at St. Anne's and Alice brought her and the baby back to San Francisco on the *Harvard*, a boat that sailed the coast between Los Angeles and San Francisco. I drove back from Los Angeles and met them and we took Sally to St. Elizabeth's Infant Hospital, where Sally left the baby. A few weeks later, she finally signed the papers and gave the child up for adoption, but in the meantime there was no veil of secrecy or partitioning babies off from their mothers. She could visit her baby as often as she wished. I've always wondered why recently many women haven't even asked to see their babies before giving them up."

Sally and the Adamses never were able to find out where the baby went after its stay at St. Elizabeth's, but that experience gave the young Phil Adams a taste of the need for help a woman had in arranging a humane adoption for her baby, as well as the need for the baby to have its advocate.

In 1943 Phil Adams, young attorney-at-law, handled his first adoption case as a licensed professional. As is usually the case in direct adoptions, he was the only attorney involved and represented the interests of all parties. The young woman in this first case had been referred to him by a local physician and was already past four months of the pregnancy when Phil met her. She wanted an abortion and her physician, who couldn't by law perform one, thought an attorney might be able to find the woman help. She was fortunate to have met Phil, as it's not difficult to imagine what might have been her fate had she insisted on an illegal abortion done quite late in pregnancy. Figures for maternal deaths in the first forty years of this century were still alarmingly high and a large percentage of maternal mortality was the result of complications of abortion, either attempted by the desperate women themselves or done by physicians or lay practitioners who practiced in back rooms.

Phil knew where to send his client for a late abortion under the best possible, though illegal, conditions. One surgeon in San Francisco had a reputation for competence, but because of the increased risk to himself and to the woman from a late abortion, there was an $800 price tag, which was well beyond his client's means. So Phil offered her an alternative.

"I asked her, 'Have you ever thought of dropping four months out of your life and having this baby? I could find a nice place for you to stay until after the birth, and a good home for your baby.' When she said she'd like that, I took her to meet the woman she would be staying with, someone I'd helped in a similar situation a few years back, and then I referred her to a good obstetrician."

It was also Phil who drove the woman to the hospital in labor and, when the admitting clerk asked for her surname and she hesitated, he who jumped once more to the rescue. And so she was registered as Mrs. Adams. He then left her standing in the lobby with her suitcase and drove off, a typical father for those days, when fathers were not permitted to be present at the births of their children or even with their wives during labor. Meanwhile, the physician and attorney had put their heads together about finding a good home for the baby and had come up with the name of a mutual friend who'd had a succession of miscarriages and very much wanted to have a child. The couple was telephoned and said yes without pause. And they would be delighted to take the baby as soon as it could leave the hospital. They also agreed to pay all of the woman's hospital and physician cost, which, in those days, Phil remembers, was all of $95 for the complete *fourteen-day stay* in a two-bed room.

"That was how long a woman was expected to remain in hospital after birth. The medical opinion of the day said it would be *two more* weeks before the new mother was supposed to venture to put her foot on a flight of stairs!" With wartime nursing shortages her hospital stay was half the usual and when she was ready to leave, Phil and a friend came to pick her up. The new parents went to the hospital to collect their baby, and the adoption was simply and speedily accomplished to the apparent satisfaction of everyone.

The second time Phil Adams arranged an adoption he and his wife drove to the hospital themselves, picked up the baby from the nursery and drove to the home of their friends in a nearby town who had agreed to take the baby. It was the beginning of a long career of "being a professional wet nurse," a role he admittedly enjoys.

Phil Adams's third adoption occurred within the year and his specialty in adoption cases had begun. "A friend called me up saying she needed my help. Her husband had been away in the war and had just returned. She was a normal, lusty young woman suddenly made a temporary widow by the war and when she crawled into the percales with one of their mutual friends in her husband's absence, lo and behold, she found herself pregnant. Of course, the only 'honorable' thing to do would have been to get a divorce so she could marry this baby's father. But unfortunately it was complicated by the fact that she and her husband already had a child eighteen months old at home. Besides, they were well-suited to each other and it seemed like a crazy idea to get a divorce just for one mistake." Having recently finished his second adoption, Phil was full of creative ideas; he suggested that his friend and her husband needn't wreck their first child's youth or ruin their own lives by rushing into a divorce. Why not, he suggested, place this coming baby for adoption?

"The idea knocked her over. She was a married woman and such a thought had never entered her head. It was just *never* done!" But the solution Phil offered was better than anything they could think of and it was the choice they made.

To further complicate the tale, the woman's older sister soon moved in with them, and shortly before her due date the married friend called Phil to say, "Guess what?!" It turned out that her older sister, Suzie, had been seeing the manager of the War Production Board, whose wife was committed to a mental hospital in another state. The plot thickened. "In those days you couldn't get a divorce on grounds of insanity. So Suzie was seeing a married man and had gotten herself pregnant! But everything coordinated perfectly. Suzie simply stayed home from work and took care of her sister's toddler while her sister went into the hospital for two weeks. When Suzie herself went into the hospital three months later to give birth to her baby, her sister helped her. That baby too was given up for adoption.

"In those days, I was busy playing God. By then I'd personally handled three adoptions and, heck, that was three more than anyone else in town. It is interesting, all three of my first cases were adult, Caucasian females and one of them was even married. Don't let anybody tell you this is the problem of the poor or people of some other color!"

By the time World War II ended in 1945, there were about 4,500 adoptions (excluding stepparent adoptions) in just one year in the State of California, or more than four times what had been the average a decade earlier. By 1948, the number had risen considerably; nearly 80% of the adoptions were direct, independent but legal placements, and the two tiny adoption agencies in the state were inundated with babies. There was suddenly a surplus on the adoption market and attorneys like Phil Adams were kept busy trying to find homes for children.

From the beginning of his work in adoption law, Phil Adams had seen his role as including that of counselor to the mother planning to relinquish her baby, and assisting in the logistics of the transfer of the child to the new parents. Because of the conscientiousness of people like Phil Adams, it became an unwritten rule that the attorney in a direct adoption would assist the pregnant woman in finding housing and paying her bills, a job that in agency adoptions was taken over by the many homes for the unwed that were then in existence and filling up with young women hiding out or just needing a home until their birthings were over. Phil took his job seriously and today, almost forty years later, he still maintains an up-to-date file of people willing to take a pregnant woman into their home while she awaits the birth. The file was stuffed with names from the mid-1940s right through the 1960s, and it was well-used.

By the late 1960s, society was no longer being quite so unpleasant to women who got pregnant without being married. In fact, in the '60s and '70s a number of well-known women in the United States, Great Britain and Europe wore their out-of-wedlock pregnancies and bore their out-of-wedlock babies with pride, more often than not also choosing to keep the babies and raise them, alone or with unmarried partners. The trend of the 1970s and beginning 1980s for unmarried mothers of all ages, races, religions and social standings has been to keep the babies they bear, rather than to give them up for adoption, though this may not always be a wise thing for mother or baby.

The fragmentation of the family that has been partly responsible for society's new tolerance for unmarried mothers also means that the single mother is often particularly alone. What might at other times have been supported by close family life is today occurring in a vacuum. This has meant additional hardship for the mother, as she usually must leave the baby in the hands of strangers while she goes out of the home to earn their living. For the baby it has meant being deprived not only of the father, but of its mother's presence as well. Mothers who choose to stay home and receive state aid must live below poverty level, finding it very difficult to get housing and carrying a considerable social stigma for collecting aid at all. The new trend of single women and teenagers keeping their babies against all odds has also meant hardship for infertile couples who want children and are vying for babies to adopt from an ever-decreasing supply.

When he wrote the book on adoption (which also appeared in a text on family law for California's attorneys,* as a section entitled "Adoption Practice in California"), Phil Adams tried to envision the varied situations that could arise in adoption. The philosophy he expressed there is still considered unconventional. One of the controversial sections is "The Personal Meeting Between Adoptive and Natural Parents, Where the Child Is Not Yet Born." In it, he tells why, in his view, such a meeting should occur.

In the great majority of cases, real enthusiasm and happy acceptance will be mutual between the adoptive and natural parents. When the petitioners have explored the background of the child's parents, they will look forward to the day when the child comes into their home with increasing eagerness and a feeling of security born of full knowledge of the situation. The natural parent, in turn, will have progressed from the first moment of dismay and panic to relaxation and serenity, knowing she has selected an appropriate home for the child. What, then, will more securely and permanently cement this decision than for the petitioners and the parent or parents to meet each other and to prove by personal acquaintance the rightness of the decision?

The adopting parent who is haunted by fears of future attempts by an irrational parent to contact the child in its new home or to disturb the serenity will have such fears rapidly dispelled by seeing that the parent is a normal individual, acting with intelligence in a time of stress and quite obviously incapable of taking any action that would be to the detriment of the child or its new home. The natural parent will be reassured on seeing the adopting parents as warm, flesh-and-blood people, who are eager to give the child the love and affection it needs. Occasionally, such a meeting will demonstrate to one or another of the participants that the plans which appeared on paper to be acceptable have a serious flaw. This, too, redounds to the ultimate benefit of the child and the parties involved and can only result in the making of other plans which are better calculated to promote the best interests of the child and the parties.

* *Family Law for California Lawyers,* Berkeley: University of California Printing Department, 1956.

His view that knowledge is good and promotes more responsible decision-making—and that ignorance breeds harm—is everywhere evident in his writing. He dispels common myths that have perpetuated a closed-file, agency-directed system of adoption for the past half-century. Most people still assume that the anonymity peculiar to agency adoption is necessary and normal to all adoption. This is not in the least true, according to Phil Adams. The fact that it developed in agency adoptions and was made into law in a number of states after a strong lobbying effort does not mean that it is right or necessary. Despite the common argument that only with anonymity can the best interests of the child and all parties involved be served, anonymity, Adams writes, is "not so much an end in itself as a necessary byproduct of the most fundamental rule of an adoption agency, that it must be free at all times to make the ultimate decision of where a child will be placed." He notes that in 1954, two years before his book on adoption was published and accepted as the standard reference on the subject in his state, there were 4,000 direct adoptions in California. In just under half of those cases the biological parent was acquainted with the adoptive parents. The practice of biological parent and adoptive parents' meeting each other was one that arose spontaneously and naturally in the history of adoption, he argues, and reflects a genuine need for firsthand knowledge and trust between the parties. It is Adams's contention that the real reason the practice of anonymity in both agency and some direct adoption has been encouraged is that it enhances the status of the person or agency who stands between the various parties.

"To 'play God' in acting as an intermediary is an intoxicating experience whether one be an old friend, a relative, a physician, a lawyer or social worker," he writes. "The moment the principals themselves get together and talk over the situation between them, the status of all other persons is reduced to that of mere bystanders and advisors."* And that, he feels, is precisely the way it should be, his own and others' egos notwithstanding.

He recommends that the meeting between biological and prospective parents should take place not in a professional's office or clinic but in a place conducive to informality and relaxation. The best arrange-

* *Ibid.*

43

ment is for the prospective parents to meet the biological parent on her own territory, at her apartment or home, or in a comfortable restaurant. In a case where the child has already been born and might even have been living for some time with a biological or foster parent, Phil Adams believes it is even *more* crucial that such meetings occur. It is essential that the adoptive parents be familiar with the pattern of living and environment in which the child has spent its life, and this can only be ensured by having the adoptive parents make numerous visits to the child in its current surroundings prior to taking the child out to another home.*

The adoption agencies are not the only group interested in limiting the biological parents' control over the adoption process. The profession of social workers has taken the position that only they can properly assist the biological mother through the adoption and in getting back on her feet afterward, so that she is not likely to repeat the same scenario. In several states, notably Delaware, Massachusetts and Connecticut, social worker organizations have successfully lobbied to pass laws declaring that no one may file a petition for adoption without the express formal approval of that state's department of social welfare. Phil Adams sees this as "big brother" politics, taking away the right of individuals to make their own decisions. There is a real need for help when there is grieving. But apart from the ideological objections to the dominance of social workers in adoption there is the practical reality that social workers often are overworked and unable to handle properly the number of cases for which they are responsible. It is not uncommon for an individual woman to see half a dozen different professionals in the course of her pregnancy. In the State of Massachusetts, in a well-publicized case of a mother who was clearly incompetent to raise children, it came to light that her history was full of documented statements about the danger she represented to her children. Yet, a product of a battered childhood and a ward of the courts herself, she had been under no fewer than thirteen

---

* In state-arranged adoptions in Greece, it has long been the practice for the adoptive mother to come on several occasions to the maternity home where the baby is living and observe it with its professional caretaker, and listen as she describes the infant's temperamental traits, preferences and habits. Only after several weeks, when the adoptive mother is familiar with this particular baby, is she permitted to take it home and adopt it.

different social workers in a fifteen-year period and not one had had the authority to see that her children were protected. The children were neglected and badly beaten and one was finally killed by the mother's boyfriend. The profession known for its heart had utterly failed a family in need because of bureaucratic confusion, which permitted no individual professional any power to do anything.

The hold that social workers and adoption agencies have over state legislatures often makes things difficult for would-be adoptive parents, especially as most agencies today, for convenience, impose arbitrary cut-offs on prospective parents' eligibility according to age, economic status, marital status and sexual preference. Many a person who puts his or her name into an agency finds himself or herself waiting six or eight years and then suddenly being classified as "too old" to be considered any longer. When a married woman in a Midwestern state found herself unable to make any headway with local adoption agencies and turned to the solution of placing personal ads in newspapers, the local agencies responded with anger and attempted to frighten her into stopping her ads by implying publicly that she was stepping into the black market. She had received several responses to her simply worded ads from young women who were pregnant and planning to give their babies up for adoption; but in each case, after an initial, positive phone conversation, the pregnant woman was dissuaded from going any further by local adoption agencies. In that state, recent additions to the civil code have made it virtually impossible for a person to adopt a baby except through an established agency, which this woman had already tried unsuccessfully to do.

In recent decades, a number of court decisions have complicated the legal issues surrounding adoption. For example, in the case where a biological mother was not married at the time of conception, she was until recently regarded as the only person whose consent was necessary in an adoption. This was the result of a tradition disparaging of women and children that defined a child whose mother was not married at the time of pregnancy or at least of a child's birth as "illegitimate." A child wasn't by nature considered legitimate or real—it only gained legitimacy through its mother's being married. This meant that a child whose father was unknown or mother was unmarried was a "bastard," a curse not only on the mother but on itself for its entire life. It meant too that the mother was solely and exclusively responsible for her child's custody and, until the state began to offer women financial support and services for the care of a young "illegitimate" child, she either carried the burden alone, or, as was common in the early part of the twentieth century, could have the child taken from her and placed in a workhouse or other institution because of her status. The concept of illegitimacy at least gave a mother whose children were not taken away because of poverty or moral mandates the chance to choose adoption for her child and thus assure its survival. For many years adoptions were speedily accomplished with only her permission and the allowance of some legally defined waiting period, after which an adoption could become final.

Then, as of January 1, 1976, in California, and following that in many other states across the country, all of this changed. Under the Uniform Parentage Act, which was drafted by a concerned group of advocates and which, after many rounds of heated argument, is now being adopted by one state after another, *every* child is to be considered legitimate. *Every* child also has two parents. The father is placed in one of three categories. He is either the mother's husband (who is still "presumed" to be the father); or he is that man who has been identified by the mother or others as the father, in which case he is the "alleged" father; or, where there is no person identified, he is the "unidentified" father. And a number of court cases have begun to assert the father's rights with regard to his children. One major case that made it all the way to the Supreme Court of the United States on appeal was that of *Stanley* v. *The State of Illinois.*

Phil Adams recalls this case in particular because of the impact it has had on subsequent adoption cases where the biological parents weren't married. He is glad he wasn't the attorney involved in all of the convolutions and appeals of the original case, and isn't at all sure that the decision on behalf of the father ever did any good at all for a certain Mr. Stanley, the plaintiff.

There were three children, ages about ten, twelve and fifteen, all living with both their biological parents, a man and a woman who had never gotten around to getting married. When the mother died, the state took the kids and placed them in other homes. The father tried unsuccessfully to fight the state, declaring it had given him no standing or consideration, either as a foster parent or a custodian, much less a step-parent, despite the well-known fact that he had lived with, raised and financially supported all three of the children, and all the children were commonly acknowledged to be his. The U.S. Supreme Court finally agreed to hear the case and reversed the Illinois high court decision, commenting rather obscurely that the natural father of a child is at least entitled to a notice of adoption proceedings.

The legal confusion over the rights and privileges of the biological father has grown recently as it has become more common for men to express concern and responsibility when they father a child outside of marriage. They want a say in what happens to their children. Cases may now be brought to court where a man identifying himself as the father attempts to prevent the woman with whom he claims to have had inter-course from obtaining an abortion she desires. In one such case the unmarried couple had separated *after* she became pregnant. She chose to keep the pregnancy but give the baby up for adoption, and the father tried legally to prevent her from doing this. He actually got a restraining order in the state where they both lived. But all his efforts were to no avail, because she merely went to another state for the birth and pre-pared for the adoption in that state, placing the new baby with a couple who lived in a third state all the way across the country. Apparently the father's rights were terminated during the adoption proceedings when the mother insisted the identity of the father was unknown. But the man claiming to be the baby's rightful father did not stop there. He tracked down the whereabouts of the baby to its adoptive parents' home. By the time he had done this, the child and its new parents were living in yet another state. Nevertheless the father filed for custody and won a judg-ment in his favor. A judge saw this man's rights as superior to those of the adoptive parents and ordered that the child be given to him. A higher court went on to affirm this judgment, and the state supreme court, as well as the United States Supreme Court, refused to grant a hearing or change the original decision. When the adoptive parents finally gave the child to its biological father, the child was then more than two years old, an innocent pawn in a system of legal delays and unclear laws. The adoptive parents were also victims. Today the biologi-cal father continues to raise his son. Whether the biological mother knows what happened and, if so, what she feels about all this is unknown.

What has this meant for an attorney seeking to honor a mother's wishes and conclude a petition for her child to be adopted? Today both independent adoption attorneys and adoption agencies must bring a legal action to terminate the relationship of an alleged father before any adoption can proceed. The father must be served papers and given an opportunity to declare his desires with regard to the disposition of the child. Any man who has been alleged to be the father of a child is entitled to such notice if his whereabouts are known.

Thus agency adoptions do not eliminate these new problems in adoption. They merely give the illusion of greater protection for the privacy of the parties involved by ensuring greater physical distance, because the agency has stepped in and taken full custody of the child and the birth mother has relinquished her rights as its mother.

Phil Adams recognizes that the law gives the biological mother the final say. He trusts her, no matter what her age or circumstance, to be the one to make the best decision for her child's future. Of all the individuals Phil has assisted in his long career, it is the mothers who gave up their babies who have made the most lasting impressions on him. A number have become longtime friends and some have later even adopted children. It is the mothers, those who have made the difficult choice of giving up a child, to whom he has directed his expert care. Whether the mother is a thirteen-year-old unmarried girl or a forty-six-year-old married mother of five, his attitude toward her is the same.

"I regard every client as an adult, making up her own mind about things. Once a young woman is pregnant, she must be treated as a responsible adult. All I do is try to keep an eye out for practicalities."

He is purposely brusque and to-the-point with prospective clients, in order to catch people off guard so that they will reveal their real desires. And he does feel a responsibility for seeing that everyone—a birth mother, *and* prospective adoptive parents—is certain in his or her decisions.

"Mainly I want to know, 'How do you really feel about this?' and 'How are you going to live with it over the years?' If a woman comes in and she's made up her mind and I can see that she is certain, I leave it at that. Sometimes a woman feels incapable of making any decision. A child's future is at stake, as well as her own, and at these times a bit of prodding may be called for." To Phil, giving up a child is as pragmatic a decision as a person can make. Whenever a woman places her child for adoption through him he assigns her priority to receive a child, should she ever want to adopt one herself. All life, for him, is a cycle. Those who give unselfishly should receive.

From his vantage point, nearly eight decades of living through several wars and a social/sexual revolution followed by a swing of the pendulum to the right, he has had his share of surprises. It was surprising to everyone when, about 1960, there were suddenly more children to adopt than there were people to take them. Then this was followed, just a decade later, by a period when almost no children were available to adopt but the numbers of adults wishing to adopt had increased. Changes in sexual mores, changes in the law as regards abortion, and changing religious attitudes have altered both the number of unplanned babies born and what happens to them after birth. Only 3% of pregnant minors who give birth without being married currently choose adoption. The very pressures from peers and parents that led young women twenty years ago to leave town and give birth in secrecy now offer many teenagers a special status for being pregnant. And for many, when looking ahead to the complexities of being an emancipated woman with a career, having a baby seems far simpler and preferable. "Have your children while you're young enough to enjoy them and grow up with them" is the new adage among many teens. In addition to social pressures, impersonal factors such as fluctuations in the stock market have been found to have great impact upon the bearing of children and also on the desires of people to adopt. As for the future, at least in Western industrial nations, many people anticipate a further scarcity of infants of all races to adopt, in combination with increasing infertility among reproductive-age men and women.

What will happen in a world where children are at a real premium is yet to be seen. Perhaps scarcity will cause societies to value children more highly and guarantee them greater rights, more care and attention. There also may be more children left homeless in other countries who are brought to countries like the United States for adoption. The ethical and political issues surrounding international adoption are hotly debated today. But for those who seek to become parents through adoption and those who need to find parents for their children through adoption, direct independent adoption will continue to offer one way of bringing people together in a simple, humane fashion. It is the mothers themselves, women like Pàt, Katherine and Diane, who are taking adoption into new dimensions. And Phil Adams is only one of the many people today who favor adoptions in which the individuals themselves are free to make the decisions and design their own futures.

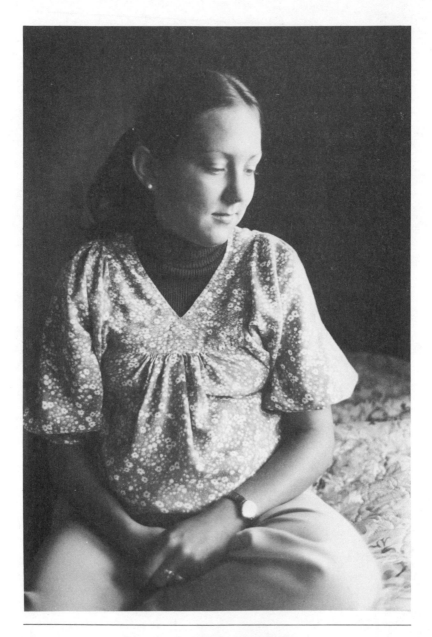

Pat, age 16, eight months pregnant

Too Soon a Mother

It was Christmastime when I first received a phone call from Claudia. She said she had been given my number by a mutual friend with an interest in childbirth and children and she wanted to apologize for taking my time. She had, she said, something private to talk about and hoped I might help. I could sense her discomfort about airing her family's intimate problems to a stranger over the telephone but she had to talk to someone who might be able to give her some advice. Her younger sister back in Florida had gotten herself pregnant at the beginning of the summer. She had only told this to her family around Halloween. Claudia, the older sister, living 3,000 miles across the country, had not been told the news until just now. The baby was due in March, just ten weeks away, and Pat needed help. Claudia told me that the siblings in her family had always hung together in crisis, particularly the three youngest—she, Eddie and Pat. I gathered it was not their style to ask for anything from anyone outside the family but this was a situation beyond their combined resources.

Claudia sketchily described her sister as a capable, bright, and intensely private seventeen-year-old. Their family was traditionally Catholic, their mother originally from South America, and neither mother nor father was given to any outward show of affection toward the children. Pat's disclosure of her pregnancy evoked outrage and shame in her parents. It was proof of illicit sexuality and, it seemed, their mother especially took it as a personal insult and a matter for private anguish. She had made it known that after the baby came, Pat was to raise it at home but keep to her room and out of sight of the neighborhood. Pat was not only obviously pregnant and single but isolated and alone, not a pleasant way to face childbirth and motherhood.

What Claudia wanted from me, I sensed, was some support for a conclusion she had already reached by herself. If Pat's parents were unable to provide the emotional support she needed, then Pat should be removed from them and brought to a place where she could live out the remainder of her pregnancy in peace and consider her options clearly. Claudia wanted badly to do something for her sister. I felt that if she could have, she would happily have taken the entire experience out of Pat's hands and gone through any amount of pain to save Pat from it. She was her big sister and felt helpless living all the way across the continent. Although she was almost the last in their family to know the story, it turned out Claudia was probably the only one who had the resources and contacts to be able to offer Pat some real support. She sounded most anxious that Pat, out of fear or a desire to protect their parents, might refuse her help. She was thinking not only of her sister but of the baby and the needs it had that were not being met.

During that first phone conversation we roughed out some possible plans, concrete support Claudia could offer Pat to entice her to leave Florida and come to California, where Claudia lived, as well as reasons to give their parents that would be acceptable. I remember asking her what kind of person Pat was. Was she the sort who, given a bit of a hand, would take off on her own? Or might outside offers of help just embarrass or embitter her and drive her into passivity? Previous experiments at being a "helper" had taught me it doesn't always work out as planned. Pat was not only a stranger with feelings I couldn't possibly know but she was also a teenager. I gathered from Claudia that she had a lot of determination and stubbornness and I didn't know if the physicians, midwives, birth educators and the like that I knew would be received well by her. I remembered how unpredictable and sullen I must have appeared some of the time as a teenager. The world I inhabited was bounded by home, school, friends and my own painfully sensitive feelings. The family home might not be supportive, but it *was* home base. Anything else existed as a shadowy form, outside, distant and something I could hardly relate to. How difficult it would have been for me at sixteen to express what was going on inside me to some adult, especially when I often could not put it into words or make sense of it for myself. However, I did recall that strangers can sometimes be easier to talk with than friends and family. They have no past shared experiences and therefore fewer preconceptions and judgments.

We ended our first conversation with Claudia determined to find some way to get Pat out to California and with me fairly sure Pat had a strong instinct for survival and would do well transplanted to a new environment if given enough support. I told Claudia I would start looking for services and people to link Pat up with. The use she made of them would be up to Pat. I would be there too. She would need a place to live, money to survive on. I imagined she had given little thought to the baby and to the birth itself and would need a lot of preparation in a very short time. I hoped she had given some thought to the health of the child she was carrying, to her diet and everything she took into and did to her body, for that would partially determine the health of this baby. She had some very serious thinking to do about her options for keeping or giving up her baby and creating a support system for herself in parenting if she chose to raise it herself. She was young and might feel alone but, as I might have been able to tell her, approximately one out of every five nineteen-year-old women in America today is a mother. This is in addition to those who become pregnant, face the prospect of having a child and instead choose abortion. Pat's situation repeats itself daily around the country.

The next time I heard from Claudia, barely a week later, Pat was arriving on a plane; and two days later Claudia brought her to my house. Standing on my front door stoop with her summer blouse bulging over a pair of poorly fitting faded blue maternity pants, she might have been any pregnant young woman. Her olive-colored skin was unlined and perfectly smooth. Her mouth was a small bow. Her brown straight hair was clean and pulled carelessly back by a clip. Her arms were lean and brown and her fingers long. As we walked inside I noticed the diffident stoop of the shoulders, which didn't match the firm set to her mouth. She was taller than I had expected and walked with her long feet turned out a bit. She was instantly likeable though she hadn't said more than "hi." I led the way up to my room at the top of the stairs so we might have a bit of privacy. I asked Pat to sit with me on the edge of the big bed. Claudia sat on the floor in front of us. Where to begin?

There was little time in Pat's life these days to spend on social niceties. Anyway, I already knew far more about her and her family than a stranger ordinarily would. So I started right in talking about what she'd need, where she might live and how she was feeling, physically. Claudia's housing situation, tiny quarters in a friend's apartment under the prying eye of the landlady, didn't offer much hope. They'd need to go apartment hunting, but with what for money? Better go to social services and find out about Aid to Dependent Children first, since Pat's being pregnant qualified her immediately in this state for some support and for Women, Infant and Children food supplements. I could taste the bitterness that suggestion left with both of them. Their familial reluctance to taking any handouts obviously ran deep, though they knew as well as I that it was the best we could do. Pat did not need to spend what little time she had before the birth job hunting. Once they had found a place to live and she had money to contribute for food, she would have to turn her attention to the difficult decisions about the birth and the future of her baby. I've seen the craziness that moving around late in pregnancy or changing homes just after birth can create in a woman of any age. Clearly Pat needed to be physically settled. She had apparently just spent a month living with one divorced sister and her child in Miami, feeling she was taking up too much of their cramped apartment space and intruding on their need for privacy. The next two or three months would barely give her time to get her life together.

California may have a decent welfare system but it is *not* known for its public transportation. Pat would have to get around the country during the day by limited bus service, since Claudia needed her car to get to school, so they felt she should find a place to live that was on a main road near one of the downtown areas. There were many thrift and secondhand shops to find clothes in. From the outset I filled Pat's head with the various possibilities I was aware of. I wanted her to know she was in a different place now and that there were real choices here and people who would support her in her decisions but not try to take the control or responsibility away from her. The conversation was supposedly between Pat and me but it was Claudia and I who did all the talking. Pat's reserve unnerved me then, as it would continue to do. She listened with a look of polite mild interest. Everything, even good news, must have sounded implausible and foreign to her ears. I rattled on about birth preparation classes, different kinds of approaches to labor, places they would be likely to find the best rents for apartments in reasonably safe neighborhoods. I would have taken her into our house that very afternoon, but not because she looked lost or needy. She didn't. She was graceful and eerily composed. Only her silence and that stoop of her shoulders beneath her deeply tanned round face could have been interpreted as need. But what she seemed to want most was privacy and the familiar company of her sister and brother. Together, I sensed, they felt they could survive anything.

I sent Pat and her sister away with a heavy box of my favorite books on pregnancy and childbirth. With everything else that had filled Pat's mind for the past months, I felt it would be a relief for her to turn her attention to the health of her baby and the birth ahead. I lent them a few dollars to do something pleasurable—a meal out, perhaps, a movie, a new maternity shirt. I knew I'd get it back and I did, within the month. It wouldn't hurt to have a few hours of play time before facing the state bureaucracy at the welfare office, the rejection of apartment managers who hate children and single mothers, and the shock of leaving her familiar, if unsupportive, home.

Early in December Claudia had received a letter from Pat postmarked Miami. In it there had been no mention of what Pat was doing in Miami—their family home was far from there and Claudia had not heard that Pat had moved away. What she read puzzled her. Pat talked about leaving Florida and joining the Air Force, about having to get out and see the world before it was "too late." Too late for what? Pat was only sixteen and barely out of high school, having graduated early.

One week later, while she was making Christmas candy for the children at her school, Claudia impulsively picked up the phone and called home. She casually mentioned the letter from Pat and asked her mother what was going on and why Pat sounded so strange. Her mother said she had no idea. Everything was fine at home, just fine. Then she mumbled something Claudia couldn't quite catch, but Claudia thought she heard the words "something terrible," and suddenly feeling panicked that something terrible had happened to her baby sister, she pressed for details. She insisted that her mother tell her what was going on. The truth came out at last: Pat was six months pregnant. Claudia was furious to think she might never have found out at all if it were not for her own detective work—when everyone knew the special love she had for Pat. Why, hadn't she practically raised her? If only she'd known at the beginning there was so much she could have done, Claudia kept telling herself after she put the phone down. But her mother said they had only found out about it a month ago and that before they could discuss what to do Pat had packed her bag, stormed out of the house and gone to live with another sister. They were planning to bring her back home to live after Christmas, when all the relatives had gone. But what would their neighbors say? All her mother could talk about was her own bitterness and humiliation. The hurt had apparently driven both parents so deep into isolation they couldn't share it with anyone, even their grown children.

Claudia knew she would have to come up with a solution. And she had no interest in participating in a coverup of the truth just to protect her parents' feelings. Her mother's final request over the phone had been that if she spoke to Pat she must not, under *any* circumstances, let it slip how she'd found out. What was she supposed to say to Pat? She sat down feeling sick. Flashing through her mind were pictures from the past, memories of the unwed mothers she'd seen when she was a high school student working in Mercy Hospital as a candy striper volunteer. The unmarried pregnant girls had always entered the hospital through the side entrance, from an unmarked building where they lived, next door to the hospital. They always came carrying a few belongings for their stay. And they always left the same way—through the side door. Alone. She'd seen them lying on recovery beds all alone after their birthings, when she was cleaning up in the delivery suite. She never knew what happened to their babies and she'd wondered at the time what life must be like for the girls when they left the hospital. Then a picture of Pat came to mind, the way she'd looked when Claudia had last seen her. Tall and tanned and sassy, with long slender legs and a childish awkwardness to her walk. Why, she was just a kid, hardly old enough to be interested in sex. She'd never really dated. Their mother was very strict with all the girls about dating. How could she be pregnant? It was a question Claudia never would directly put to her sister. But she tried to imagine Pat as she must look now. She could see Pat taking buses around Miami. Walking along the street. Alone. The same girl growing to a woman's body but wearing an unironed maternity shirt over blue jeans. What she imagined made her cry. And what could she do, 3,000 miles away, barely able to support herself alone on the meager teacher-training salary at the Montessori school? Somehow she had to get Pat out. And that one thought kept coming through.

That was when Claudia called me. The next evening she telephoned New Orleans, where her younger brother, Eddie, had been living for six months. It was his eighteenth birthday. She'd forgotten. Eddie sounded depressed over the phone—his three roommates had moved out of their apartment on short notice and left him stuck for the entire month's rent. His first attempt at independent living was already losing its luster. When Claudia asked him directly whether he knew about Pat, he didn't know what she was talking about. So she told him briefly all she knew. His immediate response was, "The three of us should be together!" So, she'd found one ally in the family.

Now Claudia was ready to speak to Pat herself. She was surprised when the voice that answered the phone in Miami was Pat's and she tried to sound casual. She said she'd heard Pat was there for a visit and how were things? From Pat she received the same noncommittal answer she'd gotten from their mother. "Oh, nothing special. Everything's fine." Pat always had said that when there was something bothering her that she didn't want to talk about. In fact, the more she didn't want to divulge her feelings, the "finer" things would be. Claudia knew her sister. When she wanted to remain silent even beating it out of her wouldn't work. She had told friends that Pat could survive a concentration camp. No one would ever get anything out of her she didn't want known; she was an expert at appearing not to care just when she cared the most. She couldn't help admiring her sister's strength of will and she respected her privacy; but this time she felt she had to pry. Pat needed help and from the sound of her flat, unresponsive voice, Claudia thought she must be feeling very low. And so the bare truth was slowly dragged out. She was pregnant. Six months pregnant. And she would admit to having made no plans at all for her future, for the birth, for the baby or for herself. From the sound of it, she had no energy to do anything but get through the days, one at a time.

Claudia hesitated before trying out the solution she and Eddie had come up with. Since Pat never did respond to pressure, Claudia suggested first that maybe she might like a change of scene. She told her how beautiful the weather was in California. This year it was particularly bright and warm. Pat had liked the West Coast when the family had taken a trip to visit relatives in Oakland a few years back. To Claudia's surprise, Pat offered no immediate resistance to the idea—but she had no enthusiasm for it either. Claudia knew if she were to get Pat out of Florida she and Eddie would have to lay all the groundwork by themselves. Pat would be no more able to participate than if she were in a coma. She sounded half dead. Claudia told her sister not to worry, that she would discuss the idea with their parents. "I love you," she told Pat. When she hung up she cried.

It took several lengthy cross-country conversations before Claudia's plan was accepted by their parents. But they had to agree that it would solve one huge problem: what to say to everyone if Pat did come home to live. They wouldn't offer any financial help but Claudia felt she'd gained a victory.

Despite Pat's current frame of mind it was Claudia's hope that the remainder of her pregnancy and the birth might become a positive experience from which Pat could grow and which she could even look back on with some pride. She began to seek advice on getting the best kind of care for Pat and the baby. Pat's problem energized her and gave an added purpose to her own work with young children.

When Eddie heard from his sister that his parents had offered no help at all he sputtered a few choice remarks and went into action. The next day he took his meager savings out of the bank and wired all of the money to their older brother in Florida. He had called and explained Pat's situation and the need for her leaving Florida for the time being and asked him to buy a ticket and get Pat onto the first available plane. Claudia would meet her at the airport.

Eddie was only two years older than Pat and he found it easy to put himself in her position. In his eyes her very survival was at stake, and her pride, just as his was, during this first year out on his own. Helping her out gave him a reason to get out of his own depression.

When Pat flew into San Francisco International Airport on New Year's Eve, a familiar face was waiting at the gate. And Eddie was already packing up to join them.

As a child Pat had periodically been given messages about what it was like to grow up. "I knew there was a certain time, maybe between sixteen and twenty-five, when you knew that from then on your opinions and decisions counted, when you would be worth something." She might not count for much at home but in her imagination it would come one day in a flash. "I wondered about it a lot, about whether I was ever going to make it to that day." And so she'd spent many hours observing the adults around her, looking at the things they did and the preoccupied, serious way in which they seemed to go about their lives. Pat never checked any of her perceptions to see if they might be true. Her life at home had made her very quiet and self-protective, and there was never intimacy or communication between her and her parents.

She had entered her teens with a sense of urgency, a need to test her parents' iron rule and her mother's old world attitudes, a need to see for herself what life was all about. Pregnancy at sixteen had put a heavy lid on further exploration for now. She withdrew deep inside herself and built tall walls to protect her feelings from all outsiders. She used this time to explore the world within herself in a way she'd never done before; but it was a lonely, isolated world and not very connected to outside reality or to what was going on inside her body.

It was her brother Bobby who drove her now to the airport, just as three months earlier he had driven her to the clinic where she'd made the appointment for an abortion she could not go through with. And in just the same fashion he dropped her off outside, leaving her to find her own way and avoiding his embarrassment at an emotional scene. It was an abrupt goodbye to childhood, to family and to home, and a lonely walk into a new future. And Pat couldn't help but feel sorry for herself.

"I stared out of the huge window at the planes and said goodbye. I could never come back." She carried with her a small dark blue canvas bag, her book bag from the eighth grade. In it she'd packed one sweater and several full shirts. She'd also put in one faded denim skirt. It would fit after she had the baby. She was wearing the only pair of maternity pants she owned, a faded blue cotton. They were a bit baggy in the seat and knees and a touch short for current fashion, but at least they didn't bind across the waist. It had been a relief to give up at last the elastic girdle she'd been wearing to hide the truth.

Her father worked for an airline and Pat had always pictured him out in some distant blue sky, a free spirit, different from what he was at home. She'd idealized the freedom of his flying. But her flight was different. Whether it was a banishment or an act of independence was debatable. At first all she felt was relief, from the pit of her stomach all the way up to her throat. The tension that had always been there, ever since she discovered she was pregnant, was suddenly gone.

No one seemed to pay any attention to the round-shouldered, brown-skinned young woman with the blue book bag and the protruding belly. But her condition was obvious, even though she was too preoccupied to think about it for the time being. Then suddenly a stranger's remark brought it home. "As I was going through baggage check, the man there said something like, 'There you go, Momma!' At first I figured he was talking to someone in back of me in line. Then he said it again. When I turned around he added, 'You better get used to it, Momma.'"

The plane was full and Pat found herself sitting next to a middle-aged woman. When the stewardess came by with drinks, Pat asked for milk and, as though this gave her an opening, the woman started talking. "I guess it was because I'd ordered milk, instead of alcohol or coffee or tea. She said, 'I see you're pregnant.' She began telling me about her pregnancies, how she wished things had been different with her births. She asked me about my husband. I told her I was going to meet him in California."

The five-hour flight marked a rite of passage for Pat. From now on both she and the people around her would openly acknowledge that she was going to be a mother, even though she might be just a teenager and wore no ring on her finger. There was pleasant anonymity in being known to no one on the plane. She could create a new past to her liking and take any identity she wished.

Yet leaving home, however positive her reasons, would be difficult. Pat couldn't simply wipe out all the training of her family and church as if it had never existed. She was bringing along herself, all the baggage of brooding and self-doubt she had carried with her ever since she could remember. It would take time to trust that things were in fact different now and even more time to feel comfortable with those differences. Her family had spent a year living in California when Pat was very young and she had some vague memories of those times. But she had forgotten how different the air would smell and feel, the different look of the trees, and the sight of rolling hills where she was used to flat land. One's sense of home and security is built of such recognition of the familiar. And so Pat arrived. She hardly dared dream of how it might be, this new life. All she knew was she was opening another door.

She stepped from the plane, walked up the tunneled ramp to the lobby and the crowd of people at the gate. There among the faces of strangers she spotted one face she would know anywhere. She had to smile a bit, seeing the anxious look and furrowed forehead of Claudia, who swept her eyes searchingly over Pat's face and body. Claudia always had been concerned about her. Sometimes that had felt like a heavy cloak Pat wanted to shrug off. But today it felt fine and welcoming. Claudia asked how much luggage Pat had brought with her. She raised the crumpled canvas bag and shrugged and laughed. Hardly anyone noticed the two women who bore a strong resemblance to each other and who left the building with their arms around each other, smiling.

Claudia had not gotten very far in making living arrangements. She was going to try to limit the number of people who knew about Pat to those whom she could really trust and who might be of help. Her landlady, a prying woman who lived in the front of the home where Claudia had her tiny apartment, didn't fall into either category. There was an immediate touch of intrigue to Pat's arrival. She would have to stay at Claudia's place until they found something more suitable, and Claudia waited until dark to bring Pat home. They sneaked in, bedded down for the night in Claudia's single bed and got up very early to leave before the landlady was up. They would not have money enough to find another place until Eddie arrived and could get a job.

Before the week was over one of Claudia's classmates told her she was going out of town for two weeks. She asked if Claudia and Pat would stay at her place, keep an eye on things, and feed her cat. The apartment was roomy and made a good temporary home for the two sisters. Using it as a base, they made trips to the welfare office and the store. Claudia brought Pat with her to class.

Just a week after Pat had arrived, Eddie came by bus, carrying his plastic waterbed mattress folded flat under his arm and a handful of clothes. The three of them bedded down in the borrowed apartment and Eddie found a job as a shipping clerk at Sears. He was able to get part of a pay check at the end of one week. They went looking for apartments and found a cramped and rather unattractive place whose main advantage was that the landlady took no apparent notice of Pat's bulging figure and obvious youth. The neighborhood was racially mixed, a blend of working-class young people and a few families. Unemployed

Pat with her brother Eddie and her sister Claudia

and out-of-school teenage boys worked on their cars and motorcycles and revved them up and down the street for the benefit of one another and any girls who were around.

The apartment had three tiny square rooms, a kitchen with a window whose light was partly blocked by a tall bush, and a bathroom. It was on the first floor of the building and faced the noisy street. Eddie took the larger bedroom and put up his waterbed while Claudia took the second. Pat said she preferred the living room, though it contained nothing but an uncomfortable old couch. She would take the cushions off at night and use them for a sleeping pad on the floor. They settled in, divided the shopping, cooking and cleaning-up chores. Pat was left on her own during the days. Claudia was busy studying for exams, and within a couple of weeks Eddie had a girlfriend in the building. Life began to fill up and take on a comforting steadiness.

Claudia had taken Pat to the county social service department the day after she'd arrived in California. The social worker who interviewed Pat was brusque. Claudia was uncomfortable and protective, Pat uncommunicative. The interview quickly turned into a grilling. The woman asking the questions wanted the identity of the baby's father. Pat refused to give any name or to talk about the man. The woman's belligerent remark, "You know, we have ways of finding out. We'll get the district attorney to interrogate you!" didn't budge her. But then the woman began to ask why Pat had not had an abortion. "We have enough unwanted children in the world. . . ." "Without people like you" was the phrase that was to follow, though she didn't say it. Pat's hands clenched in her lap but she would not be moved. Claudia barely kept control. She was raging inside; but this social worker stood between them and Pat's eating for the next months. She said nothing.

Claudia knew nothing of Pat's inner thoughts about the father, or who he might be; she continued to be unwilling to broach the subject of the conception with her sister. It must have been a bad experience, which Pat would like to forget, for her to have kept so silent about it. The social worker's prying and verbal attacks were, in her eyes, a clear-cut case of harassment and she was angry enough to take the matter to the supervisor the next day, something her natural timidity would never have allowed her to do on her own behalf. She received an apology and a promise that the worker would be reprimanded, and within three days

Pat had her first check from the state. It was little more than enough for her share of the rent and utilities and bus fares. But in addition there were food stamps. It would be enough for her to get by.

Claudia mentioned in passing the unnerving interview at the welfare office to her landlady. Feeling distaste at the woman's solicitous comments, Claudia knew she'd made a mistake to mention it. But it was too late. The next day the woman cornered her as she was leaving the apartment. She told her she'd set up an appointment for Pat with someone from her church, the Mormon church, so Pat could make arrangements for the baby to be adopted into a "good" home. At the same time the worker at social services was busy on the phone setting up a similar appointment with the state adoption agency. In Claudia's protective eyes it seemed as if everyone was willing to take the baby but no one was interested in her sister. After all, it was Pat's baby and it was up to her to decide with whom she wanted to place the child, or if she wanted to place it for adoption at all. Pat and she had only begun to talk about Pat's desires.

Though Claudia intellectually supported Pat's right to make her own decision about the baby, it was beyond her understanding how Pat, or anyone else for that matter, could consider giving up her own flesh and blood. On the bus ride back from the state adoption agency interview Claudia hesitantly broached what had been going around in her head for some time. She offered to help Pat raise the baby if she chose to keep it. Pat didn't say much, so she went on. She'd even take the baby herself if Pat would find it a help. She knew it sounded preposterous, her being single, still in teacher training and with no prospect of a decent salary for a year or more, but she had to offer. What she was really acknowledging was her aching to be a mother. She couldn't bear the thought that Pat's baby might go to a stranger. When Pat made no response Claudia didn't press further. She gave her sister credit for being wise enough to know what was best for herself.

Pat seemed to have made up her mind to place the baby for adoption, so Claudia made an appointment with the Catholic adoption agency and took Pat for an interview. She assumed their church would have a better alternative than the state agency, where things had seemed so impersonal and cold. The woman there told Pat that the baby would live in a foster home for several weeks until they placed it with a family.

Pat asked if she could see the baby at all during that time. No, it was their policy that the biological mothers not see their babies once they made their decision. Pat asked if she might be able to see the home into which the baby went. The woman said firmly that this was *never* done. Both the state and church agencies apparently took the same line. They would gladly accept her baby but they wanted as little as possible to do with Pat's needs. Claudia firmly told her landlady Pat was not interested in meeting with anyone from the Mormon adoption agency, but she wondered what alternatives were left. Pat didn't offer any help. She hardly spoke about her plans for the baby and Claudia waited for something to surface in her sister that would give her some idea of what they should do next.

Meanwhile Pat was finding things to her liking around the apartment. "The people all around us in the building were what my parents would call 'lower class.' They crowded into their apartments and it was always noisy through the walls." But she felt safe living amidst such a mass of people in a complex of apartments. Because she was pregnant she felt she had nothing to fear from strange men, and Pat always had liked to strike up conversations with strangers. Her brother and sister quickly assumed parental roles toward her and worried about her casual friendliness. As they went to work and school each day, they left Pat at home with admonishments about what not to do. "Eddie would always scream at me if he caught me talking to people. He told me that's how I get into these messes." But Pat was enjoying most of the hours she spent out of everyone's way. At the first opportunity each day she fled the dreary interior of their bare, undecorated and poorly lit apartment for the light and fresh warm air of the outside. Although it was midwinter, the weather was mild and there were several big city parks within walking distance. She had always loved to walk. "I would go to the park every day and sit in the same spot with my book." The books changed and her belly grew larger but her favorite spot was the same, a grassy knoll near a few trees alongside the tennis courts.

"People would come up and talk to me between their tennis games." Most of those who came and stood or sat and struck up conversations were men. They must have been fascinated by the young woman, always alone and wearing the same outfit, sometimes with an old brown sweater thrown over her shoulders, always with some book. She was getting browner-skinned by the day and seemed to be enjoying her aloneness. "The guys would ask me what it was like to be pregnant and what I was going to do after the baby came." With no one there to contradict whatever story she chose to make up about the pregnancy, Pat found it easier to say that she had been raped. This would inevitably bring a murmur of sympathy and usually silenced further questions, but once in a while the listener's curiosity got the best of it.

"Once a lady came over to me and started asking questions. After I'd told her the story she told me how her daughter wanted children so much and how she couldn't have any of her own. She acted really interested when I told her I was giving up the baby for adoption. She was nice enough, but I felt like she wanted to grab the baby inside me and run off with it for her daughter." Pat was to find that adoption was an emotion-packed subject and that once hearing she wasn't planning to keep the baby, people would usually launch right into a story about this or that relative or acquaintance who couldn't have a baby of her own but who would love to adopt one.

Claudia gave her the name of the physician, Dr. Creevy, who was most highly recommended by her friends as being someone who really cared about women and birth, who listened and did things the way you wanted. She went with her to the first visit and was surprised to hear her sister open up so quickly to this man. His manner was gentle without being fatherly and he seemed truly interested in Pat, not in prying at all into her privacy. Claudia heard Pat tell this stranger more in that visit than she had heard in weeks of living under the same roof. Pat talked about wanting to have the baby adopted into a loving home and about her disappointing visits to the adoption agencies. She told him her thoughts about the adoption. She might like just to be able to meet the parents, so she could feel sure about letting the baby go.

The doctor pricked up his ears at that remark. He had attended several thousand births in his fifteen-year practice and had very few experiences with women planning to give up their babies for adoption. But in each case he had offered to help find suitable parents from among a number of his own patients or acquaintances who were unable to conceive and wanted to be parents. And he had been involved already in three cases of direct adoption where the baby never went to a foster home, where no agency was involved and an adoption attorney— Phil Adams—handled all the arrangements.

At their next meeting, after the long history was taken and the physical exam was done, the physician, Pat and Claudia sat in his office and talked for almost an hour. He wanted to know if Pat had thought of having natural childbirth and to recommend it if she hadn't. He wasn't the first to mention the phrase. I had broached the subject to her at our first meeting. Claudia had been resistant to the idea from the first. She told Pat of her fear that having an unmedicated birth would be very painful, especially since Pat would be giving birth to a baby she'd never see again. A friend of hers had given up a baby years ago and her opinion was that it would be impossible to see your baby and hold it and still stick with a decision to give it up for adoption. Claudia couldn't resist interjecting her anxieties. Wouldn't it leave too deep and vivid impressions, permanent emotional scars, on Pat if she were to go through the birth awake, seeing and feeling everything? The physician did his best to reassure her. No, he said, her sister would not necessarily find the experience more traumatic if she had natural childbirth. First of all, natural childbirth was definitely better for the baby because it would have no drugs in its body in its first hours and days of life, the time when it had the job of adjusting to a new world without the food and oxygen from its mother's body. And the women he saw, almost without exception, felt natural childbirth had been one of the finest experiences of their lives. If Pat was going to make a life for herself without the baby, then her memories of a good birth experience might be especially helpful, he felt. Whatever she chose, and it was her choice completely, he did insist that she go to childbirth classes and prepare for the labor as if she were planning an unmedicated spontaneous delivery. That way, no matter what she finally chose to do, she would know as much as possible about the process and about her body. So, in the end, it was Claudia who accompanied Pat to the series of eight childbirth classes and Claudia who diligently practiced all the many ways she could support Pat during labor to make Pat's work easier. And it was Claudia who would accompany Pat right into labor, be at Pat's side, or rather her backside, throughout, with warm cloths and pressure against her spine.

Some women never experience the euphoria that is one of the many delights pregnancy can bring to those who are ready for it. Those who do talk about a heightened sense of smell and taste, a magical quality to the light, a greater appreciation for the beauty in life and a feeling of the preciousness of the fleeting moments until birth, all triggered by the growing life inside them. Emotions during pregnancy run a deep and shifting course and there are wistful times, memories of girlhood past, which seem all the more sweet for having now been left behind. For the woman who chooses pregnancy and looks forward to parenthood all the emotional ups and downs that wash over them are taken as they come. For the woman who backs into parenthood, who faces birth with fear, who never has felt comfortable with her body and its changes, or with the feeling of being swept away in pure sensation and emotion, pregnancy can be a particularly traumatic time—a constant struggle against the feeling she is losing control. In a very young woman who has experienced little of her own potential, pregnancy can seem like the beginning of a life sentence without reprieve, or a fantasy of playing dolls with a real-life baby who will always love you. Pity any woman who finds herself pregnant and not wanting to be so, who cannot make the shift of mind into becoming a parent, a *source* of love rather than the *object* of affection. Pity her all the more if she is without a mate, without the love of another adult to share the adventure with her, or without the support of other loving people around her willing to help her care for this child and respect its needs as a separate human being.

The time for relishing the sensations, changes and blooming of pregnancy came late for Pat. It had been thwarted in her home by shame and guilt and there was a void where there should have been someone else eager to share the adventure on which she was embarking. Any pleasure she might have felt was diminished by the manner in which she had become pregnant. Yet in the end the pregnancy and the baby growing inside her won out. Not long after arriving in California and settling into her life there, she found herself experiencing that giddy elatedness at last. She described it as excitement, a feeling of being fully alive. The baby had been moving and dancing inside her actively for months, but with no one to share in the magic of it Pat never paid it much attention. Considering her age and the sorts of substances teenagers in modern society fill their bodies up with, Pat ate comparatively well and kept herself free of drugs. She didn't skimp or try to diet in a desperate attempt to keep her own shape. The exercise she gave herself in walking every day was a benefit to her body and a rhythmic pattern for the baby. It was soothing to her mind, which was also linked to the baby by their shared chemistry. Her body had been pregnant a long time but now her mind and spirit were filling out too.

She found herself one morning in the apartment alone and naked in front of a mirror and liking what she saw. It was at such moments that she had begun to feel a relationship forming with the one inside. "I would do lots of things with the baby when nobody was around. I'd dance. I would put on a record of Eddie's and dance in front of the mirror." Pregnancy is a sensual time. Pat became more and more comfortable looking at herself, rubbing her skin all over with almond oil. "I liked to take off all my clothes when I was home alone. I even took a mirror sometimes and looked between my legs." She'd never dared to look before. And so she made peace with her own body at the same time that she began to acknowledge the bond with the little body inside her. One day, she began talking to the baby, and that began a game of conversation and playfulness many expectant mothers delight in. "At first the baby was just an idea in my head. I had felt for a long time, ever since I dreamed about a little girl baby trying to swim to the surface as I was drowning, that this baby wanted to be born. But it took a while to feel in tune with it." The "in tune" feeling could only come when Pat felt free to enjoy the pregnancy. "When I took baths I would think about how good it felt and I would tell that out loud to the baby, like I was talking to a friend in the room. Pretty soon we'd have conversations every day." The baby held up its end of the conversation by kicking in response to pressure from a hand on the belly, or by suddenly increasing its activity after some movement of Pat's.

"I would say, 'You know that I love you, don't you! I'm doing what is good for you with this adoption. You'll be better off for it, I know.' I'd tell her that, just like we were old friends. I never told anyone about my conversations with her because I didn't think they would understand." But by the last weeks of her pregnancy Pat spent more and more time in the apartment talking and playing with the baby. She would tell the baby all about her activities at the end of each day. "I had no one else. And she would listen. When she moved or jerked her elbow I'd say, 'Oh, so you think what I'm saying is funny, do you?'"

Pat dared to tell the baby her uncensored thoughts, not just what she thought the baby would like to hear. "I'd tell her I am looking forward to having my own belly back. 'It's nothing personal, you know, but you've got to come out. You can't live in here forever!' "

There was laughter once more in Pat's solitary life, especially when she was alone with the baby. Eddie, Claudia and Pat shared their moments of lightness too. Teasing one another began, and laughter bubbled up as regularly as did the arguments so familiar to families sharing tight quarters. Claudia noticed in particular how much pleasure Pat got from her walks and the kind of protection pregnancy did seem to bring her. She began to call her sister "Duck" when Pat's splay-footed gait became more pronounced at the end of pregnancy, as her pelvic bones shifted and she walked with a bounce. On their walks together the two women would invariably run into the same people. The neighborhood young men would always stop what they were doing, bow or nod and offer a familiar, "How're you doing today, Momma!" One of them, who was usually seen underneath the hood of his car, brought flowers to the apartment on several occasions. The nuns at the local church where Pat went every day smiled and often asked how she was doing. She had walked the streets of a big city with no one paying the least attention but in their rough, sprawling neighborhood of streetwise young men everyone made Pat feel welcome and showed an interest in the baby.

Visits to the church, like her walks to the park, played an important part in her feeling of well-being during the last weeks. "It didn't matter what particular faith it was, I think it was just the ritual of going there and thinking about the spiritual for a few minutes every day." She had gone to church every day too when she was a little girl in uniform attending Catholic school. The ritual was one of the things she'd missed in public high school. The neighborhood Catholic church had an informal feeling. "The priest would see me there each day and after a while he'd say something like, 'Good for you!' as if he were sort of glad to see me pregnant."

While the ritual of going to church gave her strength and support, Church doctrines were another matter. Pat began seriously to question the principles of her faith in the time she was waiting for the baby to come. She could not forget what kind of adoption her church had wanted to give her. She now knew a great deal about herself and what she wanted for her baby and was disappointed that her own church didn't offer her any solutions that fit her desires.

She returned to a weekly visit with the doctor and, as she had on many of the other visits, sat quietly as he did much of the talking, answering his questions with monosyllables until she had something she wanted to say. It was a surprise to her that the physician and nurse practitioner both wanted to listen to her, since she found it as difficult as ever to talk about herself. Often she wasted precious time pulling away from their questions, making them have to figure out just what kind of birth and adoption she wanted. In the curious mental construct only a teenager could make, Pat felt she didn't need to talk because anyone you needed to explain things to couldn't possibly see your point anyway. It was an excuse for continuing her pattern of being disappointed in authority figures. Fortunately for her she had picked herself several strangers in this drama who wouldn't join her game, who were determined to help her achieve the very best.

At one of the first visits her physician had given Pat and Claudia the names of several childbirth educators in town and recommended that they call the one he had found best for preparing women for natural birth. Claudia had called and signed the two of them up for the next series of weekly classes. There were eight classes and the baby was then due in seven weeks. Pat went initially because she had the sense to realize that what she had learned about birth from women like her mother wasn't useful or accurate. For her mother and her aunts, birth meant horrible pain and you needed to be unconscious or numbed with drugs to survive it. For some reason she never had believed them. "It didn't make any sense the way people were telling me you should give birth. Everyone always pushed the pain of it and the need to stop all the feelings. And I knew in the back of my mind what I wanted to do for the baby but I didn't say anything." She went along to the classes and there had her eyes opened to the possibilities. Soon she even found herself talking more easily with the doctor about what she was learning and what some of her hopes were.

Claudia had been the logical partner for Pat in the classes but her role there and at the birth was never really discussed between the sisters. She was shy about pushing or intruding on Pat's privacy in any way but it was maddeningly difficult to work with Pat in class because she seemed to pull away during every practice session. One of the major goals of the teacher was to facilitate communication between partners so that they could work smoothly together in the unpredictable course of labor—when a laboring woman often finds it impossible to talk, and she is so engulfed by sensation that she is driven out of all her rational faculties and into body language. Instead of accepting Claudia as a surrogate mate for the purposes of the classes, Pat spent a great deal of her time looking critically at her sister. She did feel they had a good relationship and were a team as they practiced the breathing and did massage for relaxation with the other six couples in the class. But, as Pat once confided to Claudia after class, they weren't a *real* couple, merely a pretend one. What she was thinking, but couldn't say to Claudia, was, "You aren't the father or my husband but I think you really want to be the mother of this baby!"

As Pat went through the last weeks, with the strange blend of awkwardness and grace so peculiar and common to women late in pregnancy, she found her belly was the drawing card for many unwanted conversations. The mere sight of her walking, usually alone, with no ring on her finger and obviously young, was enough to attract the attention of many women who have carried their own stories of pregnancy and birth around for years, unfinished and needing to be retold. They would come up to her on the street or on the ground where she was sitting reading and would pour out their own stories. Stories of pregnancies unplanned, of months and months of nausea and backaches and babies coming too soon and too close together, husbands too insensitive or too busy and births that had been traumatic encounters with fear and suffering, loneliness and remorse. They would give her unasked-for advice all mixed up with their own vivid memories and they would leave Pat depressed.

At the classes she saw a wholly different side of childbirth, not the ordeal she'd heard so much about but the personal satisfaction and the adventure of working to one's fullest capacity and learning to be in harmony with the natural process, even with pain. Claudia's presence helped, though the two of them never did break down the barriers and awkwardness they felt. The sisters struggled with unspoken communications, and touching, which was so important to Pat's relaxation during birth, didn't come easily. Claudia occasionally voiced her hurt. "What is it?" she'd say. "I know you can't stand me to touch you but can't you just say you love me?" And Pat would sullenly reply, "I can't talk now.

I don't feel anything." Even though Claudia was older and had some sense of what Pat was struggling with—and that it had nothing to do with herself—it was difficult not to perceive Pat's coldness as rejection. Pat was essentially alone but still in need of the very kind of support she couldn't ask for or tolerate. That was the hardest thing for both sisters, knowing that not only was Pat going through labor on her own with the baby, but that she would be alone after the birth and on into the future. Even the love and affection of a sister couldn't soften this truth.

As Pat grew into a feeling of kinship with the baby her concern for its well-being carried over into her dream life. During those last weeks she had two dreams, which she remembered clearly on waking. The first was full of anxiety and feelings of helplessness but ended triumphantly.

"It was daytime and I was in town driving my first car around, a goldish-gray 1963 Fairlane. Way out in Port St. Lucie there is flat land with streets but very few houses and nothing else. That's where I was. I knew I was about to have this baby and at the same time the car was running out of gas. I didn't know what to do. Should I keep going or should I try to get back to civilization and find help? Then I thought, 'How will I feed the baby?' Next thing I knew the baby was there, lying on the front seat next to me. At first I didn't know what to do with it and didn't pick it up. I felt stranded. Finally I picked it up and started caring for it. It was a girl." The dream ended there.

The second dream was a more refined version of an earlier dream, which had recurred throughout the pregnancy. First, as she told it, she was walking, striding rather, out into the hills. She was alone. Next she was bringing the baby back over those same hills, carrying it in her arms. In its final version, dreamt just before the birth, Pat saw the same hills and once more she was striding out into the distance. It was daytime again, morning perhaps, and the sun was out and the hills were green and round and empty. Over the crest of one hill and down below she spotted the small, still, blue pond. At the edge of the pond she made a bed for herself to lie in. There she must have given birth, for in the next sequence the baby was lying between her legs on the grass. She scooped it up in her arms and took off, striding back up across the hills she'd come from, as the sun warmed the two of them.

The idea of being alone, of accomplishing this thing all by herself, seemed important to Pat. Nowhere in any of her dreams did she imagine the birth as it would be, taking place in a cramped and sterile room filled with people. Always in her imaginings she was alone, with the baby and a benevolent nature. And always the birth itself was missing. But she did see herself taking responsibility for the baby, after initial confusion and anxiety. Pat had come of age and was now thinking consciously of the well-being of this baby. She felt the responsibility for its welfare keenly, another life for which she was sole caretaker.

Thus it was that by the time her prenatal visits with her physician had begun to focus on concrete options for the adoption, Pat was herself ready to voice her desires and concerns, to make decisions consciously and to picture the probable consequences of her actions.

At first there had been a question whether her labor would wait for the finish of the childbirth classes. She had a due date of late March and the series didn't finish until the first week of April. But, when the last class ended, the baby still showed no sign of coming. Pat's days were now filled. Her appointments with the physician were now twice a week. There was still more preparation to be made for the adoption. Her physician had encouraged her to participate herself in the selection of the parents. He had spoken most warmly of one couple to whom he had lived next door for several years. They were already raising a little girl they had adopted from birth and had, he recalled, been very eager for a second child. Pat thought they sounded interesting. He offered to call them and find out whether they might like this baby. Then he gave her a brief description of direct independent adoption, a legal process in California and many other states, which avoids foster homes and allows the baby to be given directly to the new parents. She would have to work with an attorney if this option interested her and he told her again of the attorney in the city who had arranged several adoptions for patients of his. Pat liked the idea that in direct adoption the baby could go directly from her to the new mother, and she wondered why no one in Florida or at the agencies had ever mentioned this possibility to her. The attorney, the doctor said, would insist on meeting her before he would agree to work with her, in order to discuss all of her rights and the legal details. He also liked to be able to confirm for himself that the woman was not being railroaded into anything that she would later regret, that she understood what she was getting into, giving her baby up and doing it without the anonymity of going through an agency. In just one office visit Pat found herself moving much closer to her unspoken goal—to be able to see for herself that the parents were good, kind people, and to be able to keep the baby from spending any time in foster care after its birth. Her doctor said he would call the attorney and set up an appointment for them to meet with him as soon as possible.

The visit to Phil Adams in San Francisco turned out to be a memorable one. Her physician took a half day off from his practice to accompany her and brought along his eight-year-old daughter, whom Pat had met before. Pat talked freely with the attorney. He seemed to have just the right blend of solicitousness, sternness and teasing to draw out a reticent teenager. By the end of an hour she announced that she was ready to meet the couple, as he suggested she should. Afterward the physician took Pat and his daughter to a park, to dinner at a Japanese restaurant, and to a concert. Things were falling into place quickly and Pat could not help showing the relief it brought her. She was playful and talkative.

Meanwhile the couple her physician had called were quite interested. The news that there might be a baby for them came when they least expected it and had put all hope for another child behind them. They too called Phil Adams, since he had handled their first adoption five years earlier. He told them Pat was certainly a healthy young woman who should have a healthy child. They could hardly have been more surprised when later that evening Pat's physician called to ask if they would like the chance to meet Pat. They would indeed. The date was set for the following Friday. The baby was due in two weeks by now, but since such dates are rather imprecise predictors of the time of birth, the baby could arrive any day or not for a month.

And so Pat found herself late Friday afternoon dressing with a bit of extra care and waiting at the apartment for her physician, myself and two strangers who were to play a key role in her life. The young woman who stepped out of the doorway, quickly crossed the street and slipped into the car seemed very different from the one who had stepped off the airplane just two months earlier. Her shoulders were hardly stooped at all, her skin glowed with color and her blouse was freshly ironed. She hadn't even considered asking her brother or sister to accompany her this evening. She felt comfortable going without a chaperone. I was only there as her advocate, in case she should need one. If the evening went well and she felt good about the couple, she told herself, she would look no further for parents for her baby.

How little needs to be said or done on momentous occasions. The simple preparation had been laid well and in spite of the short notice the evening was a resounding success. Pat talked little but was perfectly at ease. It was as if the trials and strains of the months preceding had all been leading her to this. She had found a solution to the biggest unknown—what would become of her baby—and even better, it fit her dreams.

An hour and a half slipped by quickly. Pat's physician suggested everyone might like to come to his home to sit in on an informal meeting for couples in his practice who were contemplating home birth. It would give them more time to be together with no agenda or pressure.

At the house, fifteen people sat in a large circle around the living room and they all introduced themselves to the group by stating briefly what their interests were in home birth. Halfway around the room a woman named Maria briefly told about her first birthing and what a chilling experience it had been. She said she'd given that baby up for adoption. She'd been eighteen at the time and living in the Midwest, and ever since then hospitals in her mind were associated with very negative feelings. She was trying to make this coming birthing a positive experience. As she talked, her face tightened and she didn't try to hold back the tears. Though her first birthing had been almost thirteen years ago the memory and its pain were fresh. Hers was not the only story of an unpleasant birth experience among the group. Nor was she the only one determined to do it differently this time. But it was she who caught the pregnant teenager's attention.

After the meeting Pat walked over to Maria. It was the first time in her pregnancy she had met anyone she felt might understand exactly what she was going through. Maria's first birthing also had meant loss instead of an exciting adventure into parenthood. The two women felt an immediate connection and Maria offered to drive her home so they could talk some more. Pat smiled broadly as she said goodnight to everyone. She would sleep easily this night.

The prospective parents returned to their home elated at the events of the evening. They had liked Pat right off and felt her concern for the baby and her strength and gentleness. She had even mentioned to them during the evening that she would be happy to have them at the actual birth if they would like to be there. That they would have to think about. They'd never imagined such a thing. As it turned out, there was no need to rush anything, for her due date came and went and there seemed to be no birth in sight. Her physician, having long before made plans for a weekend away with his family, was faced with having to cancel his few days of play or possibly miss Pat's birth. He was uncomfortable with not being there as he felt he could not guarantee things would go as Pat wished unless he was there to act as a buffer against the regimentation of the hospital. And so Pat was invited along on the weekend with his family, and they stayed in a suite at a motel on the coast. She played with the little girl and they all took long walks on the windy expanse of beach. Pat was quiet. Her mind was full of the curious preoccupations that make a birth both an imminent reality and a fantasy to a mother-in-waiting. In addition there must have been the memory of that incident nine months ago that left her pregnant. Now she would soon be face-to-face with the child that resulted. The arrival of her baby would be a meeting up with the past, a past she'd tried to erase from her life.

There is a belief among physicians and midwives that a woman's going much beyond two weeks past due date is cause for concern. Very late, very large babies, like very early, very small ones, may have more difficulty in labor. Impatience and pressure in the field of obstetrics and newborn care push many physicians into artificially ending pregnancy and stimulating labor with drugs when a woman is hardly a week "overdue." Pat's physician, without real cause to act and being cautious and not one to hurry when nature takes its time, felt it best to let the labor begin when it would. He did a simple test to see whether the baby was still getting enough nourishment from its placenta. It was. So he waited. But when Pat had gone two and a half weeks past his more accurate birth date he began to rumble about the possibility of inducing her labor. Pat didn't like this at all, though she wouldn't tell him so. She felt sure that the baby was going to come in its own right time and that there was no cause for concern, but she left his office on a warm spring day in mid-April with the news that, if the baby had not started labor by the coming Saturday, her physician wanted to hospitalize her for induction. Three days more. That was all the pregnancy she had left.

I stopped by the apartment unannounced that afternoon to see how she was doing. Pat was at home in the living room, deep in thought. She told me the deadline she was under. I asked if she thought there was any reason she herself might be holding up the labor. I knew it was possible for women, like the females of other species, to postpone the onset of labor and inhibit its progress from fear and anxiety. Certainly there is ample record of mammal mothers-to-be suddenly stopping labor when under stress, particularly stress caused by a sudden change of environment or the unwanted presence of a human observer. Many a family after waking the children to come and see Spot have her puppies has found Momma simply won't perform to a crowd. Pat thought about it. She said she could think of nothing in particular that was bothering her. So I approached it a different way and asked whether there might be any reason Pat could think of why she would not want the birth to happen now. She was quiet for some minutes, thinking, and said finally that she didn't think so. Only, she added vaguely, she guessed she hadn't really made any plans for herself for after the birth. It was, she said, as if everything would end with the birth and giving up the baby. I suggested perhaps it would be a good time to begin visualizing what kind of a life she wanted for herself after the birth. Perhaps her mind was holding up release of the hormones that start labor in order to hang on to the pregnancy, which had become the familiar, most stable part of her life. Of the women I've met who were without mates, or whose partners were unsupportive, or who planned to give their babies up for adoption at birth, many did seem to start into labor several weeks after they were due or had difficulty making normal progress when they did go into labor. I never underestimate the power of the unconscious mind to influence what goes on in our bodies.

Pat spent the rest of the day in the apartment, alone. She told me later she did a great deal of turning over in her mind what we had discussed. Perhaps she did have some control over when this baby came, though she couldn't imagine just how. But she had to admit to herself it was odd that she hadn't given a thought to making plans for her own future. Friday night passed and still labor did not begin. When Saturday came Pat telephoned me sounding greatly disappointed; she had not yet had even a twinge of a contraction. She was resigned to her physician's decision, but she didn't like it one bit. It didn't seem right, she said, that one minute she could be wandering around leading her life and the next minute some chemical injected into her vein could force her body to give birth. But she had to admit she probably was twenty-one days late. She was adamant that there could not be any error about when she got pregnant. And I was not about to press her about the past.

Three months in a new environment had done a lot for Pat. It had boosted her self-confidence, given her the feeling her opinions might be worth something. But it was not enough to overcome years of training in obedience to adults. No, she could not refuse a doctor's insistence. And so, after a phone call from him, she once more packed a few things in her blue school bag. She didn't forget the green handknit baby sweater that she'd been given at class. The teacher's mother enjoyed knitting and had sent enough baby sweaters for everyone in the group. This would be her parting gift to the baby. Eddie and Claudia got ready too. I went to her apartment and found Pat washing her feet in the bathtub. She had put on one of her well-worn maternity shirts over her stretched-out blue pants. Eddie drove Pat and Claudia in the van to the hospital. I followed in my car. Fifteen minutes later the four of us trooped into the lobby of the large medical center and up to the admitting desk.

Paul and Vicki waiting during Pat's labor

Parents-in-Waiting

When Paul and Vicki first decided to look into adoption it was early in the 1970s and they had been married for five years. Abortion was by then legal in the United States, following the Supreme Court's ruling. Partly as a result of that decision infants available for adoption were rapidly becoming a scarce commodity, as many more women chose to abort an unwanted pregnancy rather than face giving birth to a child they could not raise. By the time Paul and Vicki began searching for a second baby, three years after getting Amanda, babies to adopt in infancy and in good health were virtually nonexistent.

Vicki had entered married life without any great eagerness to have children. She had a career as a biologist that was as promising as Paul's, and their life together seemed complete. But after a few years they began to feel pressure, especially from Paul's mother, to start a family. She belongs to a club of women in their sixties who went to high school together in a small Midwestern town and who have met monthly ever since graduation. At their meetings they play cards, eat and talk about grandchildren. For years, Paul says, his mother had been the only one of the group who had no grandchildren to brag about and not even one on the way.

"We were told about that on occasion," says Vicki. "Paul's mother would manage to drop into a phone conversation, 'Suzie has a new grandchild! Mary has a new grandson! Kate has six grandchildren, would you believe that! And you know, it's really interesting; I'm the only one who has none!' "

It was subtle pressure, but pressure nevertheless. Paul was expected to continue the family line.

Decisions about having children and the timing of conception, even in a day of supposed contraceptive freedom and legalized abortion, are often made whimsically, as if real choice is too difficult to face when it comes to having children and the alternatives are too awesome to approach consciously and with planning. So, like many others around them, as their twenties began to slip by and their careers prospered, Paul and Vicki quietly gave up using any contraception without ever making a conscious, shared decision to become parents. But when after several years Vicki was still not pregnant, their decision became painfully conscious. In a matter-of-fact way that hints at the emotional energy beneath, Vicki describes their dilemma.

"I was twenty-nine and unable to get pregnant after trying and trying. Pretty soon we thought about adopting and it wasn't very long before our families knew we were looking for a baby." They were teased a bit. "Paul's middle sister was then dating a guy whom she liked and she once suggested to us that she had the perfect solution to our problem. 'You know, if you two paid me enough. . . .' " Surrogate motherhood was unheard of then and it caused quite a laugh in their family. But when Vicki's gynecologist, Don, called her into his office after one more visit to determine the cause of their infertility, it was suddenly no laughing matter. He knew Vicki well and felt he could put it bluntly. "Look, Vicki. I can't find anything physically wrong with you or Paul. There are some people who just don't get pregnant with a given person." Vicki asked what that meant and he explained. "I was told I had four options. I could give up on having kids. I could get divorced and marry someone else, because I'd probably get pregnant with different sperm. I could have artificial insemination with a donor. Or, we could adopt."

As Vicki saw it, her choices were more limited than that. She had no intention of ending their marriage, and found it difficult to consider artificial insemination as a possibility. "I didn't want to carry somebody else's child!" She found Paul shared her distaste for artificial insemination, and separating just because they couldn't have children together was as inconceivable to him as it was to her. That didn't leave much choice.

"We thought about our options for a long time," Paul reflects. "It didn't really bother me that we weren't having children, but the idea of adoption did at first. I guess I had the typical response of many men in my culture, that it's not *my* blood." But by now Vicki wasn't willing to accept being childless permanently.

First, as Paul recognized, there had to be some coming to terms with the fact of their apparent infertility. The process of accepting an unwanted truth is an internal one and must have been a particularly lonely one for Vicki. Paul knows this. "We talked about it, sure. And then, after a while, we didn't talk about it any more. There were times, I know, when I wasn't home, when Vicki did a lot of crying."

Then Vicki began to press Paul about adopting a child. After a while he agreed that it would be all right to adopt, but as young a baby as possible. Among the middle class and the wealthy, for those who are capable of paying the fees, who are considered neither too young nor too old, and who offer the kinds of homes that please adoption agency workers, adoption had always been a relatively easy matter. That is, it was as long as adoptable infants were in rich supply. Vicki and Paul found they lived in a neighborhood that is a virtual sea of adoption— with the people next door, the couple across the street, the couple be- hind them, all adoptive parents. They assumed that finding a child would be easy. But they were several years too late. Finding a baby proved no easy matter for them.

Their need for help in finding a child necessitated exposing the privacy of their well-ordered life and themselves to the scrutiny of strangers. Vicki began with the county adoption agency, that estab- lished agent in the adoption business, which sets standards and rules on suitability and matches potential parents with available children. She was quickly rebuffed—at twenty-nine she was considered too old. Her local agency had made an arbitrary cut-off age because they were re- ceiving so many more applications from people seeking healthy infants than there were babies available. Next, she tried the Children's Home Society, an established and respected large private agency and the only other one in their area. They weren't even interested enough to take Vicki's initial application. Shocked and very discouraged, she returned to her gynecologist's office. He might not be an adoption agency but he must have some suggestions, since he delivered so many babies. He told Vicki he'd been involved in surprisingly few adoptions in the fifteen years he'd been in practice. But he did know of an attorney who specialized in adoption whom he'd used on two occasions. He was reputed to be rather an institution himself, because he'd handled so many legal private adoptions.

Vicki didn't really know the difference between an agency adoption and an independent adoption before she met Phil Adams. But she got a quick education after she went to his office for an appointment. Paul went with her, and what they heard from their attorney was not encouraging.

"At something like seventy-five dollars an hour, he went into great detail discouraging us, saying it would be years, if ever, before we would ever find a baby. He sat there with a vile cigar, teasing us, and telling us stories about adoptions he'd handled. He wanted to know which one of us was going to take care of this imagined child, since I had a good job and Paul was also working full-time at his. I said I was, that I was going to give up my job, at least for the first few years, to stay home with the child. 'What do you mean!' He practically leaped out of his seat, he was so excited. 'My wife is a teacher, and she wouldn't dream of giving up *her* job for any kids.' I gathered from that remark that they didn't have any children, at least not together; but then he said he'd raised four in his first marriage."

Along with the story-telling Phil gave Paul and Vicki some serious practical information about the philosophy of direct independent adoption. Vicki carefully remembered everything he had told them. "Assuming we could find someone wanting to give up a child for adoption, we should get as much information as possible about both parents and we should in turn give as much information as possible about ourselves to the mother. He strongly recommended that we meet each other in advance if at all feasible. Above all, he felt we should do it all as adults, out in the open, not hiding behind doors and sneaking around." It was this matter-of-fact, commonsensical approach that attracted Vicki to Phil Adams, despite the cigars and offputting remarks. She returned home with Paul, determined to be the squeaky wheel who made enough of a nuisance of herself with the attorney to keep their cause in front of him. She chuckles today recalling her frequent phone calls to his office to inquire whether he had any news for them yet.

Although they would have the choice of accepting or not a particular infant that became available, even in direct adoption Paul and Vicki would still be taking the luck of the draw with regard to which child came to their attention. Direct adoption has its own screening process, which is an unwritten one. Only the most persistent get references in the first place, and these references usually come from friends or physicians who come across a pregnant woman planning to give up her child and pass along the news. Most obstetricians regularly get form letters from people they don't know who are searching for a child and are writing to every physician in the phone book, sending out pictures of themselves and résumés of their lives. Each person searching for a child must find his or her own best way. For some it is a form letter. For some it's prayer. Others tell everyone they know and everyone they meet. The process may be agonizingly slow, full of detours, sudden hopes and shattered expectations. A child you hear is available one week goes to another couple the next week and you are always one step away from being there at the right time. However, Vicki's persistence paid off surprisingly quickly.

"I think Phil just couldn't stand getting any more of my phone calls, so he found us a child." They had first gone to his office in December and their daughter, Amanda, was born the following May. Phil had called Vicki once in March to tell them about a woman who would be giving birth to a mixed-race child. She and Paul talked a lot about taking this baby. Then they went to see Phil, hemming and hawing and indecisive. "He took one look at our faces and said, 'Forget it! If you're not comfortable with it, forget it!'" That was that. Raising this child in the area where they live, where there isn't a Latino, black or Asian person for miles, Paul and Vicki felt, would bring too many problems upon the child. Another consideration for Vicki was the grandparents. "They come from a different generation and I couldn't see them playing grandparents to a child of a different race. I believe a child needs a full, extended family and our parents' attitudes do make a difference."

Another set of parents was found for that baby and a month later Phil telephoned Vicki saying he might have a baby for them. He had just received a letter from a woman due to give birth in six or eight weeks. She was married and living out of state and had heard of Phil from a friend. She was asking him to help her find parents for her baby—people who would take the baby home directly from the hospital, so it wouldn't have to be placed in a foster home. In her letter she expressed a preference that this be a Christian home but, more important, she wanted to be sure that the parents were healthy and financially able to raise a child. Phil told Paul and Vicki the couple didn't have enough money to pay the medical bills for the birth and that they would therefore be expected to pay them—this practice being a longstanding tradition in direct adoption. They must agree to put the estimated total needed for the hospital and physician in a separate bank account, to which only the attorney and they had access. The hospital where the woman planned to give birth would then be sent a record of the deposit. Without that guarantee that the bill would be paid, the hospital would not admit the woman when her labor started. He had to warn them that there was always the possibility that once this baby was born, the birth parents might choose to keep it themselves. In properly handled direct adoption the greatest power initially lies with the biological parents and every attempt is made to protect the woman giving birth so that she does not feel any pressure to guarantee her child will be placed for adoption prior to her signing final consent papers. But at least with no agency standing between the participants, the baby would be assured of a home with them right from birth. There would be no limbo time for the infant to spend in foster care. Paul and Vicki would have to take the risk in exchange for a speedy, humane adoption. They were thrilled at the chance.

On Monday, Paul made the necessary transfer at their bank and he and Vicki went in to work as usual. Vicki's employer was busy in meetings all day and she didn't have a chance to talk with him about her plans to give up work soon. Tuesday morning she again went in to work, intending to talk with him about the baby and her leaving the job, at least while the baby was young. But there was no time for discussion or negotiation. Immediately upon arriving at his office, Paul received a call from the attorney. He hung up the phone, stunned and jubilant, and called Vicki. Vicki could hardly believe the news.

"Our daughter was born at seven this morning!" The birth had occurred six weeks earlier than expected but the baby was not premature. They hadn't even had a chance to tell anybody they were adopting a baby, much less to get ready. This was Tuesday. They had only made the decision to get involved on Saturday. Vicki walked into her employer's office at ten that morning and announced, "My child was born this morning and I have to fly to Nevada to get her."

Vicki was in a state of shock. She'd had no time to prepare for this leap into new motherhood. No physical and hormonal changes had slowed her down and made her ready for the tremendous energy involved in caring for a tiny human being whose needs at first would seem unceasing. She could rely only on her intellect and her dreams to prepare her for the moment when she would carry a strange baby out of a hospital a thousand miles away and into her own home.

Wednesday and Thursday morning Vicki went to work and tried to be a biologist. Then she went home and frantically went around to their friends' houses collecting things they would need for the baby—crib, diapers, clothes, receiving blankets. She made a plane reservation for herself and several calls to Phil Adams. Thursday afternoon after work she and Paul drove to San Francisco once more and had a three-way conversation with the baby's father and Phil at Phil's office, to set final arrangements. Friday morning, early, Paul drove Vicki to the airport and went on to work while she flew off to Nevada, carrying an armload of borrowed baby things.

They had decided that only Vicki should go to get the baby because they thought it would be harder for the father to meet Paul or both of them together than it would be to meet Vicki alone. Vicki carried with her all the necessary legal documents prepared by Phil so that they could accomplish a private interstate adoption. There had been no time for the pre-birth meeting Phil encouraged people to have. The meeting with the father at the obstetrician's office ended up being very awkward and strained. They took a taxi to the hospital together and the one thing Vicki remembers him saying was that he had nearly called the whole thing off the night before because the baby was a girl and he had three boys. He was crying.

At the hospital Vicki was introduced as the woman who would be helping to care for the baby at home. A nurse brought the baby to them in the hallway and began to change its diapers on a gurney. She asked the father if he'd brought clothes to take the baby home in. He was at a loss and turned to Vicki, who gave the nurse the clothes she'd brought. When they were ready to leave, the father asked the nurse if she would please carry the baby to the taxi. At the taxi's door, the nurse turned and gave the baby to the father before he had time to refuse. Vicki recalls his reaction was that of someone handed a hot frying pan. He passed her to Vicki immediately. When the taxi stopped, he jumped out and took off, leaving Vicki with the baby. By the time she arrived at the doctor's office, he had already signed the papers and left by another door. Vicki never saw him again, and neither has his daughter. Vicki named the little girl Amanda, and she held her new daughter all the way to the airport, onto the plane, and home.

Certainly not the best closure to such an emotional event, even this brief, awkward encounter had given Vicki information she could pass on to Amanda as she grew up—about her birth father and the events of the day Amanda went home from the hospital, just three days after she was born. The process of absorbing and working through the experience of the transfer of Amanda was not helped by the rigidity of the law. Even without knowing any alternatives to what she had experienced in their first private adoption, Vicki sensed there had to be a better way.

When Amanda was two months old and colicky, crying unconsolably for several hours each evening, her gynecologist offered Vicki another baby. She declined without asking Paul. Their hands were full. But when Amanda was two years old they started looking for a second child to complete their family. Babies to adopt were by then very scarce. Again, neither the county nor the private agencies would consider them unless they would agree to take a hard-to-place older, handicapped or mixed-race child. And they did not see themselves as exceptional parents, able to take on additional responsibilities required for a child with special needs. Phil Adams told them he now had a file of several hundred active names of people looking for a child to adopt. In the previous year he'd only been able to place twenty-five babies and he told Vicki bluntly, "Go find your own. I'll be glad to do the legal work."

Vicki's gynecologist was called upon once more. After several months he called one day to say he'd found another prospective mother who was planning to give up her baby at birth. It turned out that the woman had taken heroin early in her pregnancy and Paul and Vicki turned down the offer. (That baby at birth appeared to be healthy and normal and was placed for adoption through the county.) No more babies came to their attention. Three years of looking passed and they began to disengage from their dream of ever finding a brother or sister for Amanda. As resignation set in, they turned their attention to the benefits of having their only child now of school age.

"Amanda was pretty grown-up by then," says Vicki. "She was in nursery school, and able to spend long weekends with her grandparents.

Paul and I were back to making love in the morning, a luxury we hadn't had in many years. We weren't all that sure we really wanted to start all over with another child. We told ourselves we were fortunate to have one." They began giving away all the baby things Vicki had stored in the garage.

Then one Friday afternoon the phone rang. It was Don Creevy. He said, "Hi, Vicki. Do you want a baby?" That was all. She thought he was being flip, so she said, "Sure!" Then he said, "I'll call you later," and hung up. The offer was casual but not offhand. Vicki figured it must have been a busy day and that her doctor was probably calling in between seeing patients. It suddenly dawned on her that it probably wasn't a joke and so she called Paul at work.

Don called again that evening when he had time to give them more information. He told her the young woman in question had just turned seventeen. She'd only a few weeks earlier come across the country from Florida. She was living with her older brother and sister and felt she could not, under the circumstances, give this child what it deserved. Like Amanda's young mother, she didn't want the baby to spend any time in foster care and none of the agencies she'd been to would offer that guarantee. Vicki was intrigued. She felt ready to jump in once more, willing to take the risk, knowing that this mother also might ultimately choose to keep her baby and that she and Paul would be the losers. She decided not to say anything about the possibility to Amanda.

The next morning she called Phil Adams. In his typical mock off-hand way he said, "Fine, sounds good! When can I meet this young woman?" Vicki called Don back and told him what the attorney had said. He said he would take it from there and bring the young woman to meet with Phil. It was up to Paul and Vicki to keep their hopes in proportion.

"We didn't have high expectations for getting this baby. There must be a great deal of pressure for the companionship of a baby if you're a young, single mother. We knew it would be especially difficult for someone like her to give up her baby."

A week passed. Don called again; he wanted to know whether she and Paul wanted to meet the young woman. They did. He made reservations for dinner at a Japanese restaurant. Vicki remembers the evening with a great deal of pleasure.

"We drove to Don's home and then all went in his car to pick her up

On the evening she met Paul and Vicki for the first time,
Pat sits with her doctor on her right and the prospective parents
of her baby on her left.

at the apartment she was sharing with her brother and sister. Paul and I waited in the back seat and soon an attractive, dark-haired, olive-skinned, very pregnant young woman came across the street. She opened the door, looked in at us and said, 'Hi!' She sat down next to me. We chatted on the way to the restaurant. She certainly was poised for her age, and friendly too."

Inside the restaurant they were seated along one side of a long cooking table where they could watch the Japanese waiter preparing the vegetables and shrimp on a hot griddle right in front of them. Vicki, seated next to the young woman she'd just met, found it easy to broach the subject of childrearing.

"Paul and I are reasonably strict with kids by today's standards. I thought she should know that. That seemed fine with her. We talked about the religious question. Don had told me she was Catholic and that she'd gone first to see Catholic Social Services about giving them the baby. I told her Paul and I were brought up in Protestant churches and that we believe a religious background of some kind is important for children."

The seating arrangement at dinner placed Paul farthest from the young woman. He stayed in the background, as he would at their next meeting too, listening and observing. He felt protective already of her feelings and sensed she might be more at ease with Vicki than with him. That didn't prevent him from forming some immediate and strong impressions of the young woman he watched.

"I didn't think of her as a child, not from the first. After all, she'd already crossed over that threshold, she'd done something that made her an adult. It was probably a painful experience, but whether for better or worse, her childhood was over, and was before I met her—just freshly over. I could see she was still learning about being an adult, but she was no child, not with the kind of decisions she was making."

For Vicki the evening felt particularly fruitful. While she would dearly like to have this baby, she too felt protective of this young woman who was struggling with a crucial decision. She was torn between personal desire and a feeling of admiration and support for the other woman. All she could do was stand by and wish her clarity in her thinking.

"We went home and for the first time since Don called me I began to feel settled about things. Up until then this young woman was just a faceless seventeen-year-old who was thinking about giving up her unplanned child for adoption. But she seemed to know what she wanted. She told us outright at dinner that she couldn't promise anything, because she didn't know exactly what she'd be able to do once she had given birth and held the baby in her arms. She felt sure that adoption was the best thing she could do for the baby and for herself, but she couldn't make any guarantees. I thought that was one of the finest things she could have said—that she couldn't promise us—because it meant she was thinking carefully about what she was doing and not blindly trying to convince herself."

By the time the woman went into labor, Paul and Vicki were feeling there was much less risk of not getting this child than they'd felt with Amanda. They knew this mother was not being pressured by the father of the baby (who was not even in the picture), by her parents, by her physician or attorney, or by them. She was making her own decisions and had people around her who would support her in any decision she made.

Paul and Vicki had never considered being asked to attend the birth of their child. They'd never heard of it and never dreamed it was possible. When the idea was mentioned, first by Vicki's doctor and then by the woman herself, both Paul and Vicki were stunned and delighted. For Vicki in particular, being present could be a profound experience. With all but a very few women in North America giving birth in hospitals, few women are now privileged to participate in another woman's birthing.

The next time Vicki and Paul met with the dark-haired young woman, she was well into her labor. The setting was a cramped, windowless room on the third floor of the teaching hospital in the same medical center where Vicki used to work. Despite the sterility of the physical environment, the experience was to become the fulfillment of this couple's dream and a profoundly emotional time for Vicki. The woman about to give birth to their second child was named Pat.

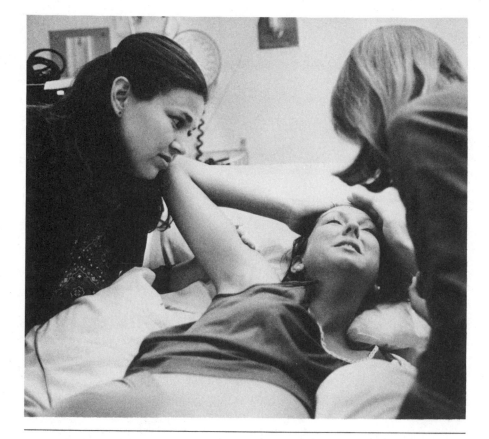

Pat late in her labor. Her sister is at left, her birth educator at right.

Invitation to a
Birthing

The day of Paul and Vicki's second meeting with Pat had proved to be further in the future than anyone imagined, as Pat's pregnancy dragged on long past her mid-March due date. Paul and Vicki went about their daily lives with five-year-old Amanda, going to bed each night with the uncertainty of when Pat's baby would be born and what Pat's ultimate decision regarding her baby's future would be. It was a waiting period for them that paralleled Pat's. Each expectant mother feels anticipation, uncertainty and some anxiety about the birth ahead. For some, the apprehension lies in what the labor will be like and how they will behave under its pressure. For others, it is concern about whether their husband or whomever they are depending upon for emotional support will be there when they go into labor. In addition, there is always the question, voiced or not: "Will this unseen child I am growing inside me be healthy and perfectly formed?" For the sensitive birth mother this last anxiety has an additional hook: "Will this creation of my body be marred in any way by my imperfections, my thoughts and moods, my actions while I have carried it?" Pat must have felt somewhat like the prized goose expected to lay the golden egg. Only after the birth was she able to express her feelings of embarrassment at having been the recipient of so much attention from the time she arrived in California. But she had chosen this path and felt right about it.

Don called Paul and Vicki one Friday night with the news that if Pat had not begun labor spontaneously by the next morning, he planned to induce her labor artificially. Vicki was ready.

They could now plan on the probability that they would be parents again within the next day or two. They found a neighbor to be on call for Amanda and we sat near the phone all day Saturday. It was dinner time before Don finally rang to say he was at the hospital with Pat and had just begun inducing her labor. He told them they might just as well get a bit of rest because, since this was Pat's first labor, even with the stimulation of artificial hormones, it would certainly take many hours.

"So we took Amanda to our next-door neighbors', in case we had to leave for the hospital in the middle of the night, and then we went to bed early. Just as we were falling off to sleep the phone rang. It was Don again, saying we'd better come quickly because Pat's labor was moving very quickly and she would soon be pushing! Already! We threw on our clothes, jumped in the car and went careening down to the hospital. It was ten-thirty. We went straight upstairs to the labor and delivery suite, walked in the door and asked for Dr. Creevy at the nursing station. Don came out of one of the rooms and told us that Pat was doing very well. Then he took me right in to see her."

Although this was the same building where Vicki had worked for eight years, she'd never been inside the labor and delivery unit and it was as strange to her as to a first-time mother. Propped up on a high metal bed, Pat was already quite far along in labor, and her appearance stunned Vicki. "She looked so exhausted!" Between contractions Pat looked over at Vicki and said hello. Then her attention was quickly absorbed by the next rush of contraction and she could give no more thought to the awestruck woman watching her so intently from across the room. Vicki politely excused herself at the end of the next contraction and said she would go sit out in the lobby with Paul.

It wasn't very long before a nurse came out to the lobby to get them. Paul and Vicki followed her into Pat's room and stood off to one side at the foot of the bed. She was working very, very hard and the contractions seemed to give her no rest. Vicki was quickly absorbed into the fast-moving drama in front of her. It was the end of Pat's labor and an emotionally fraught time for everyone.

"I'll never forget, during one particularly hard one, Pat cried out. After it was over, she sat there panting, leaning on one arm, her legs dangling over the edge of the bed. Then she suddenly looked right up at me with a mischievous grin on her face and asked, 'Aren't you glad I'm doing this for you?' I will remember that face and those words till my dying day."

Vicki had slowly moved from the foot of the bed around its side until she was standing near Pat's shoulder. Paul had felt awkward entering the privacy of the scene and stood watching from his semi-darkened corner and made no attempt to participate. He admired the strength of will and physical stamina he saw.

"I tend to do things more as an observer than taking an active part, and I was sure impressed with Pat. When I heard the wisecracks she would make between some of those rough contractions just before pushing, I knew she was tough. Not tough-hard. Pat doesn't seem a particularly forceful person. But tough-strong. Whenever she could catch her breath, she was still funning everybody in the room. Then suddenly Don was saying, 'Wait a minute! That's the head showing! We're going to have this baby here!'

"Pat had been saying that she felt the urge to push and Don was saying, 'Let's wait just a minute; I don't think you're fully dilated yet.' Then she was grunting, 'I've *got* to!' And he quickly checked her to see how far dilated she was and announced that the baby was down very low; not only could she push but she was practically ready to deliver. The room suddenly felt hot and exciting."

The labor room was only the size of a small bedroom and it was by then filled to capacity with people. There were Vicki and Paul, a young physician in training, Don, two nurses, Pat's childbirth teacher, Eddie and Claudia, myself, Pat, and the baby about to be born. The group was suddenly silent and the air hot with breathing and with Pat's urgent effort. The sweetish smell of amniotic fluid began to fill the air. The membranes surrounding the baby, in which the baby had lived all those months, had spontaneously broken, dropping the baby even lower down the birth canal. Everyone sensed birth was imminent. Vicki was amazed at how the group functioned, as if it were a single organism.

"I've heard so often about how hospitals have rigid rules for how many people a woman can bring to her birth. They say it's because any extra would get in the way if an emergency arose. I never felt I was in the way. And there was one point, just before the baby's head came out, when Don, after listening to the baby's heart, wanted to give Pat some extra oxygen. All he did was say, once, 'I want some oxygen' in a serious tone of voice and everyone stepped out of the way while the nurse reached over to hand it to him, as if we all had one mind."

Vicki's view of the actual moment the rest of the baby's body slipped out of Pat's was temporarily blocked by the physician's back as he bent over the foot of the labor bed. But as he stepped back she could then see a wet baby lying between Pat's outstretched legs, its bluish cord still attached and extending up inside Pat's body, still pulsing with her life blood. The sight of that physical connection between Pat and her baby was a vivid reminder of the unnaturalness of what was to follow. No matter how gently the cord was severed, how gracefully the exchange could be made, the baby was of Pat's body. Yet Vicki was already feeling connected to the little girl lying there on the bed with her arms outstretched as if startled at being born so quickly. It was only a moment before her little body was gathered up and lifted into Pat's outstretched arms, just long enough for everyone to see that this baby was fine and healthy. Meanwhile, Paul's view of the birth had been complete. Ghost-pale and stunned, he absorbed everything from his place in the shadows at the foot of the bed. He'd never before even seen a film of birth.

"I wasn't shocked by all the blood. It was just that I was so keyed up! So I squatted for a while just before she was born. I remember when she gave her first cry, when she was only halfway out. She didn't make another sound after that, just lay there quietly breathing. I've read that some people feel babies are affected by all the noise, bright lights and hurry of hospital delivery rooms. That makes sense to me now. To hear her give that one brief outcry and then to breathe without any encouragement! I was so very touched. It was intense and tense—different from anything I've ever seen before. You could feel the energy in the room, especially as she was coming through and everyone grew quiet. Such a good feeling."

About the crowd in the room, Paul was clear that it was a support for Pat. "I think you could put those same people together in a tent in the desert and the birth would have turned out just as well, because there weren't any negative personalities there. Well, Pat's sister did seem to have a lot of tension. I think I know how she must have been feeling about Pat's giving up the baby; but even she seemed positive about the birth itself. At the end, nobody was focused on anyone but

Pat, who was working to her limit. Then on the baby, resting after its journey."

After the few seconds it took for the physician to feel sure that the baby was breathing well on her own, in one smooth motion he slipped both hands under her wet body and brought her up onto Pat's soft abdomen, which was warm and glistening with sweat. Then he turned to Vicki and asked, "Would you like to cut the cord?" Vicki took the blunt-tipped scissors that were held out to her and cut through the spiraling, sinewy cord. There was utter silence in the room as everyone listened to the baby take her first breath independent of her mother. Don quietly asked Paul and Vicki what name they'd chosen for her.

"Abigail," Vicki said softly as she looked directly at Pat as if for approval. Pat looked into Vicki's eyes and nodded. She held Abigail closely and one of the nurses covered the two of them with a warmed blanket. More silence in the room as Abigail's eyes tentatively began to open for the first time since the birth. And as they opened she began to turn her head slowly until she was gazing directly up into her mother's face. For one brief moment Pat looked down at her and smiled. Then she reached out her free arm and grasped Vicki's hand. No one else moved as the two women shared a private smile of satisfaction. Paul hung back.

"I felt it would have been out of place if I did anything. It might have caused Pat's family pain if I came too close then. But Vicki being there with Pat seemed to be okay."

During the entire time Pat held Abigail, stroked Abigail and spoke to her, Vicki stood by Pat's shoulder, first clasping her hands at her breasts and then with her hands extended as if in waiting. No one in the room knew how the next minutes would pass and what Pat would do. It was all her decision and only hers. The medical resident and the nurses, the only strangers at this scene, seemed to understand and stood still, delaying their own ritual—the weighing, measuring, footprinting, tagging.

Then, suddenly, Pat passed a large clot of blood from her vagina followed by a rather heavy gush of blood. Her placenta, the baby's blood and food supply, was beginning to detach itself from the wall of her uterus, as her uterus contracted with the stimulation of the baby's body lying so near to Pat's breast. Time to birth the placenta. The nurse said, to no one in particular, "Take the baby." Don said, "Give the baby to Vicki." What followed happened so swiftly it seemed an apparition to everyone else in the room. Vicki took the baby from Pat's arms, wrapped the blanket tightly around its body and in one movement slipped around the foot of the bed and over to a straight-backed chair, which had all this time been sitting empty in the darkened corner of the room. There she sat rapt with little Abigail in her arms, hidden from everyone else's view. The baby had begun to cry the minute she was taken from Pat's arms; but soon she stopped. Of what happened next Vicki remembers little. She was unable to notice Pat or anyone else, except Abigail, for the next half hour.

From across the room, Pat and her sister watched Vicki immersed in discovering this little baby. Eddie was still hanging back near the other bed in the room. Pat, Claudia, Eddie, each of the faces told a different story of the mixed emotions felt; but Pat's face remained calm and curious and open. And so the first moment everyone had dreaded passed without ceremony or awkwardness. But this was not the end. Pat had granted Vicki permission, without words, to be with Abigail and to name her. It was still for Pat to make her conscious decision about the future of Abigail and she would need some privacy in which to reflect upon all that had happened in the last brief dozen hours of her life.

Paul thought he knew what lay ahead—parting, grieving and pain for a young woman he barely knew and so admired. He didn't like to think of it. "I was so glad I could be there; but I knew hard times were coming. Giving up Abigail for good, that was going to hurt. It hurt everyone."

It was then the middle of the night, though in the windowless room one could easily lose track of night and day. Everyone could use some rest. Nighttime was no time for making life decisions. Pat's doctor thought she looked tired. A nurse suggested that Abigail remain in the hospital overnight and be watched the few hours until morning, to be sure she didn't develop any problems. There was brief conversation among Pat, Don, Paul and Vicki about what to do. Vicki suggested she and Paul go home and come back in the morning. Then Amanda could be with them. Pat, it was decided, should spend the night in the hospital along with Abigail. There was no mention of how the parting would take place. Pat merely asked Paul and Vicki to come for Abigail early. In her mind the decision was firm.

The knot of people began to dissolve. Heather, Pat's teacher, who had been so helpful to her in labor, bent over and hugged Pat before she left, whispering congratulations and words of praise for how beautifully Pat had labored. She promised to return in the morning if she could be of any help, and Pat said she would like that. One of the nurses and the resident left. The remaining nurse asked Paul if she might take the baby for a few minutes, to weigh and measure and put medication in the eyes. Abigail did not make any fuss as she was moved this time but, eyes wide open, continued to look out at the world around her. I too gave Pat a big hug and congratulations, and offered to return early in the morning in case she needed an advocate. I forgot to ask Pat whether she would prefer to have Abigail remain with her through the night, an omission I later regretted. Soon after I left Don also said goodnight. It would be a short night's sleep before he had to return to check Pat in the morning, discharge her from the hospital and see that arrangements for Abigail went just as Pat wished. He could get a call to attend another birth at any time and in his haste to get some sleep, he failed to leave written orders that this baby should remain with its mother and that nurses should visit Pat's room to check on them so it never needed to leave her side. Without this, the staff assumed the baby should spend the night in the nursery along with the rest of the babies.

It was 2 a.m. Only Pat, Abigail, Claudia, Eddie and one nurse remained. Once she had finished with her duties the nurse gave the baby back to Pat. Eddie then said goodbye to his sister. He had no words to describe how he felt about what he had just witnessed, how proud and amazed he'd been, how moved, as the expressions on his face throughout the birth had shown. He merely told his sister he'd be seeing her back at the apartment. Then he picked up his guitar and left. That left only Claudia, who had no intention of leaving her sister alone in a hospital, even for a few hours. She offered to stay the night with Pat in her room, and Pat accepted the offer. The nurse began to get her ready for the move down the hall, through the swinging doors, across the lobby and into the post-partum unit where new mothers and babies stayed until they left the hospital. Claudia helped the nurse push the bed, with Pat and the baby in it. The room they gave Pat was semi-private with two beds, but she had no roommate. Claudia spotted the second bed as a place for herself to sleep but the nurse saw immediately what she must be thinking and informed her that no one was permitted to use, or even sit on, the second bed. Hospital policy, she said patly. It was clear that she considered Claudia's presence a nuisance, and felt that if she insisted on staying the night she should make do in a chair. So Abigail was whisked off to the nursery across the hall in the arms of a stranger. Pat's sanitary napkin was changed, she was shown the button to press if she needed anything, and the nurse left, shutting the door behind her. The two sisters were alone.

Pat seemed to want to be left to sleep, so Claudia made no attempt at conversation. With the lights off she too tried to sleep, sitting up in the straight-backed chair next to the window. But when her head began to nod she jerked awake, feeling stiff all over. Finally, she got up and placed her coat on the linoleum floor and lay down at the foot of Pat's bed. Thus she passed the remaining hours of the night. With no one else there to act as advocate on their behalf, the two sisters and little Abigail had been quickly absorbed into the hospital routine. The intimacy of the evening had dissolved once all the friends had gone home. There was a different set of nurses in maternity and in the nursery during the night and the shift would change again at dawn.

Pat, who has just said goodbye for her baby daughter, lets herself cry
in the arms of her sister.

PAT

How Do You Say Goodbye?

It was a fine, warm, hazy spring day that began as food and medicine carts clanged in the hallway and people rushed to and fro outside. Pat and Claudia awoke as the noise seeped under their door. Pat waited patiently for someone to come in so she could ask to have Abigail brought to her. Meanwhile, outside the hospital, day came all too soon for her exhausted physician, for Paul and Vicki, who knew many nights of lost sleep lay ahead with a new baby in the home to care for. For Abigail there was no marking of a new day. She lay wrapped in a blanket in a plastic cot in a brightly lit, noisy nursery full of babies. The room had never darkened for the night and it faced away from the morning sun.

As the sunlight slipped over the window sill into Pat's room with the spare bed still unmussed, a new nurse came in to check on Pat. Whether she was surprised to see another person there too and wondered where she could have slept, she didn't say. Pat asked for her baby. Had she and Abigail lain together in Pat's bed during the night, Pat might have gazed for hours in quiet ecstasy on the face of her child, as so many mothers before have done when left undisturbed with their new babies. That might have been one of her most precious memories. Instead, Abigail was brought in to her at 8 a.m. by a stranger in uniform who knew nothing of Pat's circumstances or of the special time this was meant to be. There was little time to be together before Paul and Vicki would arrive.

Bright and early Paul and Vicki picked up Amanda from the neighbors'. Feeling certain now of Pat's decision to give them Abigail, they told Amanda for the first time that she had a baby sister, and they took her with them to the hospital. Amanda was simply delighted. Vicki carried with her a tiny stretch-knit suit in which to dress Abigail for the short car ride home. They all three rode the elevator to the third floor and sat in the lobby just outside the maternity ward to wait until they heard what Pat's wishes were.

Meanwhile, Pat was sitting up in bed holding Abigail, just finishing giving her a bottle of formula, a final maternal offering. Claudia sat on the edge of the bed, enchanted with the tiny person in Pat's arms, amazed at the alert gaze on the broad little face that looked so much like one of their family. The two sisters explored the tiny hands and feet, and unwrapped Abigail's little body so they could see and touch all of her.

Outside, the pediatrician on duty that morning, who was to discharge Abigail after examining her, heard that the new parents were waiting in the lobby and went out to speak with them. This was the first private adoption he'd had anything to do with. Abigail was not even ten hours old and about to leave the hospital without her biological mother. In an attempt to reassure the new parents, whom he assumed must naturally be anxious, he began to recite a detailed list of instructions for the feeding and care of a new baby. He felt it was his responsibility as a professional to look out for Abigail's well-being and he had no idea to what kind of people he was releasing this brand-new baby. To Vicki, his instructions made it seem that her competence and judgment as an adult and a mother were being questioned, especially since her five-year-old daughter was sitting right next to her as visible proof of her qualifications.

Vicki was preparing to cut the pediatrician's monologue off mid-sentence when a familiar face appeared at the door. Don came out into the lobby and said that Pat was ready to see them. Paul quickly offered to stay out in the lobby with Amanda. Paul and Vicki had already signed innumerable documents, so they didn't have to deal with any of that now. It was the emotional material Paul was wishing to avoid. He said later, "I'm sure glad Amanda was there to give me an excuse for staying in the lobby, because I was really chicken. I knew it was going to be heavy in that room and I don't like heavy scenes. I just couldn't take Abigail and feel totally happy, knowing Pat would be left back there crying."

When Vicki went into Pat's room with Don she carried the outfit and receiving blanket she'd brought for Abigail. The papers Pat signed giving Vicki the right to take Abigail out of the hospital were attached to Pat's chart. Don had already spoken with Pat alone about Abigail and her right to change her mind. He would give her post-partum instructions later that afternoon. With nothing more to do and feeling he was more in the way than needed, he quickly withdrew from the room, leaving the women to talk and to orchestrate the exchange for themselves. Heather and I were there in the room with Claudia, Pat, Vicki and Abigail. Abigail's beauty was everyone's immediate topic for discussion. Pat did not seem to wish to talk about herself and enjoyed the focus being on the baby. She appeared relaxed and centered, in much better shape than Vicki or anyone had expected.

Sensing that Pat was ready, Vicki asked if she might change Abigail's clothes from the hospital's outfit to the one she'd brought. Pat said that was a good idea and laid her daughter on the bed. If she was braced inside for what was coming, she didn't give any appearance of being so, or of feeling either remorse or confusion over her decision. She watched Vicki dress her baby. Vicki felt the difference between last night and now. "In the labor room we'd all felt like one family. It was so warm and soft and loving. But in this room . . . This was a final parting."

Remembering those moments today, Vicki's face looks pained. Tears fill her eyes and emotion softens her features. "I was thinking about the leaving," she says quietly. "We dressed Abigail together. Then since there was nothing more to do, I picked her up and put her over my shoulder. Pat said something very simple. I think it was, 'Can I kiss her goodbye?' I said, 'Sure.' And I held Abigail out to her. Then she kissed her and said goodbye and handed her back to me. Abigail was very quiet but Pat was already starting to cry."

Vicki's voice is thick. But suddenly she shifts and her words take on their usual, quick, clipped rhythm.

"I don't think it would have helped Pat for me to cry too," she says. And so instead of stopping to comfort, Vicki quickly turned away from Pat and carried the still quiet little Abigail out of the room, down the hall, into the lobby to the eager faces and waiting arms of Amanda and Paul. Once outside, Amanda and Paul's excitement quickly submerged all thoughts of Pat back in her room. Vicki was too busy watching the way her older daughter responded to her new baby sister to think of anything else. And she was pleased with Amanda, her older daughter, with how she greeted Abigail with a quiet seriousness and insisted on holding her at once. Outside in the sunlight Amanda asked her mother to stop for a moment and show her her baby sister once more. In the back seat of their car, Vicki carefully placed Abigail in Mandy's arms.

In Pat's room the morning sunlight was spreading an indirect glow over the hospital bed. I had gone back in to see Pat after I saw Paul, Vicki, Amanda and Abigail off. Pat was sitting on the edge of the bed where I'd left her, leaning against her sister and sobbing quietly, her face covered with her hands. She had known that this would come, that she would grieve and the sooner the better, so she did nothing to attempt to stop the tears. But it wasn't more than a few minutes before she suddenly lifted up her head, wiped her eyes, displayed that same small grin she'd shown everyone in labor and I'd seen so many times before, and said quietly, "What could I say to her? How could I ask her to be good to Abigail?" Her voice cracked a bit as she added softly, "I *knew* she would be."

With those words said she lifted up her nightgown and began to examine her deflated abdomen, which had for nine months contained another life. She said nothing more for a long while. Then, as the bustle of the maternity floor went on outside the door, the two sisters began to whisper, heads together, arms entwined.

A reception party of one waited in the driveway as the family drove up—the little neighbor girl from next-door. Vicki briefly recalled the pediatrician's anxious warnings and, quickly dismissing them, she invited Sarah to come and peek at Amanda's new baby sister. It was the beginning of Abigail's second social whirl. Vicki couldn't believe what a stir they'd created. By lunch time they had been visited by the entire school-age population of the neighborhood.

And so they settled into the turbulence of a household with a new baby. Rituals began to order their lives. Paul recalls, "Since I do the night feedings around here, after two the next morning Abigail already felt like mine. I damn near missed the very first feeding, though, she made so little noise. We had her bed in the den across from our bedroom. I woke up and heard cooing in the dark. When I walked into her room she was lying on her back in the Port-A-Crib with her eyes wide open, looking very content." Abigail seemed at ease in her new home from the first.

One week later the newborn pictures that had been taken at the hospital nursery arrived in the mail. They were a lovely surprise. Since Abigail only spent half a dozen nighttime hours in the nursery the photographer must have worked quickly. The baby in the pictures looked indistinguishable from a million other babies except for the broad, flat cheeks that were unmistakably her mother's. The five miniature pictures were a reminder of the brief, intense time they'd shared with Pat at Abigail's birth. Vicki was surprised to discover that the pictures had been sent by Pat herself, who had carefully filled in the accompanying card with the time of birth and Abigail's weight and length. In the space marked "Baby's Name," she had written simply "Abigail." Where blanks were left marked "Parents," she'd written her own name. There was one print missing from the group. Pat had kept that for herself, one tiny remembrance of the dark-eyed, round-cheeked little baby who looked so much like her but who now brightened the lives of three other people.

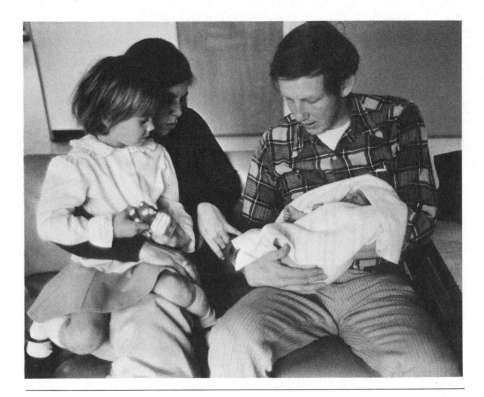

Paul and Vicki showing Amanda her new baby sister, Abigail

Adoptive Parents

Paul and Vicki have never seen themselves as different from any other parents, adoptive or not. Paul found that any initial reluctance he felt about raising another man's offspring quickly evaporated in the day-to-day business of diapering, soothing, carrying and caring for Amanda. "I think I was bamboozled when I was told how different it would be raising a child who wasn't part of me genetically. I don't know how long it takes and how difficult it is to bond to a child who enters your life after infancy; but I *certainly* know there is a bond this way. Amanda and Abby are mine and have been since almost the first week we had them. Cleaning up vomit in the middle of the night, you soon make no distinction about whose genes that baby has."

Vicki agrees. "Even with Amanda, and we didn't have her until she was three days old, I feel she is *my* child. The thing that matters, when one of them is being a brat and doing something I find totally unacceptable, is that she is *my* brat! What's genetic is genetic and I accept that. But the rest, whatever external circumstances have made her the way she is, that's *us*, Paul and me. I think it *must* be easier growing up with an infant. I can't sit back and complain, 'Somebody must have traumatized her before she came to us and that's why she is the way she is.' I think we are fortunate they were both so healthy from birth. I'm egocentric enough to look at each of them and think, 'That's *my* child and she is perfect.' "

Vicki is not talking about ownership, but about a deep sense her daughters are part of her. This is what is meant by the term "bonding" and it is the strength of this parent-child love that holds families together through traumatic times and protects the lives of small children while they are dependent upon their parents for providing for all their needs. Society could do a lot more than it now does to support the bonds of affection between parents and their children. But nature provides its own special bonding between parent and newborn infant, and Paul and Vicki benefited from their early intimate contacts with Amanda and Abigail.

In retrospect, both Paul and Vicki feel that they also benefited from the long anxious process of Vicki's trying to become pregnant, their lengthy agency search and the wait until the attorney and Vicki's doctor found babies for them. The waiting, searching process gave them time to grow and adjust to change. Paul is sure it helped them to feel so attached to their chilren so soon and so easily.

"I think if we'd gotten a child right away, when we first went to the agencies, it would actually have been more difficult for us to adjust to becoming parents. It seems important to take the time to get emotionally ready for the disruptions in your life which come with a child, rather than having to do it afterward. One thing is for sure, when Vicki walked off the plane carrying Amanda in her arms, even though I had never seen her before, she was ours, and I didn't feel any strangeness toward her at all."

It remains to be seen just how their two daughters will feel when they are older—about having been adopted, about the manner in which they came to Paul and Vicki. Those feelings are likely to be mixed and to bubble up to the surface as they grow. At least Paul and Vicki are comfortable with that fact. They have never felt they had to apologize to Amanda and Abigail or to protect them from even painful truth.

In answer to Amanda's question, when she was four years old, "Mom, did I grow in your tummy?" Vicki remembers answering, "No, dear, you didn't. You grew in another woman's tummy; but she couldn't take care of you and she gave you to us, because we couldn't make a baby and wanted to very much." Children absorb and process information like this at very individual rates. When she was seven, at the dinner table Amanda asked another question out of the blue. "How old was my mother when I was born?" Vicki again answered with only the briefest hesitation, "Your mother was twenty-one." Amanda then asked, "Why didn't our mothers keep us?" A dinner table discussion followed, first about Amanda's mother and father and their circumstances, then about

Pat, her having no partner and no money and being just seventeen. In each case Vicki emphasized that "your mothers weren't ready." That was really all Amanda asked to hear. Her next question was, "What's for dessert, Mom?" She may turn the new information over for a while before more questions surface. She is a child. That is her style.

For Abby it might be different. Such conversation might go unnoticed by her for a time more but the words are familiar and out in the open. There are many children in her neighborhood, including her big sister, who found a family the same way she did, through adoption. To her this is a normal way to begin life. She likes to have her parents read the little books about children who are adopted. These books have been around the house since Amanda came. One is even about a little girl named Abby. "Let's read about Abby," Abigail will say; sometimes she adds, "She's adopted, just like me!"

Abigail, at age six, has a distinctive and a passionate temperament. She is both enchanting and trying for her parents. Her short, sturdy legs and big, blue, luminous eyes have carried her into many kinds of mischief. She is hardly ever still and is fearless in the face of each new adventure. She has had an explosive temper since she was just a few weeks old and, though it doesn't trigger easily, it is impossible to ignore once it is unleashed. Paul was its victim on a number of occasions when she was young.

"Abigail was a hellion! If she didn't get her way she screamed, she kicked, she hollered. One morning, when she was two, she wouldn't put the caps back on the marking pens she was using. I said, 'Abigail, if you won't put the caps back on the pens, you don't get to use them. I'll take them away from you.' She lay right down on the floor and started screaming and beating the floor with her fists. When she got that way she was utterly helpless. So I just picked her up and laid her down on the couch in the living room as she continued to scream. She lay there screaming for a full twenty minutes more before suddenly it stopped. Then she just got up and went back to playing."

Paul and Vicki have worked consciously at helping Abigail gain some control over her violent outbursts. They have sometimes wondered whether she inherited this trait. But Abigail is theirs now and they accept the angry part of her along with the rest. Like the proverbial little girl with the little curl right in the middle of her forehead, Abigail has been a child of extremes. But most often she is a generous, outgoing, affectionate child whose little body, right from birth, would softly melt against anyone who held her. Paul is understanding of her extreme swings in mood. She has a lot in common with his own temperament.

"When bedtime comes, for example, there is never a fight, if I've gauged her right and she's ready to sleep. From when she was just an infant in her crib, she has always loved to sleep surrounded by her stuffed animals. She would sit up in bed and play for maybe an hour or more, until she finally fell asleep, and all the while she will be talking nonstop to her animals, singing and having a wonderful time. I used to stand outside her door and listen to her babble. It was so beautiful I could listen all night." And there are other traits he loves. "Abigail always had such gentle hands. She always picked things up just so, right from when she was a baby. She never broke anything; yet she was so curious."

Such is the patchwork pattern of being a parent. For Paul and Vicki, especially for Vicki, being parents has both altered and enriched their lives. They hardly ever think about the mother and father each of the girls left behind at birth. They are well aware of the pain that giving up a child can create. At some point, paths have to separate, and that is always a time for pain and loss for those we leave behind. For them and the girls' birth mothers separation came right at birth. There was no discussion of a future relationship. The possibility was left open. Paul and Vicki are reassured by the thought that each of the women was very young and had time to start again. One day, perhaps, there will be a phone call or a knock on the door and then their paths will cross again. And it will be right.

Some people claim that the detailed information Paul and Vicki hold about their daughters' biological parents will only cause hurt if it is given out to adoptees, at any age. It is a moot question whether open files create a desire in the adoptee to know his or her roots, or whether a system where knowledge is denied actually ensures an insatiable thirst for knowing more. Vicki's views on that question are based on her own experiences in adoption.

"I think if you *can* know something, then your need to know is not so great. A woman came from the county agency to visit us just after we got Abigail, to see whether, according to law, we were considered 'suit-

Abigail at age two, holding her favorite teddy bear

able' to be parents. She seemed very interested in our experience in open adoption and wanted to know whether we thought that meeting the birth parents and keeping the records open was a good idea. She told me our county adoption agency was just beginning to get the first crop of grown-up adoptees coming in and asking for their birth files. She said it's *incredible,* the need to know that these people have."

Paul and Vicki know much more than the average adoptive parent today about their children's heritage and the decision-making the biological parents went through in choosing to place them for adoption. They have memories to share with each other and with their daughters when they choose, and the files for Amanda and Abigail are accessible to them and, more important, to the girls as they grow. All information in them is considered theirs and they own it.

There is still much they do not know. For example, though there is a letter from Amanda's mother in her file, a letter that shows her caring, they know almost nothing about her. Both Paul and Vicki find it disturbing that the woman who carried and nourished Amanda through gestation and labored to give birth to her may not have done so with full consent. They have reason to believe that the mother only gave her written consent under pressure from her husband, that he was the decision-maker in the family. Does she know that the baby she carried so long was in perfect health? Whether she was even told the sex of her baby, they don't know. "We only know she was twenty-one years old, that this was his second marriage, and they'd been married just ten months when Amanda was born. We also know that the father had three boys from his first marriage who were living then with his ex-wife and that he was committed to paying monthly child support plus a large alimony." Paul and Vicki were told she tried to get an abortion but it was illegal then to have one in their home state and by the time they went to a neighboring state where it was legal, they discovered they had waited too long.

For all Vicki knows, that mother still has regret and longing. With Pat, she feels differently. She is certain that Pat made her own decisions. She could and did look Pat in the eyes and she could see for herself that there was a bond of trust between them. To be sure, there are blanks in Abigail's history, especially with regard to her biological father and his medical history. According to Pat he had no reason to suspect there is now a child in the world because of him. Pat has yet to search for him and let him know of Abby's existence. Paul and Vicki were cautious about pushing Pat in locating the father because they are sensitive to her feelings and the painful memories she probably still carries of her very first sexual encounter, but Abigail, they feel, has a right to know who her father is and a need to have a complete medical history. The father too may have a legal as well as an ethical right to know about the existence of Abigail. Paul and Vicki can be patient for the time being. Their girls are still young. They have heard from a mutual friend that even before Pat left California she had already considered trying to track down the father. Given her nature, which is thoughtful and responsible, they have every reason to believe she will one day do this for Abigail and place the information in Abigail's file or send it directly to them.

Every parent hopes for a child that is healthy and there is no better way to guarantee a healthy baby than to know the mother is in good health, has a positive attitude toward pregnancy and gave birth without taking medication or anesthesia. Paul and Vicki were witnesses to Pat's state of health at the end of the pregnancy. Beyond that, all they could hope for was that she had cared for herself adequately during the emotionally traumatic early months. They do know that Abigail came into the world conscious and alert. She was birthed by a mother who had prepared for natural childbirth, who did not inhibit her labor and the supply of oxygen to the baby by fear and tension. Paul and Vicki were there. That is how they know. They knew their daughter was probably not traumatized by anything done to her while she was in the hospital. She could feel safe and loved from her very first experiences with people outside the womb. The room was full of friends, and she was welcomed by Pat as well as everyone else there, stroked and held and marveled at from the first moment. She was never left to lie for days in the hospital nursery in a plastic bed under the glare of lights with her care shared by dozens of strangers, which is the fate of many babies prior to placement. She was never passed out to a foster home to be cared for by a surrogate, then taken away to yet another home with still different faces, unfamiliar odors and sounds. Indeed, there is much Paul and Vicki can look back upon and be proud of.

There will be more for them to know, more for both girls to discover. Paul and Vicki do not plan to throw everything open to them at once. While they will support any search either of the girls initiates, at this time they feel that they will set the structure and guidelines when that day comes. Vicki plans to insist that the girls go through a third person, such as Phil Adams, for the initial contact with their biological parents. She expresses this in terms of protecting the parents' right to privacy, even to remain hidden if they choose to do so. Perhaps when they are actually confronted by a tearful daughter of, say, sixteen, who desires to search and comes up against a wall, their loyalty to the biological parents might change, but not now.

Has Pat's knowing their address and did her having lived so near them for such a time following the birth—more than a year, off and on—create a threat to their own security? No, they say, nor have they any worry about trouble from that quarter in the future. They trust Pat not to change from the person they came to know before, during and after the birth—honest and considerate. They expect she might contact them periodically, perhaps may even want to see Abigail from time to time, though they have not seen or heard directly from her since she sent them the newborn pictures of Abigail.

They feel that planning ahead for various possibilities helps. Vicki has even imagined a scene where Pat, unannounced, arrives at her door one day and asks whether she might see Abigail. Paul has doubts whether he would give in to such a request, but Vicki suspects she might just invite Pat into the house, welcome her as a friend and tell Abigail who she is. Such a scenario would frighten and outrage many adoptive parents today, and might have sent waves of mistrust and fear through Paul and Vicki several years ago. But they have grown to trust in their capacity to face whatever comes to them.

Direct adoption fostered a realistic attitude in Paul and Vicki toward their daughters. They were never able to pretend the biological parents did not exist or that there would be no future encounters with them. They were never offered a guarantee of protection in the way state and private agencies in the past have made promises to adoptive parents and biological parents alike that files would remain closed and identities hidden. Without an agency acting as an umbrella over them, shielding them from knowledge and the possible future consequences, they were able to grow into each new step, first meeting Pat, then being present at

Abigail's birth, then taking their child directly from the hands of Pat, and finally preparing for possible meetings or relationships in the future. Their attorney might have acted as a protective shield in the same way the agency system is set up to do. They could have asked for that and found an attorney who would have behaved like a guardian. But what is important is that there was nothing in the legal structure of private adoption to make secrecy or paternalism a requirement. Flexibility is in the nature of private adoption and it is up to everyone involved to determine how loosely or tightly they wish to construct their arrangement. Independent adoption assumes a respect for the parents, biological *and* adoptive, that *they* know what is best for themselves and for the child.

Those who support the standard adoption claim it protects everyone involved by always keeping files closed and sometimes by placing the child in foster care until the birth parents have relinquished all legal rights. Since Paul and Vicki not only met Pat before the birth but actually had Abigail in their custody for the entire six-month period before the decree of adoption was granted by the court, they had to live with a measure of risk every day. At any time in those six months Pat had the legal right to change her mind and ask for Abigail back. If that happened, short of legally proving her total unfitness to be a mother, there would be nothing they could do. Only by accepting this risk as part of the ground rules were they able to participate in the birth and start life with Abigail from the beginning. And they feel strongly that they saved her from unnecessary trauma by taking her directly from Pat's arms. This is what made the risk worth it. It has already been shown that promises made in the past cannot guarantee laws will not change to erase those promises. Adoption is full of risks and uncertainties. But Paul and Vicki are at least prepared to expect change, which adoptive parents in standard closed-file, agency-directed adoptions may not be prepared for.

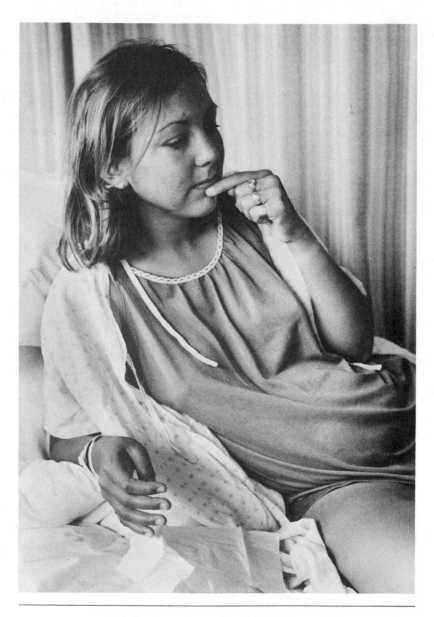

Pat's first hour alone after Abigail has gone.

Grief

When Abigail was carried from Pat's room at the hospital Pat's entire life shifted once more. She was no longer the young woman with the swollen abdomen of whom everyone felt protective. She was just Pat, a girl grown up too quickly, facing an uncertain future and a new beginning out on her own in the world.

Most women in modern societies do some mourning after giving birth. Some mourn the loss of their pregnant status and the attention it brought them. Some mourn the loss of being pregnant, particularly those for whom pregnancy was a heightened feeling of well-being, a special robustness. Some mourn the attention and kindness they received from those who cared for them at the birthing but which disappeared once birth was over. Some mourn their loss of dignity in giving birth and suffer from feelings of humiliation which traditional childbirth practices too often bring today, the loss of the dream that birth could be a miraculous experience. Some mourn the loss of independence, in having to be responsible now for another's life. There is usually something to grieve for amidst the headiness of new motherhood.

Pat had many things to mourn, above all the loss of Abigail. Only a mother who has lost a child can know this sort of sorrow. But it had been Pat's choosing and the bitterness of her loss was eased by the knowledge that she had done what she felt was best, and had done it out of love for her child and understanding of a child's needs and her own lacks.

She did not have to grieve over the birth. It was simple, uncomplicated and spontaneous; she had been surrounded by loving people. But now life moved back to its normal pace. It was all over so suddenly, that which had taken most of a year to build to climax.

All the people who had been so solicitous of Pat's welfare and on behalf of the life she carried were now busy with others. She couldn't expect to take the same place in their lives now that she had given birth. Her birth educator had new classes of pregnant couples to think about, her physician other pregnant women to absorb his attention. Even her sister and brother had other things to return to. Much as they loved and were concerned about their sister, they could no longer set aside their own needs.

Pat left the hospital with Claudia and Eddie only a few hours after Abigail did. It was in the apartment she did her grieving during its most acute phase, alone and in private. Those first weeks were a particularly solitary and dark time in Pat's life. She never had been one to talk very much about herself; it had always been nearly impossible to draw anything from her that she didn't want to share. So Claudia and Eddie could only watch the unenviable process of grieving and healing that her body and mind had to go through. She seldom left the apartment and spent most of her waking hours in her nightgown.

Milk filled her breasts right on schedule, despite the medication to suppress the flow, then was slowly reabsorbed as her body realized that there was no need for it. But this took time—and swollen, tender, hard breasts were for several days painful reminders of the loss of Abigail. The bloody lochia, discharged remains of the placenta, still had to flow from her body. Her uterus had to remain firm in order to grow steadily smaller. Without a baby in arms and at the breast to stimulate the release of hormones to do this shrinking naturally, Pat had been told that she would have to massage her abdomen frequently every day until she could no longer feel the hard round mass underneath her navel.

There was no longer that living, moving being inside her with whom Pat could converse. She could only talk to herself now and have conversations in her head. She belonged to no group of women like her with whom she might have shared feelings. There was in her case no loving parent to turn to, no chance to place her head on a comforting lap and sob and be held for as long and as often as it took. Claudia would gladly have filled this role but, except for the few hours immediately after Abigail left the hospital, Pat would not unburden herself to her sister.

She lived some miles from all the people to whom she had grown close in the past weeks. She had no car to get around in and made no effort to reach out for companionship. There was so much to go over in her mind. The sensations inside her body heralded its drawing inward, shifting the balance of weight on her spine back to its pre-pregnant state. Pat had to regain her balance more ways than physically. Everyone gave her a lot of space in those weeks—perhaps too much, but she would never be the one to say so. She'd never been one to criticize, any more than she was one to ask for help. Perhaps that was why she found herself daydreaming about going back to Florida, though it was only a few weeks after the birth and she had hardly begun to heal. Life without pregnancy, without Abigail, didn't hold much for her in her new home and the void loomed large inside her.

When I visited Pat late one morning about a week after the birth, I found her in her nightgown, sitting slackly on the edge of the couch. Her shoulders were hunched and her hair was uncombed. There wasn't much I could say. Pat herself had said that life after birthing would be difficult, especially because she'd made no plans. But that realization had come such a short time before the onset of labor there had been no time to begin to dream and make plans for herself. All that had waited till she had come back home to the dingy, empty apartment, where Claudia and Eddie went off to work each morning and left her alone with nothing but her thoughts. She made no apologies for her appearance, her lack of animation or conversation, and I asked nothing of her. I merely wanted to see how she was getting along, to let her know I and others were thinking of her, to sit with her.

Pat may have been hoping to hear how Abigail was doing, to hear that Paul and Vicki were taking fine care of her. Her arms may have ached to hold Abigail, to hold anyone. She never said so. All she did say was there were days when it hurt a lot. She knew she could have phoned Paul and Vicki or written them. She had their address. They lived only a few miles away; but when she sent baby pictures to them, she chose not to include a note. When I said goodbye, hugging her softly and reminding her I would love to hear from her at any time, she thanked me for coming and said she was fine, really. Those were the same words she told her physician when he had phoned each day during the first week after the birth.

When she returned to his office for her scheduled post-partum visit a month later, well-dressed and looking slim and a bit tanned, she smiled and told everyone there she was fine. She also said she was leaving. Abigail had come and gone only six weeks before, yet Pat had made the decision to go home at once. Everyone to whom she told this news begged her to wait at least a little longer, to give herself more time in peace before moving back into her parents' home. There was no rush. She needed very little money to live on. Why not get a part-time job nearby, spend time walking in the sun, visit museums, go to the beach, have dinner with friends? But it was as if she couldn't bear the quiet of her days and the calm of her life now. So used as she had been to being in the center of a storm, to years of fighting the authority of parents and school, and recently to the mounting excitement of the final months before the birth, that the time after Abigail was too quiet. She did not take our suggestion that it might be better first to spend some time in counseling, to resolve some of her feelings about her home life and the birth and Abigail's adoption, before going home. Instead, she waited only until several of us had left town for summer vacation. Then she packed up her few belongings and slipped from sight. She left behind on my answering machine a short message. She was going home. She was sorry she couldn't say goodbye to anyone in person but she hated good-byes and she just had to go.

It was nearly six months before she wrote to anyone but Claudia and Eddie. Her letter to me was brief. She said things were difficult back at home, but didn't explain. She was working at an office job and still living with her parents. Her letter had a wistful tone but no self-pity. Life, it seemed, was what it had always been for Pat, a continual struggle to feel good about herself in the face of constant criticism and her own guilt. She did say that the people who were around her during the last months of her pregnancy and for her birthing still meant a great deal to her. She said also that it had been very hard to endure the kind attention she had gotten from everyone. Why was she the recipient of so much kindness? Surely, she implied, she didn't deserve it. How could she ever repay everyone for all they'd given her? She didn't know but she hoped there would be a way. Perhaps, she wrote, she might become a childbirth educator and work with other young pregnant women and pass along the help she'd received from others and some new-found insight. It wasn't until I got her telephone number from Claudia and phoned her that Pat mentioned Abigail to anyone. She said she would like to know how Abigail was doing and how Paul and Vicki and Amanda were. I was able to tell her, because I'd seen them recently, that they were all doing well.

In the spring Pat wrote once more. She was thinking, she said, of coming back. Claudia was no longer at the old apartment—she'd taken a job in a Montessori school in the Virgin Islands, where Pat had just visited her for a month. But Eddie was still around, and she supposed they could get an apartment together.

She didn't call me or anyone until she'd been in town nearly a month, and had found work and a place to live with Eddie. When she did call we made a date to meet at her physician's office downtown on her lunch hour. I arrived a few minutes late, opened the door into the waiting room and looked around. Across the room someone rose from a chair. I hardly recognized her. She was wearing heels and a sleeveless printed cotton dress that was open at the neck. Her bare legs and arms were smooth-skinned, just as I'd remembered, but a richer nutlike brown than I'd ever seen them. I'd never imagined how exotic Pat could look when she was tanned and feeling good. I'd never seen her glowing, supple and slim. I couldn't take my eyes off her. We hadn't seen each other in nearly a year. I was looking at a lovely poised young woman but in my mind I was seeing Pat the way she'd first looked when she arrived at my door, the way she'd looked at birth, the grace and dignity with which she'd relinquished Abigail and the way she looked in her grief.

She was dressed for job interviews. She had taken work with a temporary-help agency to get quick money. She had her own car now, Claudia's old blue one. She wanted me to know from the outset that she hadn't come back to try and connect with Abigail or Paul and Vicki. She didn't even ask how Abigail was, though she must have known I would still be in touch with Paul and Vicki and could have told her anything she wanted to know. It was clear that she didn't intend to live around the edges of Abigail's life. She'd returned simply because she missed the ease she'd felt when she had lived here.

The one bright spot of time during the year back home had been the month she'd spent away, with Claudia in the Virgin Islands. That, she said, was the most peaceful period of her life, the first time she felt whole and right with the world from when she woke up in the morning until she fell asleep at night. The warm sun, the friendliness of the islanders, the bubbling laughter and play of the children at the Montessori school, it all added up to a taste of paradise. Her experience on the island left her changed and wanting more: more peace, more time and a chance to explore life and express herself without pressure. But there were very few jobs to be had and Pat had few skills, so when her visit came to an end she'd decided to return to school. And so she had returned to California, because here was a place she felt she had been accepted for who she *wanted* to be, as well as for who she was. She said she hoped to learn some job skills and to prepare herself for going back to Florida in the future, where she thought she would like to teach young children.

Pat found work soon, in the billing department of a small company, and within a month had charmed the entire office with her wry wit and her ability to do her job while being able to laugh off every annoyance. After several months she was promoted to head of the payroll department. She was only nineteen years old.

At the end of summer Pat enrolled in a course. An institute in San Francisco offered a one-year program in childbirth education. She thought she would like to help other pregnant young women have good experiences in birth. The school brought her in touch with a small group of women from all around the country, many of whom hoped to become midwives. They were mostly young, but Pat was the youngest— though by no means the youngest in experience. This group of women and their instructors formed a kind of family for each other during the next year. Pat had to drive an hour each way to get to class, while most of the other students had found housing and jobs near the institute. Her full-time job, the long commute, living apart from everyone else, didn't offer her much chance to socialize; but the education proved nourishing. She was there to learn how to support and counsel around a very important time in a woman's life. It was considered essential that the students do a lot of introspective work in order to be sensitive to other people. Several of the classes were run as seminars whose purposes were interaction as a group and self-discovery. Pat found herself in an environment like none she'd ever known, a place where it was not only safe to explore feelings but where such exploration was encouraged and supported by everyone. During the next six months she found herself going back to her experience of pregnancy, looking at things she'd never faced herself or told anyone, and also going back to her lonely childhood and her confined life under her parents' harsh control.

After months in this environment where there was no competition Pat slowly found herself able to trust what was happening. At first she found it difficult to find any strong emotions inside, so used was she to using her mind to shield herself from her feelings. In class whenever things became very confrontational or conversation turned to her, she would retreat into a familiar "spaciness," watch herself as from a distance, and listen to what words came out of her mouth as if they didn't belong to her but to a stranger. But she stuck with it, attending every seminar and class despite the frustration of often being the only one in the room who could find nothing "inside" of which to speak. Somewhere she'd found the inner strength to get through life thus far. Now she could take some time to examine how her defenses had helped and how they now inhibited her.

Pat liked to credit everyone but herself with her gains. She wanted the group to know it hadn't been she, Pat, who had found the strength to give up her child out of love for her. She attributed a special power to Abigail as she grew inside her, and called her the source of the strength, saying it had been Abigail who'd kept her from harming herself during the early months of pregnancy. She had felt Abigail's presence all along. "If Abby could survive all my doubts about wanting her and my smoking early in pregnancy, even the circumstances of her conception, then she must be a special spirit." She described feeling as if her life in pregnancy had been a cresting wave, rushing headlong to crash on the shore—until she'd found supports: friends, parents for her baby, a physician for herself and the baby, and an attorney who helped her create the kind of adoption she'd dreamed of. It was others who had given her the necessary strength to balance on the crest of the wave and ride it through without crashing.

She talked on many occasions about how strange and embarrassing it had been to be the recipient of so much kindness and attention. Yet that had been what made it possible for her to do what was "right." What she had been striving for above all else had been to do what was

Pat, two years after Abigail's birth

"right," what Jesus might have done in the same circumstances. Feeling certain she was doing the best for Abigail was what had sustained her through the end of the pregnancy, made the last weeks a happy time, and carried her through labor and birth and through her grief. Only once or twice was she able to put her head on the lap of a classmate and cry. But the friends she made in school made her feel so welcome and comfortable that she found she could go to them with her pain. She still missed Abigail deeply. But giving her up to Paul and Vicki was something she had no regrets about, just an aching in her most private places inside. And time, she found, was softening the memory of what she had given up, blurring the edges, soothing the aching.

I talked to Pat often and could see the growth she was making. There was one thing I felt I wanted to offer her. Although she had given birth herself, had been fully awake and conscious through it, she had never had the chance to see what birth *could* be—when the joy is not mixed with sadness. I asked her if she might like to come to a birth with me sometime, as an extra support for the family, not just an onlooker. Since she was planning to work with women who were going to give birth, it would provide valuable experience for that as well. She was excited at the idea.

The next birth I was asked to photograph seemed appropriate for Pat to attend. The woman was having her second baby at home with midwives. She had invited her own parents and her sister to be present and hoped her two-year-old daughter could be there too. She appreciated the offer of another woman to help with the little girl and said she also could use a little extra support herself in labor. Labor began late one evening. I called Pat and she was at home. We drove the hour to the house together and talked about what she was going to witness, how she might be of help. I hadn't needed to prepare her at all. Once inside the home Pat went and sat on the couch next to the woman, who was resting. As I took out my cameras and talked to the midwives and the little girl and her father, I watched Pat slip unself-consciously into the role of support person. Soon she was stroking the woman's forehead during contractions, breathing with her, giving her a back rub.

Labor went on slowly all night. At dawn the grandparents arrived with their younger daughter. Pat moved from supporting the laboring woman, who now had two midwives and her husband to be with her, to supporting the grandmother, who was nervous and anxious for her daughter's well-being.

When the baby was finally born the two-year-old was sitting curled in her grandfather's lap, and the woman was sitting against her husband, and the grandmother had her hands clasped tightly together and Pat's arm protectively around her. Everyone shed tears of relief and delight. Pat was ecstatic. She bubbled about the birth all the way home and she knew her presence there had made a difference for that family. It must have rekindled memories of her own experience and all the love and support she had around her through labor and afterward. She said she couldn't wait to go to another birth, to be at another woman's side during labor.

At the end of the winter semester Pat made the decision to return to Florida once again. This time she was sure things would be different. Her parents had left for an extended vacation, so Pat could stay in the empty house. She enrolled in a week-long childbirth educator workshop in Atlanta as a stop on her journey. When she returned home this time she would have a certificate as a childbirth educator, part of her dream to return to Florida bringing some skills she could offer women and babies in her community.

Abigail was almost two when Pat left. Before leaving, Pat remarked that had she been pregnant *now*, she thought she would have made a different decision about Abigail. *Now* she felt ready to be a parent.

Pat's life is very different today from what it would have been if she had chosen to keep Abby. She has had the time to experiment a bit, to learn more about trusting men, to learn about herself as a woman, in her strength and her vulnerability. She is learning to view herself with compassion. She has learned about herself as a sexual person as well. And she has done all of this without subjecting a young child to the difficult process of her own growing up. True, she could have grown too through the raising of Abby, though it would have been a forced maturity and hard on both of them. Abby would have borne the brunt of Pat's inexperience and youth. That may be the way many of us have been raised and have gone on to raise our own children, especially a first child. But who among us would say it is the best or even the only way?

Today Pat is a woman, a woman who still carries an old picture of a new baby in her wallet. The pregnancy, the birth, holding Abigail in her arms, these were momentous events in her life; but they were neither the end nor the peak experience. They were in fact a beginning. It was a strange and difficult initiation into adulthood but nevertheless a way in which Pat discovered herself while doing her best not to hurt a child in the process. And because her decision brightened the lives of two other people who were in the position to be good parents, who would call what she did a mistake?

Pat could be your daughter. She could even be you or me. You would, I think, be proud of her. Pat chose not to use having a baby as an answer to her own personal problems and she has chosen not to try and fill the hole Abby left by having another baby before growing up herself. She has a past she can be proud of and a future to look forward to. She is on her way.

Katherine, two weeks before she gives birth

A Conscious Choice

Katherine was twenty-one years old and eight months pregnant. I had never met her but heard from friends she had a serenity about her that did not seem to fit with her decision to give her baby up for adoption at birth. Unlike Pat she was not a teenager, nor was she unprepared for the responsibility of having sexual intercourse. At a time when most of her high school friends were already having their second child, Katherine was choosing not to be a mother. People who met her casually found it difficult to comprehend why she should have made the decision she did and some were quite unsympathetic. But Katherine isn't living her life for the benefit of other people's opinions. She takes the requirements of parenthood seriously and she also has her own dreams, which she intends to pursue. Pregnancy simply caught her off guard and totally unprepared. She wrote in her diary, "It's funny because I was pregnant once before, when I was sixteen and had just begun having sex. I think I'm pretty aware of my body. Yet I didn't even consider I might be pregnant this time." Katherine's periods had always been irregular, so she didn't worry about missing one. She had always used a diaphragm on the few occasions she'd had intercourse. That is how it was possible for her to be ten weeks pregnant before she even went for the test that confirmed the pregnancy. And by that time the young man involved was nowhere to be reached.

The first person she told was her roommate, Linda, a young woman her age who was also single, with whom she shared a cottage near downtown. She was relieved to tell someone but it was still a tremendous blow, just one more in a series of blows over the last few months. First her grandfather's death, then a bicycle accident, which sent her to the hospital with a severe concussion. And now she was pregnant!

There was no doubt in her mind who the father was. She had been celibate for over a year until she started a relationship with a graduate student two years older than she. Their brief and intensely romantic affair had hardly begun. They had been seeing each other steadily for over a month, drawing closer and closer in the magic of new love, and they'd let their feelings build long before making love. A few long passionate nights together was all they'd had before he left for a month of field work in Nicaragua. They planned to continue seeing each other as soon as he returned; but this month apart was an opportunity for each of them to take a break from the breathless intensity. They were both cautious people in relationships and no vows of love had been exchanged.

Katherine had begun feeling odd even before their last day together. She had written in her diary, "I feel strange things inside me. I'm so afraid to feel this intensely about him, afraid I'll lose myself. I've cancelled our date. I want to spend more time with Linda. She always has been the one I can trust. I'm looking forward to the time he'll be away. I have to sort things out." He was due back after the new year. That would give Katherine enough time to go home to her family in Utah for Christmas, and time to think.

They had never talked about what to do if she got pregnant because they both were so careful about birth control. One thing she'd liked about him right off had been that before they ever made love *he'd* brought up the subject. He told her she should let him know if she ever wanted him to use protection instead of her. It only made the pregnancy seem even more unreal. But unreal or not, Katherine would have to make some very hard decisions and there was no partner to share the process with her. She would bear the responsibility alone.

In relationships even the best of beginnings still need time and freedom from external pressure to deepen. Unplanned pregnancy at this stage left Katherine feeling hopeless about their chances for a future together. Since he'd said he would be moving from town to town for a few weeks and would send up an address as soon as he got settled somewhere, as far as her needs were concerned he was nowhere. "Anyway," she told her friend Linda, "like it or not, I am a woman. *I* am the one who ends up carrying this life."

It was only right that he should know, and had he been within reach his participation might have changed her most basic decisions about the pregnancy. But she could not live in dreams of "might" and "if only." At ten weeks, it was already quite late to begin thinking about whether to keep the pregnancy or not. Without thinking about what it meant, Katherine made an appointment at a clinic for an abortion. Later she was to say, "I did it automatically. I thought, 'I should do this before I go home so I can use Christmas to recuperate.' But all the time I was on the telephone making the appointment, I had a feeling inside I couldn't quite define."

Alone that evening she sat with her feelings, and her own answer was there. "It was clear, the clearest, most absolute thing I've felt in my life. I just could *not* do it. I've had one abortion already and I believe in it as an option; but I had this overwhelming sense that this child wanted to live."

The decision to have an abortion for the first pregnancy had been made in a different set of circumstances. Although only sixteen at the time, she had shown maturity in being able to act in her own defense, by not pretending that pregnancy would solve her need for love. She was a child and she knew it; and she had no business thinking about raising a child of her own. Even then abortion had brought up feelings of remorse but hard reality meant making a painful decision. "That time it was a matter of survival, my survival. This time was different. I'm much stronger now. To have an abortion now feels like murder."

She'd made her decision, the first in a long series. If abortion was unconscionable, then Katherine knew she was choosing by default to carry the pregnancy to its conclusion, a baby. "That was my first decision. Not 'I'm going to be a parent,' but 'I'm going to have a baby.'"

She was taking things in proper sequence. Choosing to keep the pregnancy did not necessitate being a single mother. Whether or not to keep the baby and what to do if she did were separate and distinct choices that needed to be taken one at a time. Whatever she did was bound to affect the possibility of any future relationship with the young man she cared so much for. It might even destroy it. She spent the rest of the evening thinking in a rational manner. The next morning she walked into Linda's room and told her the decision she'd made.

"I said, 'I can't believe it, but I'm going to have this child!' Linda looked hard at me and then said she'd sensed that was what I would decide."

From the moment she knew she would be giving birth Katherine began searching her memory for anything she might have done or not done during the first ten weeks that could possibly have damaged the growing fetus. She had smoked marijuana several times in the early weeks when her stomach was upset and she was feeling so confused. It had helped her to relax. Would that cause damage to the baby later? She hoped not. She recalled several times when she'd taken laxatives. Could that? She'd studied some biology in school and knew the brain and nervous system, fingers and toes all were formed in the first weeks. She regretted that she hadn't known she was pregnant when she'd taken drugs, but there was nothing she could do about that now.

She cancelled the appointment to discuss abortion the day after she made it. Instead, a few days later she bought a train ticket to Utah, packed a few things, and left town, feeling very pregnant and very ill. That journey, thirty hours of enforced solitude, altered the course of her life.

"I was so sick I sat up the entire trip. I had the worst cold I've ever had. I was nauseated morning, noon and night. My nose ran constantly and I was in absolute misery. I'd already entertained the idea of being a mother, of raising this child. I say 'entertained' because it didn't seem any more real than that, like some picture on a postcard of a place I'd never been. I would be thinking of something else and suddenly my mind would snap back and I would realize, 'I am going to be a mother! Every minute of every day will be radically different.' "

With no distractions and nothing to do but watch and think, Katherine used the train ride to observe mothers and their children and to notice every detail of their interactions.

"There was one family with three kids sitting in front of me. The children were shouting and running up and down the aisle, whining and complaining to their parents, who seemed patient beyond belief. There was another woman with a very young baby sitting alone across the aisle. Watching all of them through my own physical misery, the romantic image I had of me as the young mother, caring for, holding, feeding and constantly being with this child, suddenly disappeared. I found myself thinking of all the other things I want to do in my life, the things

I've already postponed, which I would have to put off further to be a good mother to an infant. Could I go back to school with a baby? What kind of job could I get? What would the two of us do, day after day, together?"

The train pulled into the station in Salt Lake City at 5:30 a.m. and Katherine's father was there waiting to meet her. She'd pictured herself standing at the edge of the track as the train pulled away telling her father that she was pregnant and planned to have the baby. He would have his arms around her and she would be leaning against his shoulder. Their reunion did not go as she had planned.

"Instead my dad looked at me strangely as I got off and asked how I was and I just couldn't tell him. My face was all puffy from no sleep, my nose was red and I must have been fifteen pounds heavier than when he'd last seen me. And all I could say was, 'I'm fine. I've just got a little cold, that's all.' Poor Dad, he looked so concerned. But all I could think of was getting to my mother's house and getting some sleep."

Katherine's parents had separated when she was twelve and her father has remarried, but her mother and father still live near each other. He drove her to her mother's house and she went straight upstairs to bed without awakening her younger brother or her mother. First, though, she went to the bathroom to look for something to take for her cold.

"I took out a bottle of cold pills and read the label. At the very end, in fine print, it said, 'Do not take if pregnant unless under a doctor's supervision.' I stood there looking at the bottle thinking, 'I'm dying! I've got to get some sleep!' And I took the pill. It was the last time I took any drugs the entire pregnancy. After that no wine, no coffee, no soft drinks. When I'd slept a few hours I went downstairs and told my mother the news."

Katherine considers her parents both to be loving but very rational people who will always try to accept any decision she makes in her life, however difficult it is for them to understand. They pride themselves on being liberal. They are also very proud of their attractive only daughter, who has been independent and largely self-supporting since she left home after high school. Confiding in them, especially her mother, has always been easy, even though their relationship never did include a great deal of physical affection. Katherine told herself it would be easy. But later to Linda she admitted how brutal her frankness had been.

"The way I brought it up was to say, 'Mom, I'm pregnant and I'm going to have this child. Then I am giving it up for adoption.' It was the first time I'd said the words out loud, even to myself. I made the decision, adoption, during the train ride but the word, when I told my mother, sounded so cold and unreal. She started to cry. It was awful."

Katherine hadn't intended to shock her mother. She was partly trying the words out to hear how they sounded. She also thought it was what both her parents would have wanted her to say. She didn't expect her mother would want her to raise a child alone, not when she wasn't ready for the full responsibility of it. She was amazed that the first thing her mother said was that perhaps she should consider an abortion, but she did appreciate the concern expressed in that statement. (Katherine has a pronounced curvature of the spine, which she was told to expect to worsen in pregnancy and perhaps prevent her from ever carrying a baby to full term or giving birth vaginally.) Her mother also suggested that she think about having some professional counseling before making up her mind. A few days later, Katherine saw her father again and poured out the whole story of her pregnancy. He too was shocked.

"He could hardly speak a word but he did manage to say right off, 'I can't tell you how much I admire you, Kate, for choosing to carry this child and then choosing not to sacrifice either of your lives for the sake of sentimentality.' "

Katherine's parents' first reactions were unconditionally supportive. But the anger and disappointment each of them also felt had to surface. Within a few days her mother was taking tranquilizers, her father had retreated to silence. Christmas was ruined.

During those first days home Katherine doesn't remember having thought of the father of the baby even once, so much was happening. It was all inconceivable to her. How could she connect this nightmare with her memory of the slender young man she'd fallen in love with and their intense philosophical conversations and passionate encounters. Her world had been transformed by her feelings for him and the everydayness of life had seemed brand new and shiny clean. Each day had magic. Now she was spinning in the eye of a hurricane and he was nowhere around. She hadn't seen him in over a month and the sound of his voice, which had given her chills when he telephoned, the details of his face, which had seemed so perfect to her, were beginning to blur and fade in her memory. From the outset she had had to handle everything about this pregnancy on her own and time was putting an even greater distance between them than the physical miles of separation. She also had her doubts about what he would do when he did hear the news.

Not long after she arrived in Utah her mother's fiancé had a heart attack and died. Katherine felt her own life crumbling at the edges but she tried to comfort her mother and made the decision to stay in Utah for a while longer to help. Perhaps, she thought, they could lean on each other in their misery. She knew it would be difficult because they had an emotionally volatile relationship when they spent any amount of time together. As Katherine describes it, "We love each other very much but we live together horribly and always bring out the worst in each other."

The pregnancy, begun unwittingly in a moment of beauty, was slipping quickly downward into daily misery. Katherine had given up her job in order to go back to Utah. Now she felt stuck at home, sick and ugly. She saw her once clear and beautiful olive skin breaking out, and felt she was sinking in a hole. Looking back later she would recall it was a period of unrelieved self-pity and depression and wish she had taken her mother's advice to see a therapist. During the third and fourth months of the pregnancy she remained in Utah, and the baby felt like a growth inside her constantly making her sick. Everyone in the family was contaminated by Katherine's constant misery.

"They all seemed angry with me. Even Linda. I called to talk with her and she wasn't sure she wanted me to come back to California because she was depressed herself and she had no energy to give me. My brother and I weren't getting along. One day we were having an argument about how he never did any work around the house and left it all to my mother and me to clean up after him. I told him he was being irresponsible; and he turned on me and said, 'Well at least I'm not fat and pregnant!' I called my father one day when I was very down and he said, 'None of this would have happened if you weren't sleeping in other people's beds!' And my mother and I were having terrible fights. We could turn anything into an argument. We were both tired and upset and would say horrible things, scream at each other. I would get so frustrated I'd lock myself in the bathroom. Once I even began to cut at my arms with a kitchen knife. The scars are almost gone now. I can't believe I did that. It's not like me, the way I am when my mother and I are arguing. With everyone else I am quiet and thoughtful and never say horrible things."

She was aware of the possible effect her emotional turmoil might have on the baby. "All I could think was that this baby would only know upset and hate. I never felt any anger at the idea of the baby but I felt so sorry that this was the world he was coming into."

It was a bleak hard winter in Utah. Preoccupied with her own body and emotional changes and her domestic conflicts with her mother, Katherine gave little thought to trying to track down her boyfriend in Nicaragua. Not that she could have traced him if she wanted to. That country was in chaos from recent revolution. Once she phoned Linda and asked her to call his roommate in town and find out if he had an address where she could write him. The message came back that the project was going so well in Nicaragua that he had decided to stay at least another month. He had written but left no address and there was no message for Katherine.

Without planning to, Katherine began to distance herself from the dream she had carried of their being together again someday. She turned her attention to finding out everything she could about adoption. Trips to the public library filled the void. Even before she had finished all the material they had on adoption she knew she didn't want to work with an agency and she began to form definite ideas about just what she did want for this child.

To her diary she said, "I want more control. It seems like in a private adoption I could design what is going to happen, choose the kind of people I want for the baby, spend the pregnancy as I want and have the kind of birth I want."

She was thinking about natural childbirth, which she'd seen mentioned in a few articles and books but which she knew nothing about. To her, the birth was light years away and completely unreal. All she knew was that she wanted to give birth in a warm loving environment and she couldn't imagine going to a hospital for that.

She was forming her own dreams for the coming birth and beginning to visualize what she would like it to be like, the first step toward preparing for labor. It became increasingly clear to her that she wanted to go back to California, but first she wanted to feel she had accomplished something. Perhaps she could at least locate parents for the baby. She didn't want her own parents to have to support her financially through the pregnancy. Perhaps the parents she found would help her until the birth. She began to ask relatives and old friends how to find couples interested in adopting a new baby. She had never felt awkward about expressing herself and being thought odd, and her parents didn't once make her feel that she should keep the pregnancy a secret.

She knew she didn't want her child adopted in Utah so she called California and talked to a doctor she knew there. He said she would have no trouble finding people, that the number of people who want children far outnumber the supply of babies, and he gave her some names right off. He suggested she should write to them. He also promised to let people he knew know that there was going to be a baby and that they should contact Katherine at her mother's through their attorney. She then told her stepmother, who is a nurse. Within a few weeks suddenly the whole world seemed to know about the baby.

A cousin on the East Coast had kept his word to let friends know. Her physician friend had kept his word too. Katherine was beginning to get phone calls from people claiming to be attorneys from as far away as Pennsylvania. She still had not even written to the original set of names her physician friend had given her.

She couldn't believe it. She didn't have to look any more. Instead she was faced with a greater decision than how to find couples—how to choose one from the others. At the age of twenty-one, never having given much thought to what kinds of people make the best parents, Katherine had to arrive at some way of screening all her calls. As usual she would rely first on her intuition; but she was able to think of several attributes she thought might help insure a couple were likely to be good parents of an adopted child.

She didn't want anyone who had strong religious preferences and would force their beliefs on a child. "I was raised without that, to think for myself, and I think I was treated with great respect growing up." She felt it would be nice but not necessary if they were college educated, at least intelligent people who thought a lot. Most of all she wanted a healthy couple, in their early or mid-thirties, because that seemed like a time in life when a couple would be more ready, when they might have an abundance and want to share it with a child.

She knew she would be turning people down, good and loving people. "I feel sad that I can't provide more babies for more people," she wrote Linda. "What I have here is an incredible gift."

What she had was also what many people considered a commodity on the market. It didn't take her long to spot an arrangement that might have been illegal or unsavory, and she called Linda about an incident.

"I got a call today from a man who is supposedly a lawyer and says he has a couple who want a child badly. He told me they would like to pay me $10,000! That was the way he opened the conversation! I told him, 'This child is not for sale!' He says what he is proposing couldn't be considered a sale, just an exchange. 'They are finding it almost impossible to adopt a child,' he said. 'They are willing to pay well for one, that's all.' I told him, 'I bet they pay *you* well too!' There was a long pause on the phone and he said, 'My fee is not up for discussion! I just want to know if you are interested.' I told him it did not interest me in the least and he hung up."

For the most part the calls she received seemed legitimate. The problem was she could only get dry bits of information about the various couples from respectable-sounding persons claiming to be attorneys. They would say where they had gotten Katherine's name but reveal little else to her. Typically their clients had been interested in a baby for five to ten years. The calls became a jumble in her mind. No one couple stood out and so she decided to go back to the original suggestion and write a letter, a letter that expressed her feelings, and to send it out to the people who sounded most interesting. She wrote the first two and mailed them. In each she asked for a letter from the couple in return.

Dear Prospective Parents,

I have been informed that you are interested in adopting the baby that I am carrying. Because I've been contacted by several couples and the decision is not an easy one for me, I've decided to write to each of you. I feel the only way I can really find out about you is to hear from you directly via letter or phone. First, I'd like to tell you a little about myself, so you will have an idea of what I want for my child and what decisions I have already made.

I discovered I was pregnant when I was about ten weeks along, and I made the decision almost immediately that I would carry the child. I briefly considered keeping the baby but, because of my marital status (single) and my financial status (no career or well-paying job) and most important, because I lack the stability and maturity I feel so necessary for raising a child, I have decided on adoption.

I am now four-and-a-half-months pregnant, in good health and being very careful to eat well and do to everything I can to grow a strong, healthy baby. I have decided on having natural childbirth and I will have the baby in California, where I live, though you may get in touch with me here at my mother's until April.

There are so many things I want to know about you. Of course I'm interested in the obvious things—your financial status, religious beliefs, where you live, whether you have or plan to have more than one child, your education and your plans for a child's education. Some answers will fit my "blueprint" better than others; but the most important question I need to ask is one I can't easily phrase. It has to do with why becoming a parent is important to each of you and why you have chosen the difficult path of adoption. What do you feel you can give to a child and what do you feel you can learn from raising a child?

We are living in strange and difficult times, we can't be sure there is a future for our children or whether the earth will be a fit place to live on by the time they are grown. What can you do to help ensure a child has the chance to live a full, happy life? I don't know any answers to these questions but I want to know your beliefs and feelings. I don't want an impersonal report filled with facts; I want a sense of who you are. This is the reason I have chosen private adoption. It is hard I know. It requires more personal contact and effort on both sides. My choice of parents is the most important thing I will ever do for my baby. I hope you understand and I look forward to hearing from you.

Thank you,
Katherine

One reply came back. She rejected it because once again it said nothing about the couple except what schools they had attended, their height and weight and ages. She received two phone calls from a lawyer saying his couple had received a letter from her and they were trying to write a response but were having a difficult time writing directly to her. Wouldn't she consider working through an agency? Katherine found this request curious. If they felt uncomfortable having contact with a mother why then were they dealing with an attorney instead of an agency in the first place? To Katherine it meant they didn't want her to enter into their lives in any way. Once again it was only the baby they wanted, with no strings attached and no mother to have to deal with. She wrote in her diary, "I don't get the feeling from any of these people that they want to meet *me*."

Then her cousin back East ran across an unusual social worker who specialized in the placement of children with handicaps in adoptive homes. Perhaps this woman would be a good source. Katherine called New York and found in the woman a completely different attitude from any she had encountered up to then. At last she had met, though only by phone, someone who she felt understood. She felt that this stranger had a heart, that she cared about her and this child inside of her. The social worker gave Katherine the name of an attorney she liked to work with. Katherine tried to contact him but he was out of town so she left her name and a message with his secretary.

It was late March. Katherine was at the end of her fifth month of pregnancy. The baby had been moving inside her for almost a month. It was all slowly becoming real to her. Her dreams had become vivid and were now full of images of babies and birth, and cats. In her unconscious the baby often appeared in the form of a cat, her favorite animal. Then one day she got a call one day from Linda who said that Katherine's cat, Mouse, had been hit by a car. She had barely managed to drag herself up onto the porch of their cottage before dying. The vet had performed an autopsy and found her uterus full of tiny kittens, but all of them were dead. Katherine was heartbroken at the news. She wrote in her diary, "My own death seems very real to me now. Sometimes I can see my brother or someone else close to me dying, but mostly it is *my* death; and always in my dreams there is a lot of violence. Sometimes I dream about the baby, and there is something wrong with the baby and me. A lot of times we are on a journey, just the two of us, and I know we aren't going to make it."

She wrote about a dream in which she told the baby she knew

neither of them was going to make it because there was just too much against them. In it she repeated over and over, "I'm sorry. I'm really sorry. I did try. I really did." Her dreams were a mirror of her daily experiences and her gathering sense of gloom. She was growing more unhappy with each day.

She had planned to remain at her mother's until the lawyer from New York called but she found she couldn't wait. She woke one morning in early April, looked out the window on another wet, gray day and knew it was time to return to California. She booked a reservation using the last of the money she'd saved from her old job and flew home to Linda. In her mind that day marked the beginning. It was as if she turned a corner and started down a new path, green with promise. She was at last looking forward to the baby and able to make preparations for her birth. It was a complete change in attitude that Katherine attributed to finding the right place in which to go through her pregnancy. Her diary read, "When a woman is pregnant she is so sensitive to everything and everyone. Back in Utah it felt all negative. Perhaps not for other women, but it was for me. Coming back here I feel I can be proud of my pregnancy and maybe even enjoy it. I walked into the house and Linda looked at me and told me I look wonderful. I guess I do. I feel radiant!"

She had asked her mother to relay the message to the lawyer, should he call, that Katherine had gone home and was waiting there to hear from him. Time was growing very short and there had still not been one single contact with the baby's father. He did not yet even know there was a baby. Katherine felt embarrassed calling his roommate and kept hoping he would return and call her or at least write.

With each passing week and each decision she had to make on her own, the young man she had fallen in love with became more and more a faceless shadow. She was proud that she was doing so well on her own, yet there were times, she knew, when it would have been so much easier if he had been there to support her. How could he ever catch up with her now, when every day that dawned she was growing and experiencing new things and the gap between their lives was only widening? It had become her pregnancy now, not theirs. It had taken her three months to discover and face the fact that she was going to have a baby, another two to find that pregnancy could be a lovely time. Even were the baby's father to return or give her support from a distance, she figured he would still need a lot of time to learn to live with the reality that a child of his was going to come into the world. She wanted to give him the chance to be part of it, of what was left. Several days after she was back in her own home she phoned his apartment. The thought of hearing his voice at the end of the phone, for she was certain he would be home, left her numb and her heart beating fast. But it was his room-mate who answered. No, he wasn't back in the country yet. His project, helping to clean up after the revolution and working on a national literacy campaign, had become too exciting to leave. He didn't know when they could expect him back and Katherine thought by the sound of his voice that he was annoyed she had called.

She told Linda, "I've been fantasizing how I was going to tell him. I was so drawn to him last fall. How do I say I have a five-month-old child inside me, that it is part his and that I am giving our baby up for adoption?" She believed when she heard his voice it would all be easy, just like when they used to sit in the coffee shop and talk. Only after his roommate informed her he hadn't even set a date for his return did she have to admit to herself she was carrying around a dream.

"I've had an image," she wrote in her diary, "of the two of us sharing an experience that few people can have, going through the intensity of watching a child grow inside me, loving it and then letting it go. I don't feel getting in touch with him would change my decision about adoption or make our relationship permanent, but I've always thought we would share the end of the pregnancy and be together at the birth."

For several days Katherine reeled from the blow. She was alone, and it felt as if she'd been abandoned for the second time. First it had been with the news of the pregnancy, at having to make the decision to carry the child and the decision to give it up for adoption alone. Now she would have to face giving birth alone too. She could not wait another day. She had to tell him, even if it was in a letter. His roommate had given her an address at which a letter might reach him. She was then entering her sixth month of pregnancy, her belly protruding under all of her clothes. To Linda she poured out her feelings and her decision.

"It is his right to know. I put everything down in the letter. It feels so easy to talk to him in writing, just as it used to be. I said I wasn't writing to ask for his financial support or even to ask him to guide me through this. I told him I feel strong and know what I am doing, that I haven't chosen the parents yet but I will soon. As far as I can see I've made an irrevocable decision, and I will give this child up for adoption. I told him I am healthy and I hope he will feel a sense of joy, as I now do, that there is a new life. 'You can participate in any fashion you like, by keeping in touch with me or coming back and completing the triangle. Pregnancy is a triangle and there is a part missing without you. The decision is entirely yours but I think you have a right to know everything.' "

She mailed the letter April 10. The phone rang two days later. It was the attorney from New York. Glad at last to have found an intermediary whose judgment she instinctively felt she could trust, Katherine was open to his first suggestion of a couple who would be overjoyed to take the baby. What impressed her about him was that he didn't seem like an attorney at all but a concerned friend. The conversation lasted an hour and a half and she couldn't wait to tell Linda all about it.

"We talked intimately about my pregnancy, the changes in me. It turned out that he adopted a child himself in addition to having one by birth. He says he has a couple who will love my child in the way I do, and can carry through raising it as I can't. He said he feels they will be the kind of parents I would want to be and that he can recommend them without any reservation whatsoever."

The couple he had in mind fit the few criteria Katherine had formed. They were educated, had been married a long time and in addition had started up and were now running a successful small business together. She agreed to having them phone her. So much had been done by telephone already she was comfortable opening up that way. The initial contact felt clean and clear and warm and she felt certain they were the people for her child. Without the embarrassment of having to face one another in person they all spoke freely.

"They were so excited," she told Linda, "but also anxious to comfort me and to let me know how much they appreciate what I am doing."

The couple also revealed to her what would become over the next few months the greatest source of their own insecurity and fear and what would later cause Katherine much pain. A few months earlier, after eight years of trying to become pregnant and then looking for an infant to adopt, they had been given a baby several days old. They had contacted the mother through their attorney and no agency was involved. Suddenly, two weeks into parenthood, and without warning, the birth mother demanded the little girl back, claiming her decision to allow adoption had been a great mistake. They told Katherine the loss of this little baby was like a death in their family for which they were still grieving. Katherine understood completely their concern that she might not go through with the adoption and she found herself reassuring them that this would not happen in her case. She did not realize that having to support them would later on be a demand on her emotional strength and that from the first conversation she was placed in a support role when in fact it was she who needed support. But she was feeling strong and sure. The baby growing large and active inside her body was filling her with confidence.

The couple in turn assured her that this child would have the life she would like to give it and that they were whole-heartedly ready to be parents. In later conversations they might disagree on exactly what was best for a baby in such things as feeding, but her major criterion was fulfilled, that they would be loving, attentive parents. She did not consider how closely their attitudes and life values matched hers. She did not think of it.

Over the last three months of her pregnancy Katherine spoke with the couple once or twice a month. The trust she initially felt with them was confirmed by their continued interest in her well-being and her feelings. Their anxieties about the actual adoption increased as the birth approached but she continued to assure them of the certainty of her decision. It had not been made rashly but had grown from the knowledge of her own needs and her understanding of what commitment and resources were necessary to be the kind of parent she felt every child deserved. The conversations began to include some discussion of the details of the birth and she thinks it was they who first suggested that they take the baby as soon after birth as possible. They had been given their first child four days after its birth and it was important to them to make the connection as early in the baby's life as possible, as soon as Katherine felt comfortable. She too wanted this. She began to share with them her vision of how the exchange might take place. It was still a rather fuzzy picture but she knew it was essential that she see this baby who had lived inside her, to count its fingers and toes, to complete a cycle for her. "I want to give him my blessings, to know who this child is and to whom I am saying goodbye." The details would have to be worked out later but in theory their visions matched.

When she was at her mother's home she had taken out from the library some books about the birth process. Several of them clearly explained and illustrated labor and discussed the various kinds of breathing techniques that are sometimes useful in natural childbirth, where no medications are used. In the midst of all the turmoil she was feeling then those books had heightened her anxiety. She placed on labor all her unnamed anxieties about having a child. Distracted and divorced from the reality of her everyday life, and with no one around her who was going or had recently gone through childbirth, her birthing had filled her with terror out of all proportion. Now she began childbirth classes, with Linda as her labor support. Sometimes she also brought her brother, Tom, who had come out to live with her and Linda, or another male friend to the classes. Her diary read, "We are having a great time because none of us knows anything about birth. I've been saying the words 'natural childbirth' all along, but without knowing what they meant. In class I've learned that this birth can be an incredible, beautiful, though difficult time. By the end of these classes I think I'll be rather looking forward to the labor."

She had wisely selected a class with a teacher who had many years of experience attending births, who inspired self-confidence and emphasized the need to trust in the process and the body's ability to guide a woman and her baby through safely. Katherine also heard of yoga classes for pregnant women and so began doing exercises at home to strengthen and stretch and prepare for the work of labor. She was more attentive about what she ate. She walked miles every day and found a neighbor's swimming pool to swim laps in. She was doing all this as much for the pleasure it began to give her as for the good she knew it was doing for the baby. Perhaps, she thought, it might make up for some of the awful period they'd both suffered through in the early months.

The phone calls from New York became a ritual and Katherine would inform the couple of all the small things she was doing. She loved the interest she heard in their voices. She still didn't even ask their last names but they were feeling more and more like family. Sometime during the six weeks the childbirth classes were going on she began to visualize more concretely just how she might like the exchange of the baby to take place. She even began to imagine what it might be like to have the couple at the birth itself. That would mean they would have to meet face-to-face. What would it be like? She couldn't quite picture it but it felt all right.

At about that time, the intricacies of interstate adoption began to surface and Katherine found there were many small details surrounding an adoption where the adoptive parents were residents of a state different from hers and from where the birth would take place. The adoptive parents and their lawyer asked her please to come to New York and have the baby there. But to this request she had only an emphatic *"No!"* She told the lawyer, "I've already experienced what it is like living in the wrong place during this pregnancy. These last months have become especially happy for me and I know I must stay where I am happy. I hope that my refusing this won't change anything in the adoption because I do want them for the parents. But I know that what I have to give this child is the time of gestation." They asked once more but she was adamant and they did not press her further.

So far Katherine only knew the couple's first names. She was told that their full names and their address would be on the adoption consent she would sign. The idea of knowing who they were and where they lived felt right. As with other unexpected requirements of the pregnancy, when the time came for each new development and decision, Katherine was ready. She had taken each previous step in sequence, looking neither back nor ahead. She had much to be proud of in the way she worked through each phase.

Though she was long past feeling hopeless and depressed, her pride and pleasure were often tinged with sadness, not only for the inevitability of having to part with this baby but for the fact that in everything she was doing she was alone. No matter how much she trimmed away at the original dream—the baby's father returning to take some shared part in this experience—she still clung to pieces of the dream. Hope was briefly fanned early in May when a letter postmarked Nicaragua came in the mail. Had this letter come much earlier in pregnancy it might have altered the course of her life.

In it he wrote that he was full of concern and awe at her news of the "miracle" and had been thinking a lot about her. His work was fascinating and it was work that held him there because he really felt involved in the rebuilding of that country. The letter concluded, "I can feel nothing but pure delight at what you've written!"

On the first read-through she felt giddy. Perhaps he would want to have a part in the remainder of her pregnancy. He *was* the same sensitive person she had loved. The letter said he would return at the beginning of June. He also wrote that he was "100%" behind her, including her adoption decision. She was charmed, particularly by his asking her to write him everything, her hopes, her fears, all *her* feelings so he could be part of it even at a distance. She read again and again the section where he told how sorry he was that he couldn't be with her just then.

She had been feeling good before but now she was buoyed up by the confidence his praise of her strength instilled. She was feeling strong and even imagined that she was at last supported. She sat and wrote him a very long letter, with details of the direct adoption—her plans to meet the parents as well as to hold and feed the baby herself before she gave it up.

She was to hear from him only one more time before the birth. That too was by mail. In that briefer letter he expressed all of the confusion her shocking announcement had really filled him with. He no longer spoke of coming back in June or even of being with her at the very end of pregnancy and for the birth. And in this letter he cautioned her firmly against meeting the adoptive parents and strongly urged her not to see or hold the baby because it would then make it too difficult to give the baby up. He seemed to be shielding himself from any emotional involvement with her or the pregnancy, much less the child he'd shared in creating. Katherine easily read between the lines. He was frightened and his fear overshadowed any real concern he might have for her needs or the baby's. All her hopes for the last weeks were crushed. But even at such news she could not stay down for long. The pregnancy itself was carrying her along now. Life was carrying her.

Two weeks after receiving the second letter she took a bus up into the country to stay with a cousin where she could be alone and take leisurely walks through the hills. Her times out of doors in nature reassured her that the world was still a safe place and brought peace to her troubled mind. She was grateful to be granted the luxury of time to spend alone with the baby out of doors. It was something made possible by the prospective parents, who had been sending her a small living allowance to cover food and shelter through the birth and for three months afterward. In her diary she wrote about how important the time away from the city was for her and the baby.

"If I were ever to have another pregnancy, it will be at a time when I can arrange for long stretches where I have the freedom I have now. I see so many women, even in my birth class, who are working full-time right through their pregnancies. Part of me admires that they can do it. Yet I think they are missing so much. It's not only the cataclysmic changes but the subtle ones. I've been fortunate to be there through all of them because I haven't been preoccupied with the pressure of having to deal with the everyday working world too much. How often do you carry another life inside you?"

The pregnancy had brought her squarely into womanhood, something she had always skirted as she hung on to her girlhood body and freedoms and feared what becoming an adult in the world might do to her dreams. To Linda she confided, "I've never really accepted my womanness and my capacity to bear children. I've never liked the idea of pregnancy, birth or having children. Since I never have had regular periods I've never really felt in touch with the reproductive parts of my body." Perhaps some of that cautiousness was due to her witnessing what parenthood had done to her parents' creative urges. Their desire to be artists had been hindered by the practical considerations of raising two children with little money. Katherine saw herself as an artist too, a writer. Everything had been second to that goal. Unexpectedly this pregnancy had brought her pleasure in her maternal side. She was enjoying the traditional occupations of women; she was caring for the earth, gardening, being out of doors. Slowly, without realizing it, she was beginning to dream about what it might be like not to give the baby up but to *be* its mother. Entertaining thoughts of motherhood was a way of re-examining her decision to give the baby up.

She'd made the original decision in the early months of pregnancy, when this baby was barely a bump inside of her, something she hardly felt and couldn't relate to at all. It was natural that she should have to make the decision again, with the child now big and a vital moving part of her. So she was really asking herself, "Have I evolved to the point where I am now a mother? Can I even go on after this experience and *not* be a mother? Have I not changed so much that it is no longer possible for me to go on without this child?" If that were true, then the answer now would be clear, that she should keep this baby.

The decision had to be hers alone. It was not that Katherine could not be a competent, caring mother. She knew she could be. It was whether she fully *wanted* to enter this commitment and do so completely, consciously, with all her heart. Looking back months later she described the process she went through when she imagined keeping the baby.

"I felt as if the overwhelming sense of loss and pain I had lived with, knowing I was going to give this child up, disappeared. I passed through it. I think it was an honest reaction to being immensely, enormously pregnant, filled with life, living with it totally day in and day out that made the worst of the pain go away. Yet even the pleasure of becoming a mother, giving birth, did not change the facts. Rationally and emotionally everything still stacked up on the side of adoption. When it came right down to it, and this was hardest to admit, I did not want to keep this child!"

Knowing she had once more made her decision, or, rather, found it, didn't lessen the sadness that realization brought her. She knew she still had to face other people, and their criticism for choosing not to be a mother. Katherine wanted a few more years for her own growth. She also wanted her child to have his or her years, too, without having to share them with a mother who was trying to find her own way. She had given a lot of thought to how great it could be, just the two of them, mother and child, living together, traveling around together, growing up together. They could go through it all as a couple. But when she thought about how important it had been for her that she had a basic security in her childhood, at least until her parents were divorced—how that had remained with her—she knew she couldn't give her child that, not now. "I just don't *have* it yet. I *can't* manufacture it, no matter *how* much I would like to," she wrote in her diary.

Love was another matter. That would be easy for her to give. She already loved this child. It was *herself* she couldn't fully give because what was simply not yet developed in her could not be given. That is what she was saying when she told the baby, during one of her many conversations at the end of pregnancy, "I love you but I don't want to raise you. If I really did, then I would do it. But I am doing what I know is best for us both."

And so the major decision of her pregnancy was made for a second time; and this time it was not a girl's decision but that of a woman.

I first met Katherine when she was nearing the end of pregnancy and her decision to give the baby up was firm. We had heard about each other from mutual friends at the birth home. I don't recall who called whom, but we made a date to meet at the home of Linda's parents, where she and Linda and Tom were housesitting for several weeks. She greeted me at the door wearing a long loose summer dress. I had no picture of what she might look like but I was stunned by how small, how slender she was, how strong and high her cheekbones were, how perfectly almond her eyes, how small were her hands and bare feet. There was a refinement about her even at her advanced state of pregnancy. She talked slowly and with articulate precision. We went through the house and I was introduced to Tom. Linda was at work. Katherine carried a kitten in her arms. We went out and sat in the yard and she began to tell me her story.

"I know so many children come into the world as a mistake or an excuse. There is some ulterior motive for having them. Once I was able to admit to myself and this baby that I didn't want to raise a child, then there was no question about my decision. I know I will go through the pain of my attachment and my loss but I'll be okay." I already knew that no amount of preparation would protect Katherine from the physical pain of the loss when it came, or from the long months of grief after her detachment. But the strength of her decision and the solid foundation on which she had based it, I felt, would carry her through the experience, that and her sense of trust.

Having remade the adoption decision she was ready at last to prepare for the birth itself. It was time to work out the details for the exchange, to consider whether she did in fact want to invite the parents to her birthing, to agree upon whether they would meet and if so how much time she would spend with the baby and they would spend with her before they took the baby. She had become deeply connected to this child. She couldn't have stopped that process had she wanted to; yet after she let go she would still have to disconnect. I wondered just how she would face that. We talked about it that day in the sun, and about her options. Once again Katherine had begun to have vivid dreams. Whereas most of her dreams in Utah had involved fear and death, these dreams toward the end of her pregnancy were full of hope. Her brother had insisted she get the kitten to replace the beloved Mouse. She told me that the baby of her dreams now took the form of a kitten.

"I guess I transferred my desires to hold and carry the baby to her. I've carried her around a lot and stroke her all the time and my dreams now are lighter and happier." One recurring dream told her this kitten, her baby, could never be happy with anyone besides her. But each time, at the climax she would hear herself saying to it, "You'll make it without me, I know you will." And each time she would awake feeling confident the baby would be fine.

During her days she was practicing visualizing the scene of her birth, imagining the kinds of feelings that she and the couple would have, picturing the gestures they would each make. She could see herself placing the child in their arms, watching them hold the baby, and in these visions she felt connected to this couple. What she was doing was gaining some mastery over the event that would have so much importance to all of them, this baby's birth. And going through all the motions and the feelings ahead of time was preparing her to accept it when it came.

While she knew she could never have complete control over the interactions she had with the parents, she did want to design her labor. That she could do. Because her physician did not feel her spinal curvature warranted medical intervention, there were a number of alternatives open to her for her birthing. She could give birth in the nearby university teaching hospital. In addition to the labor and delivery room setup there were now two special birthing rooms. If she chose one of these and had no problem in labor that required moving to the delivery room, she could labor and give birth in the same bed in whatever way and with whatever people she wanted there. She could have the baby with her from the moment of birth until she gave it directly into the hands of the couple or an agent of theirs either at the hospital or somewhere else. She could also have a home birth with one of several local midwives, all skilled in normal birth, using the hospital for medical backup. What appealed to her about giving birth at home was the orientation toward normal unmedicated birth, which she knew the midwives had but which she felt she could not count on in a hospital environment no matter who her doctor was. Before deciding where to give birth, she thought she'd better choose her birth attendant.

She had heard there was a variety of physicians around to select from, a few family physicians as well as obstetrician-gynecologists, but she had put off seeking care for as long as possible, hoping she would not face the same situation she had in Utah. There she had felt the obstetricians didn't want to answer any of her questions and didn't care about what she wanted. She was determined to find someone she could trust and who at the very least appreciated her point of view and her desire to make all the decisions around this birth. She had not been seen by any professional for more than four months and the baby was due in about six weeks when she finally started to look for a midwife or doctor. Then she heard about The Birth Place—a home not connected with a hospital, but licensed by the state, where a woman could give birth using either a physician or midwife of her choice. At a resource center run by the same group she looked through the files of questionnaires filled out by dozens of physicians giving their interests and their practices. Then she looked through the midwives' files. She decided first to try a physician whose questionnaire she liked and who was recommended by the people who worked at the resource center as someone who was a strong advocate of women's rights as well as natural childbirth. He attended women both at the hospital and at the birth home and had also backed up some home births of the midwives in the area. He sounded just right.

His office was just two blocks from the resource center, so she walked to his office to make an appointment. The receptionist asked Katherine when her last period was. When she heard that it was in August she looked shocked and said, "That means you were due yesterday." Katherine told her that the date of her last period was not really a reliable index, since she was very irregular. But the receptionist looked at her size and made an immediate appointment for her with the nurse practitioner and another one for the next week with the doctor.

Katherine went to her first two appointments alone. She was impressed by the orientation of the practice and felt that she had made the right decision, especially when the doctor said he was sure she didn't need to have a Caesarean. Forms were already arriving in the mail every week from the East Coast, technical papers to be signed in preparation for the legalities of the adoption. A sum of money had been sent to cover her physician's fees. Although she was very late to start care she impressed both the nurse practitioner and the doctor with her state of health and her state of mind.

Summer was getting hotter and her abdomen was growing heavier. She wished she could escape from all the bustle and hurry of life in town. She treasured every moment of time she had with the baby. There was still no letter from Nicaragua and as the days passed she seldom thought about the father. She was excited when she went to the open house at the birth center. It surpassed even her best dreams of a place to give birth. There she felt at home. There was a living room, a kitchen, a wooden deck off each birth room, even a back yard with fruit trees. She became a familiar sight at the doctor's office and at the birth home classes, almost always alone yet radiating the same sense of calm self-assurance. The other women who volunteered at the birth home found her easy to talk with and she often stopped by after having a snack at the coffee house down the street or on her way back from shopping. She was so healthy and radiant-looking everyone noticed her. Some wondered if she could possibly be as relaxed and positive as she seemed—they hoped it was not just a façade that would crack once the work and pain of labor began. She felt she was finally part of a close community of people like her who cared about shaping their birthings and gave one another support. Her friend Linda and her brother could not give her the same feeling of support that being around other pregnant women gave. She brought Linda around to see the room she hoped to use, with the doors that swung open onto the back yard. She felt so comfortable here; she hoped the baby's new parents would feel as she did, because she was now certain she wanted them to be at the birth.

Just when the parents would arrive had not yet been settled. One thing that had begun to assume major importance in her mind was the idea that this baby should have the advantage of some breast-feeding. Her mother had breast-fed Katherine and her brother at a time when few women were doing so and when it was almost universally discouraged by doctors. Katherine recalled having read something about a woman being able to prepare herself in some special way to breast-feed an adopted child. She wondered if the woman in New York had con-

Katherine during labor, walking with the midwife
in the back yard of the birth home

sidered trying to breast-feed and during one conversation on the phone she brought up the subject. That had produced a shocked silence on the other end of the phone. The woman said she'd never heard of any such thing and said she really had no interest in the subject! Their pediatrician, she told Katherine, had already suggested to them a wonderful formula and neither she nor her husband felt breast-feeding to be that important. Their idea was that they could share equally in feeding the baby, she and her husband, and formula made it all so easy. Katherine was surprised and disappointed at this reaction. She had never before found an area where they could not at least listen to each other. She had sensed from the beginning the couple she'd chosen were not particularly liberal or adventuresome, but they had always before been willing to listen to each of her ideas. I saw Katherine shortly after this conversation and we talked about how different they were likely to be from her.

"I know I can't set up this adoption to be perfect; but breast-feeding seems so important to me. I am going to put this baby to my breast. At least for the few hours he is still with me he will be breast-fed." She was adamant that the baby should get the benefit of her first milk, colostrum, to protect the baby from infections and allergies. And I was glad to see she would assert herself. It would mean there was less chance she would compromise the most important features of the birth and adoption when the time came.

When she told the couple of her plans during their next phone conversation, she could hear them bristle. When I next saw her a few days later, Katherine was still feeling annoyed. She said the phone calls had now become strained, and though they did say they felt they had no right to impose any restrictions on her, she felt their criticism.

There were other details to discuss. They agreed that Katherine should call or have someone else call their attorney as soon as she thought she was going into labor. They would then attempt to get the first plane out to the West Coast and they would call for directions when they arrived, rent a car and drive straight to the birth home. They had apparently never heard of such a place to have a baby, though there is a well-known similar center right in New York City. They, like most people, associated birth with hospitalization. Katherine said they'd sounded very relieved to hear that she had at least chosen a physician, not a midwife, to attend her. She smiled as she told me.

I didn't see or hear from Katherine again until labor. Our time together had given her a few extra things to think about. And she had called to invite me to be there at the birth and to take photographs. Two weeks later, eleven days after her most accurate estimate of a due date and a full three weeks after the date she first thought it would be, Katherine's labor began. She spent the first part of the day at a friend's house and a midwife friend was with her. By the time they packed up her clothes and food to take to the birth home and called her physician and the rest of us to meet them at the home, Katherine was well into labor, growing weary and feeling dazed but excited and unafraid.

Katherine holding her son, not long before the arrival of
Tony and Ellen, the baby's prospective parents

Fear of Knowing

They arrived on the 11 p.m. flight and went directly to a telephone as agreed. The phone number they dialed was The Birth Place, an alternative birth center thirty miles away. It was there that their baby was waiting. Not theirs yet, but soon to be. They had booked return reservations for the 7 a.m. flight the next day and they wanted to pick up the baby and leave as soon as possible. That was what all their friends and relatives had told them to do. "Don't get involved," they warned. "It will only make things more difficult."

They had received the call from their attorney at dawn that morning telling them that the doctor had phoned to say his patient was in active labor and that she would like them to take the first possible flight out. Katherine had not actually wanted them at the birth, not after she heard their fear and mistrust over the telephone when she suggested it. The presence of anyone who didn't believe fully in what she was doing could only distract her from her commitment to labor and give birth to this baby spontaneously, with no drugs or intervention. That was why she'd chosen the birth home rather than the hospital. There she could have the run of the entire house, the kitchen to get food when she was hungry, the bathroom to take hot baths or showers if it made her more comfortable, the deck and the yard with fruit trees she could look out on or wander in. Without any rules restricting her behavior in labor she could have as many friends around her as she wished and could orchestrate her birthing and her leave-taking from her baby to her own satisfaction. There, after the birth she could at last meet the parents she'd chosen and formed a trust with long distance, could talk with them in privacy and share the baby's presence before she turned this part of her flesh over to them. That had been her plan for the last months of pregnancy, that and having some time after the birth to spend alone with the baby, to lie with him, to feed him at her breast, to relish every moment of the last few hours they would have together.

But that was not Tony and Ellen's plan. Their plan was to leave without knowing any more than they had to, without facing her, as they felt any meeting could only be a confrontation, with pain, guilt and remorse for everyone. They had friends who had adopted babies and not one of them had ever heard of what this young woman had in mind. Some of their friends told them it might be a trap. "Just get the baby and leave," they said. "We'll meet you at the airport, take you home and *then* we'll celebrate."

And so they came to town. And so she waited for them, waited with her son, to whom she had passionately given birth after an exhausting labor that had demanded every ounce of her attention and strength. The stages of her cervix opening had gone so very slowly, like slow motion, that she thought it might never end. Linda had been there from the first sign of labor, as had other friends and a midwife who offered extra support. When they had finally brought her to the birth home she was making good progress and losing all thought of time. They had all stayed with her, walked around the home with her and sat with her on the big comfortable bed with their arms for support, their backs to lean against, hour after hour. Her brother, Tom, had been there too. He had labored beside her, struggling with his own fears about her pain and misgivings over what she was going to do. He loved his sister very much. In the absence of the baby's father he had felt himself especially connected to this child his sister carried. But when she at last began to push, smiling between the urges and the bearing down, he had slipped quietly away and taken refuge on a couch in the living room, where he fell deeply asleep. Perhaps he'd hoped he would miss the birth entirely and the grief he knew his sister would face afterward. But Katherine had noticed his absence toward the end and sent someone to fetch him like a mischievous boy to her. She *needed* him. This was no time for him to be running away.

The baby had long black hair. It slipped out of her, one shoulder slightly tearing her as it came, out and up into her outreaching hands and onto her deflated abdomen. And so he had arrived. A baby boy with a round face and dark eyes peering open at her from the moment of birth. So this was what it had all been for.

Tony and Ellen, the parents-to-be, had given no thought to those first moments. They had been so caught up with the fear they'd carried with them through the past three months of waiting, the fear that somehow they would lose him as they had lost the other, they hardly thought of his birth. Just six months earlier they had a daughter. She had come to them when she was four days old. She had been with them for two brief weeks before the mother claimed her back again, as she was legally entitled to do, and she'd walked out of their lives carrying their little girl and their hearts. The pain Tony and Ellen had felt then, after all the years of trying for a child, after the miscarriage and the tubal pregnancy, seared like a branding iron. It had felt to them like a death when the woman had taken their little girl from them, back to the grandparents who didn't want her to keep the child, back to the friends who knew she was in no position to raise it herself. She had fled clutching the baby like her security blanket, leaving no trace behind. That was why they were coming now in fear. It had been such a short time ago and they were determined not to let another young woman hurt them again.

They knew they were taking a risk, that legally this mother too had six months in which to change her mind and ask for the infant back. They would have had to take that risk even in an agency adoption unless the baby was placed in a foster home or institution during the waiting period. They had gone to agencies first and there had been no baby found for them. Direct adoption seemed the only alternative. It hadn't been so bad, having to talk with the young woman by phone. They *liked* her. The papers they would sign and she would sign would necessitate their knowing each other's full names. But that was all. To how much more must they subject themselves in order to get a child?

But Katherine knew her rights, and she knew what she wanted for her child's sake. She hadn't spent the last nine and one-half months growing this baby inside her, refraining from anything that might harm it, loving and communicating with it for nothing. Certainly not to have the cycle abruptly cut off and the process aborted. Her way would give her the time she needed to complete the loving and begin the letting go. She intended to drink in every moment she had with her son and she was doing just that even as the couple were driving their rented car from the airport to the birth home.

She hadn't slept for two days. There would be time enough for that soon. Now she was too busy being enchanted with this small, fragrant little boy lying against her in the darkened room. It was after midnight. They would arrive in less than an hour. The nurse came in to check her and suggested she might like to take a warm bath and let her clean Katherine's nightgown from the stains of the birth. Sitting in the bath she held him close but out of the water, wrapped in a blanket. And she talked to him, chuckling with pleasure at his changing faces and the sounds his lips made as they pursed and his tongue explored the air.

If they had known what she was up to they would have feared her even more and never believed she could go on and give them this baby. But then they didn't know her. They hadn't lived inside her mind and heart for the past many months as she made and remade her decision. Tom wouldn't have believed it either, had he seen her at midnight with the baby in her arms in the bath. He had excused himself earlier in the evening, saying he needed some fresh air, perhaps hoping to miss meeting the couple when they arrived. He had been gone five hours now and no one had heard from him. Katherine sensed he was angry at her for what she was about to do. The baby looked just as he had in his baby pictures. This child was a part of *their* family, she knew he must be thinking. Why did she have to give him up? Couldn't they all raise him together? Their parents would surely help out. But Tom was still a teenager and the support he could give would not be enough for her in the next years were she to attempt to raise this child alone. She knew that, no matter what anyone else might think. She could deal with her brother's hurt and resentment later. She was being amazingly clear-headed. Here she was, purposely keeping her baby out of the warm water in order that the wonderful fragrance of his skin from the birth might still be there for the couple to know. She had thought of them at every step. If they were to love him, she'd reasoned, they would need to know him right from the beginning; and though they hadn't seen him born—seen that magnetic open-eyed first gaze—still, she would give them his newness.

She fed him from her breast. The two of them were brand new at this game of suckling and they were clumsy together. He couldn't find her nipple. She didn't know just how to position him most comfortably in her arm. He made such funny noises as he sucked, as if he were sucking candy. She was giving him the sweet first milk called colostrum, a protection as potent as antibiotics. And she was loving him.

It was nearly one in the morning. In the living room the midwife, Katherine's roommate and I sat and nervously waited for the lights of a car to shine down the driveway. Tony had called once to say they had taken the wrong turn and gotten lost. I had arranged for a room for them at a local motel. That way, even if Katherine gave them the baby immediately, they could have some time, perhaps even sleep with him, before they had to drive to the airport and catch the long flight back home. Their departure shouldn't be frantic. For such an event time is essential.

At 1:15 headlights lit up the driveway. The midwife greeted Tony and Ellen warmly at the door, introduced them to Linda and me and invited them in. She went to make them a cup of something hot and we all went into the living room. We had anticipated their anxiety and Tony had been honest about it when he'd called the second time. They were coming to a strange home in a strange city to meet strange people who, they could easily imagine, would be standing *between* them and their baby. It was too late in the night to bother with small talk. "Is the baby here?" "Yes." "How is *she*?" "Just fine, very well." "Can we *see* him?" "Certainly."

First we felt they had to hear what *she'd* planned for them. The idea of a motel and waiting until tomorrow to take the baby was out of the question, they said in unison. They had a plane to catch that was leaving in just five hours. If they took the baby now they would have time to return to the airport motel where they'd left their bags. As we sat and listened to Tony, looking small and stiff, and watched his crossed leg jiggling up and down, we sympathized with his and Ellen's discomfort. We were there to put the two of them at ease, to hear *their* needs too. But we were also there to make the needs of the woman in the back room known, to break the news gently that she had plans that required something more of them than they'd counted on.

We talked about the plane back to New York. Both of them were adamant, it was the only flight with available seats for the next several days. It seemed that the idea of staying the night in a strange community was more than they could possibly bear. They were inflexible but they had to listen as we gently pointed out to them that, regardless of their intentions for how the exchange would take place tonight, the desires of the mother in the other room would have to take precedence. She was in control; but they should understand that hurting or frightening them was not her intention. She merely needed a little time and she wanted to meet them. They didn't seem to hear what we were saying. They kept bringing up the plane they needed to catch as if that were their only hope of escape. We again brought up the idea of a meeting with Katherine. Why? they asked. They knew all they needed to know about her. They had great respect for what she was doing for them, for what she had done for the baby. For the grief she would surely feel, they felt profound respect. But having to meet her, having to see *their* son while he was still *her* son, in *her* arms, this they did *not* want to face, not for *anyone*.

There was more quiet talk as we leaned toward Tony and Ellen and spoke to them of Katherine. We painted a picture of an exchange she planned that might enrich everyone's lives. They listened and said no. They didn't think such a thing would enrich anyone's life, certainly not theirs! They could see no need to carry the memory of her face back home with them. They had her voice. That was enough! They spoke about the terrible suffering they had endured when they lost their little girl. It was not clear what they now feared most, *their* reactions upon seeing and sitting in the same room with Katherine or *her* reactions seeing them with her baby. Or was it the unspoken possibility that she would not be able to bring herself to let the baby go?

It was now two in the morning. We had all heard the baby's cry once or twice in the distance. Linda went to see if all was well in the bedroom. She was eager to get away from the tension in the living room. Now Katherine's midwife, a large, soft-featured older woman, started to speak about the grief Katherine would have to live with after she gave them her child. She wanted this couple to know this would not be the same as the grief of a parent whose child had died, since Katherine had freely *chosen* adoption. It would be more like the kind of grief any mother of a grown child feels when it leaves home. Katherine's time with her son would be brief and her experience with him compressed, but not lost. They should know they need not pity her. The couple seemed to hear what she was saying. Still they did not bend in their insistence that it must go *their* way.

I watched their unwillingness to yield and had to speak up, to say that in the final analysis the full decision of just how this exchange took place rested with the young woman in the other room. Legally and in fairness, I reminded them, it was in *her* hands whether they caught the first plane and whether they even became the parents of her child. Tony and Ellen both stiffened at the harsh truth of what I had said and braced for what I might say next. I told them that I didn't want to coerce them but was asking them to step outside their own perspective just for once. All Katherine was asking for was a little more time, that and one brief meeting with the people to whom she was entrusting her child. She would have only this one day to look back on, whereas they would have her child to look upon all their lives. She wanted to create a memory she could take pride in and she had every right to stage these last moments to suit herself. Moreover, I added, knowing well what the impact of my words might be on this sensitive couple, what they were really asking her to do was to hide in the background as birth mothers have been asked to do for years. By asking her to have no identity they were only reaffirming the judgment that birth mothers have no value except as passive vessels out of which babies emerge for other parents to own. That's what adoption has traditionally asked of mothers relinquishing their babies, that they remain hidden. This young woman, I said, is fortunate to know what her rights are, that it doesn't have to be that way. That was the reason she selected them to be parents of her child. All the other couples she had heard about or spoken to had only seemed interested in the baby, but *they* had expressed caring for her as a person. Were they now going to prove her trust in them wrong? I could see that this last remark hit the target I had aimed for. Tony and Ellen both saw themselves as caring people. They sat back hard in their seats, perhaps for the first time seeing the entire adoption in a new light.

I offered a choice to soften the blow. Given Katherine's strong desire to meet them, which would they prefer—to see her alone first, without the baby, and see the baby after, or to see the baby now in her presence? Given the two options, neither of which they wanted, they both chose the less difficult path. They would, they agreed, sitting upright on the edge of the couch, prefer to meet her first without the baby.

Katherine stood at the bathroom counter with Linda changing the baby's diaper, chatting excitedly. It was his first stool, the inky sticky meconium that had been like a plug in his intestines during his intrauterine life and its passage marked his readiness to digest food independent of her. When I came in they stopped what they were doing. Katherine had heard none of the disagreement out front, but she had sensed from the time it was taking that there was resistance to what she wanted. When I suggested her meeting with the couple first without the baby she tensed and her mouth set firm. She could understand their fears about seeing her with the baby, she said. She could sympathize. She'd been doing that anyway every phone conversation with them, whenever they acted afraid she would not go through with the adoption. But she would *not* give in to their fears now. These were her last few hours with her son and she meant to retain all power over this exchange. Maybe, she said in a low flat voice, it was just a sign that they were not the right people to have her baby after all.

I slipped an arm around her tensed shoulders, and whispered that perhaps this was not too much to ask, that she let them face her alone first. She was quiet a moment, looking down at her son. Her shoulders relaxed. Then she said she guessed that would be all right, to meet them first without him. But they would have to see him with her after that.

I went out with the news. The couple relaxed just a bit on the couch. Tony uncrossed his legs and Ellen began to speak with concern about Katherine's feelings. The nurse told them both once again that they needn't worry about her. She had come to her own decision and had the support of many friends and her family. She was not desperate like the mother of the little girl they lost, but a self-confident person who had thought through what she was doing very carefully and had much to be proud of in the way she had gone through pregnancy and birth. She had spent the past fifteen hours happily with her son and she was ready to begin the process of saying goodbye.

To change the subject to an easier one, the nurse asked them whether they had chosen a name for him yet. Their account of their difficulty in selecting a name for a boy, of watching the screen credits of the movie on the airplane hoping to find there the name they were looking for, made everyone laugh including them. In the middle of this light moment, the first since they'd arrived, Katherine herself suddenly walked unannounced into the room. Everything stopped. She greeted the couple warmly and smiled at them through her exhaustion. They stood up, stunned at her appearance and put out their hands to her. The nurse and I stood off to the side. The very sight of Katherine standing in her nightgown before them seemed to change everything. She was no longer the massive unseen threat they'd lived in fear of but just a slender, very young-looking woman with shoulder-length straight dark hair, high cheekbones and extraordinarily clear almond-shaped eyes. Someone broke the silence by remarking how alike the two women looked. They were both petite and dark, each with small arched noses, prominent cheekbones, slender necks and shoulders. They smiled softly at each other in acknowledgment.

Everyone sat together in the living room. Katherine seemed to be enjoying Tony and Ellen's attention and, after accepting their praises for how well and strong she looked, she began to talk about her labor and her son's birth. She was proud, like a warrior, though her birthing had not been a battle. She had given in to labor with a single-mindedness which had surprised all of us. She had a desire to tell them about those hours and she smiled as she spoke. Someday they could tell him.

It had been difficult, she said, like nothing she had ever known before, but they needn't have had anxiety for her well-being or the baby's. A natural birth had been what she had wanted, to be a part of *everything* that went on, not to lose one precious moment of the experience. The labor was thirty hours and she told them she didn't regret a minute of it. She had been surrounded by friends, some old and some like her midwife, physician and me, whom she'd only met near the end of her pregnancy. She knew everyone at her birthing was totally committed to her goals. She had never before felt so much love and attention. Then the moments of his emergence from her, lifted up by her hands while his legs were still inside her, those moments had been the peak of the painful, difficult journey of labor. And, she told Tony and Ellen, the time and work of birth had helped prepare her for what was yet to come.

Now as she sat across from them, feeling their respect for all she had done for them, she appeared small. The strength that had poured into her during labor was ebbing; two nights without sleep and the effort of the birth left her dazed and feeling fragile. She spoke briefly about her plans for the exchange. She told them simply how important it had been to her that she meet them. She had only realized in the last weeks of pregnancy that meeting them would help complete this cycle for her.

She only wanted a little more time so as not to waste the preciousness of her last hours with him on sleep-deprived senses. She needed to sleep a bit, to wash and get dressed. Then she would gladly meet with them again, help them give him his first bath and spend just a little time alone with her son before he left with them. In her presence, finally realizing how little she was asking for, Tony and Ellen glanced quickly at each other and Tony said he would change their morning flight to a later one.

Then Ellen asked her when they might see him. "Right now," Katherine answered, smiling. She left the room and was only gone an instant before she returned carrying him, wrapped in a light blanket in her arms. This time the pair remained seated, unable to move. She walked quickly over to them and placed her son in Ellen's arms. Although she would spend a little more time with him before saying goodbye, that gesture, one she'd rehearsed in her mind so many times, was her first step in letting go. She stood back and watched.

His beauty was striking, silky black hair down a wide forehead, a broad face with extraordinarily well-formed features and eyes that gazed up at them when Tony and Ellen spoke to him as if he knew it all. Katherine then spoke. She told them the scent of his birth was still on his skin, that they could smell it. They bent close to his face.

With that the room began to buzz with conversation, none of it important, all of it significant—the kinds of things people say when words won't do but must be said anyway. Katherine sat on a couch opposite the couple and watched them play with him. She smiled. She said later it was *then* she knew they were his parents. After a few minutes she suddenly stood up to leave, pleading exhaustion. She said she would like to take him back to bed. They stood and gave him back to her in one smooth motion. Before she went the three of them set the time to meet, ten the next morning, there at the home. Then Tony and Ellen kissed Katherine goodnight, leaving their son with her.

The two left the house amid the good wishes of everyone. The night was chill. Thinking it must always be summer in California, Ellen had worn only a sleeveless dress. But then so many things were different from what they had expected. It would be an hour's drive back to the motel by the airport where they'd left their belongings. They were leaving in the middle of the night, empty-armed yet confident and excited. They had come in fear with fantasies of disappointment and plans for escape. Now they too felt Katherine's certainty in her decision to give them this child. Giving her this one night to lie with him seemed easy now. They drove off.

In the warm light of the morning they arrived and greeted Katherine, who was ready for them. Though she hadn't slept at all she felt refreshed by the privacy of the night she'd spent with her son. Even her brother, Tom, had returned to meet them. First she handed the baby to Tom and Linda, that they who had supported her so well and felt such a strong connection with this baby might have some moments alone with him to say their goodbyes. Meanwhile she led Tony and Ellen back to her room, the one with the French doors, which were open to let the warm air in. There on the bed where Katherine had given birth they sat and talked.

She told them all the little things she had discovered about his nature in the past twenty-four hours and the nine-plus months he'd spent with her. Then they prepared a warm bath together and when Tom and Linda brought him in they unwrapped him and placed him in it. Lying there on his back in the water, held in two pairs of women's hands, he was relaxed and alert. The bond of affection for him had expanded to include two more people and he showed no fear. This would be the way Katherine remembered him best. It had not been a whim for her to spend the first night with him and then to bathe him with them this morning. He opened his body like a flower in the warmth of the water and the hands that supported him, and she felt she could read his future in his face. He would be all right with them. It was Linda's last-minute suggestion that put a borrowed camera in the hands of the new father. He, who hadn't wanted to see or know the woman from whom his child came, now took half a roll of film of the two mothers bathing their son, blurred unfocused images in black and white that Katherine would treasure. Then together they dressed him in the clothes the couple had brought while they told her they would call her after they returned to New York, after they had chosen his name, so she could know it too.

They left him alone with her for a few minutes as she had asked. For the first time she explained everything to him, why she was giving him up, who his new parents were, and how this would mean goodbye for the time being. She needed to say it out loud and as she held and talked to him she found the words came easily. It was like a conversation, though he merely watched her calmly. This moment, their leave-taking, was precious, she told him, because it might be their last for a long, long time. But it was no more precious than her life with him had been while she carried him. He should remember that. Soon there was nothing more to say. She chose not to go back through the house but to take him out into the green back yard and in through the side door. The ceremony of it seemed important to her.

Everyone was waiting there. Even as she had taken the short walk around the house she began to cry and, at seeing her silently crying with the baby in her arms, Tom, Linda, the midwife, myself, Tony and Ellen, standing in the entrance hall, were also moved to tears. Her gaze first fell on Ellen. She placed him in her arms. It was time for congratulations and wishes for a safe journey. There were hugs all around and only the baby had a dry face. We walked Tony and Ellen and their new baby outside to their car and waved a final goodbye as they drove off. Then everyone but Katherine went back inside the house.

Katherine stood for a moment in front of the house, watching the car. Suddenly the magic of the last two days dropped away. All she knew, standing there alone on the asphalt in the warm sunshine, was she was achingly, crazily exhausted and felt like screaming. There would be time to sort it all out later and people she could call on to help her. There would be lots of time. But first, first she had to sleep.

Katherine, six months after the birth of her son

KATHERINE

Letting Go

Most traditional societies have ways to help a person in grief. There is no expectation that one must put "a face" on for the outside world. Often noise and movement are encouraged, even ritualized, to give expression to the feelings of shocked numbness, helplessness, anger and hopelessness. And there are things one must do, rites to be followed, for that too helps. Something prescribed to pass the seemingly endless time when the grieving person feels like an outsider to all of life, until life begins to flow again.

Modern city dwellers that we almost all are, we tend to grieve silently and alone. Some try to deny grief's existence altogether and are called strong for doing so. But that is just another fiction, for one does not send grief away by putting a mask over its face. Grief takes its own time and has its own rhythm and its own cleansing. The grief a woman feels following the adoption of her child, like the grief felt for any loved one gone, is undeniable; but it is not unendurable or unending if it is recognized and lived. Sometimes it needs to be expressed and heard.

As private and solitary as Katherine had always been, she found her period of mourning was the third time in a year she had to have the support and availability and presence of friends. She had found she needed it during pregnancy and in birth. It had made all the difference in those experiences; and she needed it again now that she was alone once more.

In the weeks after the baby's leaving she kept to home, unable to face acquaintances around town. Her time was absorbed by the needs of her heart and she spent her days crying, recollecting, daydreaming, accepting the visits of close friends, crying some more. Crying had always been difficult but was now easy. But where sleep used to comfort her, it no longer did. She slept fitfully; though her body was exhausted, her mind would not let her rest. Eating was now difficult. Her knotted stomach recoiled at the thought of food. With the help of one of her friends she found a simple nourishing diet she could digest—Japanese miso soup, fresh fruit. She had to remind herself that she needed to keep her physical strength up, especially now, because not eating would only complicate matters. She needed to grieve, not to punish herself. And so she ate, without wanting to.

Why mourn at all? She might have thrown herself back into life and been able to crowd the pain out of her consciousness. But one thing she had learned from her pregnancy was to do things in their proper time and sequence. Katherine wanted no nightmares to erupt years later from feelings she'd suppressed. Better to go through it now, while it was fresh and she could cry, while there were friends around who had been through the experience with her to understand and make themselves available.

Katherine faced her most difficult challenge yet—time. More time than she'd ever had and less to do, with less reason to do anything than ever before. Labor had taught its lessons well. She discovered in the course of those hours that allowing feelings and sensations to crescendo would bring rest for a time before they swelled anew. She had learned to pay attention to the rhythm inside her, for there was a rhythm. It was not constant pain; and it took more out of her to fight it than to follow its lead and go wherever it took her. It was even possible to find a sort of solace in what was taking place in her body. The highs were so clear they were startling—she was stunned at how content she felt sometimes. At those times she worried whether it was right and fair to her son that she, having walked away from him, should feel so good and right. She asked friends about it, but she knew the answer. It amazed her how irrepressible life was, especially the life force inside her. And when she felt no strength within to draw upon there were still warm summer days and cloudless skies around her to remind her that life existed and everything changes. Even pain.

She found herself awake every two hours through the night with uncanny regularity. She sensed the cause but had to wait seven long days for confirmation in a telephone call. Ellen kept her promise to telephone Katherine and let her know the name they'd chosen for the baby. Christopher. At first Ellen sounded anxious. But soon, hearing Katherine's interest, she was talking easily of all the small details a new parent loves to share. To Katherine this was proof that she had made the right choice for her child. Her greatest fear, throughout the pregnancy and in the week after he was gone, was that his parents might not really be able to love him wholly, just as he was. But she needn't have worried. Ellen said he was the same calm baby he had been when they first met him, and she told Katherine that both she and Tony felt it was her gift to them, his contentedness. She was reassured. If he could be so comfortable in his body and feel a trust in the world he would surely continue to be easy for them to love. And the more love they gave him the more he would certainly thrive. She hung up the phone and felt like dancing.

Katherine had bound her breasts tightly when they first became swollen with milk. She had refused a shot to dry them in order that he should be able to drink of her first milk. Now her breasts were small again and leaked milk no more. But when she put down the telephone she noticed dark wet stains on her shirt front. Tears, she thought. But it was her milk, dripping freely, turned on by a voice 3,000 miles away. So, she was still connected to him. Ellen had told her how he awoke every two hours through the night for feeding. Her waking every two hours each night; it was on *his* schedule. Across the distance of a continent, while one mother awoke to give her son a bottle, another awoke to give him her breast.

Their conversation left Katherine elated for hours. It had come on Monday, the hardest day yet. Christopher had been born the previous Monday. It was not that she had felt the urge to reverse her decision— she knew she was no better able to care for a child now than when she had first decided to give him up. But Monday had been different, from the moment she awoke.

Three days later she received another phone call from New York, this from the attorney. He told her Ellen and Tony had agreed to send her $300 for the month of September to help her out, but it was all they could handle, though they had previously agreed to support her for three months after the birth. She asked when she could expect it, and he said he'd send it right out. Three days passed, then four, and then it was

Monday again. Mondays were the hardest. Katherine screwed up her nerve and placed a call to the attorney. Where was the money? His response was a mumbled apology about confusion in the office; he'd wire it that very afternoon to her bank. He had something he wanted to tell her, and tried to say it quickly. Ellen and Tony didn't want her to have any further direct contact with them. They'd called him after speaking with her and asked him to handle any future dealings with her. She was stunned as if struck and could say nothing.

Her mother flew in from Utah to stay for a week. Katherine had been looking forward to this visit. But instead of feeling she could let go and be a daughter again she found the presence of her mother stifled her. She was on stage, not daring to be herself, and she was relieved when her mother left. Their time together brought them closer; but it put an artificial stop to her grieving.

Still no money arrived. She called the bank each day and felt guilty for doing so, as if she'd asked for a handout. Her mother left what little she could and friends loaned her a bit. And she waited, wondering whether it was the couple themselves who were delaying and didn't want her to have the money.

While she needed to grieve, she also needed to be lifted out of herself at times. People began to encourage her to join them in everyday things: shopping, watching television, coming over for dinner. She found herself stopping by at the birth home just to be in the presence of pregnant women and mothers with new babies. She always carried pictures from the birth. Her favorite was a picture of Christopher, newborn and still wet-faced, lying against her breast. His features crumpled, his dark eyes alight with recognition as he gazed directly up into her face. And there was one showing her first efforts at feeding him. It made her laugh just to remember. They had both been so clumsy as they connected. Her friends listened, noticed how distracted she was in conversation and understood.

The third Monday caught her unawares. She was downtown on a busy street when she remembered what day it was. Tears fell especially hard all that day, downtown, back home, in bed, and on into the morning of the next day. Tuesday began with no relief and she could not understand why this day too felt so difficult. She had forgotten. It was her birthday, the twenty-second anniversary of her own birth. And all she could feel was anxiety about the unfinished business with Christopher's new parents. It was the first time she had felt anger toward them since the night of the birth, when they'd come to the birth home to get Christopher and tried to prevent her even from meeting them. She imagined them now, trying to push her away again. She forced herself to call the attorney once again. He apologized, made some excuse and said he'd get right on it. And the couple, he attempted to reassure her, had just been frightened by her show of interest in their baby and were afraid of what it might lead to.

The call only made her feel worse. After all they had been through with her during the pregnancy, meeting her, their crying and laughing together, how could they now deny the trust they formed? It had all been for nothing, Katherine told herself. All afternoon she talked about it to two of her friends. Why had she chosen this couple anyway? Why had she not held out longer, for people more like her, who would have understood her values, generous people, not emotional cowards! What did this mean for her son? How could they be so stupid as to try and wrench all connection with him so soon! She was not asking to be a part of their lives, only that they recognize he was still a part of hers. The smallest link with them, a letter now and then, a periodic phone call at first, that was all she needed. And they were denying her that just as if she were a piece of refuse, useless to them now that they had the only thing they wanted from her.

Her friends waited until the heat of her anger subsided, till she had no more to say, and then asked her if she could recall how much she had liked them at first. She had to admit she had liked them. And, more important, they had fulfilled her most important criteria for being parents to her child. She knew she could never find anyone who would match all her dreams. She also knew in her heart they were acting now in fear. Still, she felt the sadness.

She telephoned her doctor late in the afternoon and related the events of the day. Had he had any similar experience before in dealing with direct adoptions? His response was different from that of her friends. To him Ellen and Tony's actions showed that they were living in the natural anxiousness that she was going to evaluate any interactions they had with her, and that no matter how hard they tried they would be judged and fall short. They probably imagined she was even considering going back on her decision to give them Christopher. He asked Katherine to have a little extra understanding for their situation, since their worst fears were undoubtedly being bolstered by the people around them. Something he said brought a smile to her face. She was recalling a conversation she'd had with Ellen months before the birth. She had told Ellen then that she would always be there for this child she was carrying, no matter what happened in her life. They must have recalled her words later and thought she must have meant she would always be a haunting shadow over their lives, watching, perhaps hoping to snatch him from them; for a full month after that conversation they hadn't called her. She could smile because she now understood. A pity that they couldn't or wouldn't try to understand her as well. Katherine, who had already given so much, was being asked to give still more—more compassion, more understanding—while they, who had received so much from her, were afraid to give and were finding support which bolstered their fears.

It was time to celebrate her birthday. There was a dinner in her honor. Her brother, Linda, several friends, her doctor all came. They sat around the table with candles and flowers, drinking a toast to her coming year. Then they danced. Finally they curled up on cushions and listened to quiet music. Katherine was given a back rub and the tension of the day was massaged from her shoulders. In twenty-four hours she had come full circle. She went to bed calmer than she'd felt in weeks, ready for a full night's sleep.

Saturday following her birthday she walked to the park to listen to some music. There were people she knew there, among them Dan, a friend. Dan pointed out a slender woman with blond hair down her back. Her name was Claire. He'd spoken about her to Katherine before, about how she had chosen to raise her baby as a single mother, and about the difficult time she was having now that her little girl was an active toddler. Another of their mutual friends also had told Katherine about Claire; in that friend's eyes Claire was a shining example of all that a single mother could do, even without much money. She'd held her up to Katherine as a model who represented everything Katherine was turning her back on by giving up her son. Katherine wanted to meet this woman she'd heard so much about. She walked over and sat down on the grass and introduced herself. It turned out that Claire had also heard about Katherine. They looked at each other a minute before speaking. Then Katherine, seeing the little girl playing nearby unwatched by Claire, asked simply how things were going. Tears began to fill Claire's eyes and she started to talk. A tale of frustration, pain and self-doubt poured out.

When she had become pregnant, by the young man she loved and with whom she had had a relationship off and on since high school, she was depressed. They had used birth control consistently. The depression turned to despondency as Claire saw her dilemma. She had told herself she could never have an abortion, because that would be killing life. Yet she knew too that the young man who was the father would have no part of being a parent. He had other ambitions and they involved embarking on his own business, not starting a family.

Motherhood was as unreal as abortion. She knew she was not emotionally ready, much less ready financially, to be a mother, especially a single mother. So she sought help from a man she looked to as her teacher. A respected man in the community, he was the person who had inspired spiritual yearnings in her, and she looked up to him for his wealth of experience and knowledge. His answer was clear and simple. Claire should carry the baby, give birth and raise it, with or without the father. The pregnancy, he told her, was a sign of life. Why, he asked, won't you let life come through you? Claire was touched by his answer and when she protested that she had no way to raise a child he promised that he and his wife would help her with the baby, financially and in every other way. Claire was in a dream. Practical matters, such as how she would support herself with a baby or where they would live, only entered her thoughts occasionally, in the form of anxiety, and she felt powerless to create what she would need. Her teacher's words carried the day. Others, including her parents, had urged her to consider having an abortion, or at least to think of giving the baby up for adoption, but she was too overwhelmed to listen. When she sought her boyfriend's opinion, his only reaction was that this is your problem; you deal with it. As if to make pointed his reluctance to get involved, he consulted a lawyer, who told him that if he moved out of the house he shared with Claire and another friend, he could effectively deny paternity. Finally he was so uncaring that Claire simply left.

All during her pregnancy Claire thought seriously and often of giving up the baby for adoption. She still could not imagine how she could be a good enough mother alone, without any resources of her own. Yet she felt she could not survive the wrench of giving her baby up, and adoption was thus never a real option. Friends continued to see Claire as having tremendous inner strength. But Claire's own self-image was far more fragile. Motherhood was her only choice because she knew she was not mature enough to make the decision for anything else. And she felt alone and unsupported as she faced it.

So Claire became a mother. She had an uncomplicated birth at home with a midwife and several women helping her. Labor had been so quick it hardly gave her time to prepare emotionally for the baby who was placed wet in her arms. Then, suddenly, she found herself truly alone, more alone than she'd ever been, living round the clock with a new baby, the only one to meet its continual needs, twenty-four hours a day, day in, day out. When she turned in her unhappiness and hopelessness to friends and family for help, a bit of babysitting, some conversation, money to help make the rent payment, they all kept their distance. She was no fun to be around. What Claire needed to raise her spirits and give her the energy to cope was daily help to share in the care of this new life. And she found precious little. The father of the baby kept his word and carefully avoided her and the baby. Claire was driven to establish his paternity legally; there was no doubt about his ability to help her financially, and she desperately needed that help. She began receiving some child support. Despite his promises, her spiritual teacher never offered a bit of help, even after she went so far as to ask for it; he simply brushed the matter off, as if the whole thing had all been some sort of joke and she was learning the lessons she needed to learn.

Now Claire's little girl was bigger. She crept, then she walked and now she could run. And like most children eager to discover what lay beyond their mothers' arms, she took off in any direction as fast as her chubby legs could carry her. Claire did her very best to stay calm and treat her daughter lovingly even when her nerves were raw, but day to day reality wore her out. She could not gain any perspective on their relationship as mother and daughter and it was increasingly impossible for Claire to have any life of her own. As she told Katherine that afternoon in the park, her every waking hour was occupied by a tiny human being whose will seemed stronger than her own, whose energy depleted every bit of hers, and whose very existence now threatened her own. Eighteen months after giving birth, Claire had not yet accepted her status as a mother. She felt inseparably connected to this child she'd borne, yet hated the reality of that connection; though she never wanted to harm her child, she often felt like running away from her.

Claire and Katherine immediately realized their kinship. They were both women in need of comforting. But Katherine at this point appeared the more fortunate because at least she had no one dependent on her, no one whom she might hurt out of her own pain. The entire time Claire had been talking, holding Katherine's hand and crying, Katherine kept an eye on the little girl. She sped around the park as if on wheels, first lighting on someone's lap, then suddenly darting to the edge of the busy street. More than once Katherine interrupted Claire to go rescue the child. Claire seemed to veer from complete inattentiveness to sudden anxious concern for her little girl. She was desperate for the attention Katherine offered, even at the expense of her own child's safety. She told Katherine she loathed her life. There was never enough money to take care of the two of them and she was so worried and frightened she couldn't find any enjoyment in being a mother. She asked Katherine to come over that evening, sensing that they shared some deep under-standing.

That evening Katherine went to Claire's apartment and saw more of what she'd seen in the park. The little girl was overtired, running out of control, and a distraught Claire was at her wits' end and exhausted. The bedtime ritual was the worst. First she demanded the child stop playing and come to her to get ready for bed. When the little girl ignored her, Claire turned to Katherine and began to talk about herself. Then sud-denly, remembering her daughter, she rushed to where her child was playing and grabbed her arm. As soon as Claire touched her, she burst out crying. The tears seemed only to frustrate Claire more. Wasn't damage being done? Wasn't violence being communicated in every word and each touch? Several times Katherine went over to the crying child and picked her up. By now her arms were aching to hold her own son, and the feelings of loss welled up until she thought she would have to run out of the house and see and hear no more. Yet she could not pretend that she might not have acted like Claire were she too a single mother. Part of what held Katherine there was the recognition that she was being given a glimpse into the future she might have had.

As she held the crying child and attempted at the same time to comfort and reassure the troubled mother, she was frightened. The friends who had admired Claire as a model of motherhood's endurance must have seen the tremendous effort but ignored the anguish and the sadness Claire felt. Out of the sight of friends and the rest of the world, this well-intentioned, caring young woman was not so quietly going mad. Only rigid self-control had enabled her to provide for the most basic needs of her child. But self-control is never enough in the face of overwhelming pressure. The stresses were tearing Claire apart.

It sent a chill over Katherine when, during the evening, Claire told her, "I wish sometimes I had done what you did. I envy you your freedom. Sometimes, even now, I think I'll *have* to give her up for adoption." Katherine returned home shaken. Only once in her life had she experienced what Claire must be feeling often, that she was completely out of control. That had been right after Christopher's departure when she stood in the driveway watching the couple drive away with him. Then she had felt it, that black swirling void sucking her down into its depths. She had thought at the time she must be going crazy, but she'd managed to hang on to one slender thread of hope—that those terrifying feelings were partly a result of her exhaustion and lack of sleep. For her madness had been a temporary feeling. But she had no child needing her each day, needing and demanding from her when she had nothing left inside from which to give. While this woman felt trapped and was turning into a twisted version of herself, filled with self-loathing and sorrow, Katherine had been granted a second chance. She could only weep for Claire and for the suffering of Claire's child.

The following Monday Katherine stood in my kitchen talking. Her own doubts were again eating at her. She wasn't sleeping well. In the absence of any communication from either the parents or their lawyer, and after his strong insistence that she not press them, it was becoming difficult even to recall what she had first found in them that caused her to select them for her baby. She remembered they had not believed in direct, open adoption in the first place. Their sole desire was to get a baby any way they could short of buying one. And she'd begun to ask herself whether the way they were treating her was indicative of the way they would raise her son. She didn't want him raised in fear and mistrust of every new thing.

I had one suggestion. Perhaps if she could talk with a couple who had adopted through direct adoption, tell *them* her feelings, and hear from them what it was like to be on the adopting side, she might be able to understand better what was going on. I called Paul and Vicki, the parents of Abigail, and asked if they might have a few minutes to meet with Katherine. She spent most of the following afternoon with them at their home. Their two daughters were still young and Paul and Vicki recalled for Katherine quite vividly what they had felt during their first months with each of the girls. They had several thoughts that hadn't occurred to any of Katherine's friends. First, they said, she should re-member that this couple were new parents. On top of all the anxieties involved with the adoption and the feeling of being in limbo until the final papers were signed, they had the countless nameless anxieties that beset new parents. Vicki could recall the apprehension with which she had viewed the prospect of any interaction with Pat, Abigail's birth mother, after Abigail's birth. Although she'd told Pat she was welcome to call, even visit, to see that Abby was well and well-loved, she was not prepared for any more contact, not at first. She said this was even more true when they first got Amanda, their older daughter. Feelings of possessiveness ran strongest during the early months. Looking back now, from a distance of several years, Vicki said she would feel quite comfortable if either birth mother were to knock on her door tomorrow. She could welcome her because she was today secure as a mother. But that wasn't so in the beginning. For Vicki, private adoption and being present at the baby's birth had at first seemed odd. She had probably shared the rather conservative upbringing that Christopher's new par-ents seemed to have had. She was able to bring a reality about Chris-topher's life to Katherine where previously there had been none. Vicki and Paul suggested that Katherine's impressions of the couple before the birth were likely to prove true in the long run. The ungracious behavior she was now experiencing was, in Vicki's eyes, likely to be short-lived and *not* a predictor of Christopher's future.

Ellen and Tony fulfilled Katherine's most important criterion, that they be able to love and care for a child. Should she be faced with the same decision all over again, Katherine now knew she would have additional criteria for prospective parents to meet. She might try and find people more like her in their view of the world and in their style of life. But though this couple was not of her world, they were good people and they loved Christopher. Katherine returned home with her mind untroubled for the first time in weeks.

A large chunk of grief seemed to dissolve that day. Katherine was beginning to release Christopher. There would be more; but she felt relieved that a massive weight was now gone. The smell in the air meant summer was passing. Her daily walks could be at a brisker pace now that her body was getting back its strength. The stretch marks left behind from pregnancy on her thighs and abdomen would eventually fade. She could almost, but not quite, zip up her old blue jeans. She'd bought new ones anyway, one size larger, and was rather enjoying this new body of hers. She was no longer a 97-pound girl, but a woman, with a body that bore some scars of living.

With the small amount of assistance promised her by the attorney still nowhere in sight, she resolved to make one more call to New York, even though it made her feel cheap. His secretary said he was out of town for the afternoon and made a promise to see that the money was wired to her bank as soon as he returned. The money arrived the next day.

She was planning to visit her parents and was looking forward to the train ride to Utah, the hours of nothing to do but watch the landscape slide by her window, a chance to be a traveler. Her father had offered her the use of his small studio outside of town and she was glad she would have it all to herself for the short time she was to be there. Eight months ago this train ride had been the scene of the biggest decision of her life. Now, lulled by the train's motion, she thought about Christopher's father. It had been almost a full year since they'd slept together. She no longer remembered clearly what he looked like. But she still had a cycle to complete with him and she told herself she'd try and contact him when she returned. She knew he felt some self-pity, some guilt. He had missed out on everything. She wasn't sure how she would feel seeing him again but it was something she had to do. They would sign the final adoption papers together. That would be the end of it. And next month she would enroll in school and start work on becoming a writer.

I met her at the station when she returned. Standing with hunched shoulders, looking bewildered in the crowd and much, much thinner than I'd seen her, Katherine seemed a child lost. When she saw me she smiled quickly in relief. In the car we rolled up all the windows to shut out the noise of traffic and the city heat. Her shoulders sank back against the seat. It had been a good visit, she said; it gave her the rest and solitude she needed. But she was so glad to be back.

The first few days were a difficult readjustment. Her roommate Linda was in love; and her work kept her away from home till late every night. Often she wouldn't come home until after Katherine was asleep, and when they did cross paths Linda had little energy left over to give her best friend. Linda's happiness only underscored Katherine's sadness. But she was determined to get back into life. In the next week, visiting the coffee shop, the bookstore, shopping for food, she renewed old acquaintances and made new ones. She was thin and pale but her face could always light up in conversation. Men found her attractive. Several asked her out. She went once or twice, but felt distant and awkward. She wasn't ready, she told herself.

Standing sideways in front of a long mirror, she examined her fading stretch marks and her bloated abdomen. She still had not resumed her period. And she was feeling guilty that she hadn't thought about Christopher in two whole days. He was drifting away from her. Even the birth was fading in vividness. Would she soon have nothing left? Yet, she fretted, she didn't want to spend her life carrying a dead memory, never starting a new relationship, not daring to risk for fear of losing. In a way she felt the grieving more difficult now than ever because now she could and had to function in daily life. She knew it was time to look for work, before she could afford to enroll in school. Yet she was so distracted. She was forgetting appointments, standing up friends for dates. What job could she hold?

She made a phone call one evening to the roommate of Christopher's father, to ask if he knew when he might be returning. To her shock she found out that he was back in town and he had been for more than a month; but he wasn't in just then. The next few nights she couldn't sleep, just lay in her bed going over and over the events of the past year. She knew that he knew where to reach her; yet he had never bothered.

And so she called him. The anger welled up inside her when she heard the familiar voice on the line, then dissolved, and she found herself eager to see him. He was friendly enough and they made a date to see each other. She told her friends she was doing it for Christopher's sake. Christopher deserved to have his father know as much about him as possible. She admitted she had hopes that he would become interested in his son after hearing about the birth. She would share the pictures with him. If he only cared, then he might stay in touch with the attorney in New York, keep a current address. For Christopher's sake.

But it was for her sake too that she would see him. I saw her the morning of their planned meeting. She'd dressed with care and looked lovely, though frail, in a blue jean skirt and embroidered Mexican blouse. Looking at her, who would have guessed how big her abdomen had been only two months earlier? She was feeling as if her heart were stuck in her throat. If only the sound of his voice had brought the old feelings of excitement back, what would it be like being with him again? She carried the pictures from the birth with her to their meeting.

I spoke to her that evening on the phone. She was still in a state of excitement, but felt disappointment too. He looked just as he had when she last saw him. She'd felt the pull immediately. She didn't know whether he felt it too; but he certainly didn't feel it for his son. She hoped her description of Christopher, the pictures of the birth, would bring him alive to his father. They hadn't. He had reacted no differently from anyone else who hadn't been there. Except her parents. Her father had been visibly overwhelmed when she'd shown the photos to him, and her mother had cried. But her parents had seen in the small images their daughter and their grandson—their only grandchild, lost to them. As for Christopher's father, Katherine said, he seemed aloof and distant looking at the pictures. She tried to control the disappointment in her voice. Why should a dozen squares of shiny colored paper kindle deep feelings? To him, nothing at all had happened in the months he'd been gone. How could he really think or feel otherwise, when she sat across from him looking exactly as she had when he'd last seen her? She hadn't shown him the stretch marks. Anyway, she excused him, he had his life all mapped out. Being a political activist, working for the good of mankind, he'd mapped his life out long before he graduated from Harvard or met Katherine. He didn't want to take any detours. A man, whose body wasn't touched by bearing a child, he had the luxury of not having to take any detours.

It was, she said, as if everything she had done this past year, carrying and bearing Christopher, choosing a home for him, was all somehow trivial when compared to what he had seen while working in Latin America—revolution, tortured children, death on the streets. He had told her a bit about it, about how he'd been part of a national literacy campaign to give peasants power and the vote and asked her to try and imagine what it must feel like to see a sixty-year-old man sitting alongside a fourteen-year-old boy who is teaching him to read for the very first time. He'd seen his efforts bring hope into that man's eyes. Katherine's admiration for his principles was clear. *His* cause was noble, his vision inspired. But what was *she?* Just a woman who had given birth, a woman who had never known real poverty or ill health, whose belly would never go empty. She had told him what it felt like when she gave birth, the overwhelming love she'd had, the realization that she would gladly have given up her life then for Christopher. His response was a curious remark about how what she'd done was socialism in its purest form. No, Katherine bridled, it's nothing of the sort. It's a mother's love.

They were worlds apart. All they could do now were the practical things, signing the papers, exchanging addresses. He had offered to pay the costs from the pregnancy, half of everything. But Katherine couldn't take him seriously because she knew it was only an idea for him, just a matter of principle.

Eight weeks after the birth Katherine had her first period in more than a year. With it came a renewed longing for Christopher and for the intimacy they'd shared, for someone or something to fill up the deep hollow inside her. What followed in the next month was another brief period of enchantment with Christopher's father. Katherine saw him regularly and he too seemed infatuated with her. They began to show affection, hugs and kisses, walking hand in hand. They talked about Christopher. They went out alone together some evenings, but they never attempted to spend the night together. Then he told her he had begun seeing the woman he'd gone with when he was a student at Harvard, before he'd met Katherine. She continued to see him anyway.

Then one evening at a party she left in his backpack her notebooks and the diary she'd been writing in since the pregnancy began. It seemed a bad omen that he didn't bother to call her about it; but when she called he said he'd like to come over and see her house—he hadn't been inside. They planned a breakfast meeting. Katherine felt she needed him, for she was hurting badly. But how, she asked herself, could the imbalance of the past year ever be set right, the year of her life she'd given to their son? She knew they could never start a new relationship on the roots of the old and that Christopher would forever be a shadow between them. Yet she needed something from him, his affection, his consolation.

She had heard nothing lately from the attorney in New York. She'd given up on having any more help with living expenses from the couple, but there were still some medical bills outstanding from the pregnancy that she couldn't pay without their promised contribution. And she was still waiting for the written agreement the attorney had promised to draft, have them sign and then send on for her signature, an agreement that she would receive a picture and a brief note on Christopher's progress every six months until he turned eighteen. The attorney had been the one who suggested it and told her it would be easily arranged. They would send the picture and the report to him and he would forward it to her.

She had already signed the adoption papers and needed only to have Peter, the biological father, sign them before sending them to the attorney. It wasn't yet six months, the legal period she had in which to change her mind, but she knew she never would, no matter what happened. For Christopher's sake. Still, it had occurred to her that as long as she held the papers she had one thing they needed, something to make them keep their agreements to her. She had called the attorney early that week to ask where the agreement was and to remind him, for the third time, that she had yet to see the check to pay the long-overdue bills. She was now getting weekly notices and threats to turn her account over to the bill collector. He had sounded stiff and cold over the phone and had asked her whether she was holding on to the adoption papers as leverage. She could hardly answer, she was so close to tears with frustration and anger.

So the last days had been especially difficult, with Linda still hardly ever at home, and the unpaid lab bills sitting in a pile on her table. She had been unable to eat and now weighed well under 100 pounds. She felt too anxious and depressed to cook for herself and asked Christopher's father if he'd please bring over a sandwich when he came.

He arrived to find her standing in the driveway, elated for the first time in weeks. The formal agreement, signed by the couple and binding them to send photos and status reports on Christopher, was in her hand. There was no mention of money for the bills but this was cause enough to celebrate. They ate and she felt strong enough to confront him about his not having called her to say he had her diary. She said she was sure that if she had not called him he would not have bothered to contact her. Not one to lie when faced with facts, he admitted he probably wouldn't have called her for a while. He apologized, as he always did, and then began talking about his relationship with the other woman he was seeing. Katherine didn't want to hear the details. She told him all she wanted from him was friendship. Then he signed the adoption papers and she showed him the pile of overdue notices. He wrote a check for two hundred dollars made out to her, and sat with her as she wrote out checks to pay most of the bills.

After he'd gone, Katherine told Linda she felt as if she had just said a final goodbye. Charming as ever and still immensely attractive to her, he was not what she wanted in a man or as a father for a child. He was too ready to run, too riddled with guilt, too full of his own self-pity, too righteous about his work. Yet she felt he did care, about Christopher as well as her.

She sent off the adoption papers as soon as he had signed them. By now she had begun referring to Ellen and Tony in conversation as "the parents." She was distancing herself one more step. But the longing for her son continued. Though not ever-present, it was there like a shadow at her shoulder. She seldom cried any more. She was working again, at a part-time job in a clothing store, and she'd volunteered to be labor support for two single mothers at the birth home. But everyone noticed how pale and thin she was, and she seemed to have a constant cough. People urged her to slow down and take it easy. How? she wondered.

She kept pushing herself to do more. She became closer with Claire and took on the responsibility of a godmother to the little girl, caring for her for one evening a week so Claire could go to work as a waitress. She felt that Claire and her daughter were both perhaps a bit calmer for her presence in their lives. Claire had even begun seeing a therapist and was now trying to seek other mothers to spend time with instead of all her friends who had no responsibilities, who couldn't appreciate her needs as a mother. If only she weren't tired all the time Katherine felt she'd like to do more, for Claire and her daughter and for others. Finally, at the suggestion of a friend, she made an appointment to see a doctor. She was shocked but a little relieved to find out that she had pneumonia and would have to rest in bed for at least two weeks.

As the cool coastal winter set in Katherine felt her life was at a dead stop. Nothing was working. She had lots of time to think about Christopher now, to go over in detail each of the negative reactions she'd gotten from people whom she'd told about giving Christopher up. Not her friends, at least not most of them. But it seemed that the better she had begun to feel about herself and her decision, the more she had drawn criticism for what she'd done. A woman who worked at her physician's office said, behind Katherine's back, that she found the thought of actually choosing to give away one's own child repulsive. She was too discreet to tell Katherine this to her face but the word had got back to her. A young man at a party had called her decision selfish and asked her bluntly how she expected to live with herself over the years. "Is this what my life will be like from now on?" she wondered gloomily. Thinking back to her friend Claire, who despite improvement in her life was still having a very hard time, she wondered whether this was what society would prefer. At least sick in bed she didn't have to face the critical judgments of other people for what she had done. She wished someone had warned her, told her that she would be breaking a great social taboo by giving a child up for adoption.

Her mother wrote to say she was coming out in late December to stay for a week and help out. By the time she arrived Katherine was out of bed but still feeling physically more exhausted than ever before in her life. And it was like a weight pressing down on her, the cloud of depression that hung over her. She was barely able to speak. She managed to pull herself together for the visit, but it was a painful effort. Her mother fluttered around the house, busily doing and talking, urging Katherine not to go back to bed. She must have felt her daughter's exhaustion but perhaps not knowing what else to do, she thought she could force Katherine back to health by keeping her on her feet. When she finally went, after seven hectic days, Katherine looked like a ghost. She seemed frantic too, pacing around the house, beginning and abruptly ending conversations in a strangely agitated and distracted manner.

Linda drove Katherine's mother to the airport and Katherine went out for the day to the ocean with her friend Art. She told Linda after she returned that in Art's company and near the sea she had felt normal for the first time in weeks. What she couldn't tell anyone was that she knew the calm wouldn't last. By morning she was in the midst of a full-fledged depression. All she knew, as she made an effort to withdraw from everyone in her world, was that she felt numb and isolated and desperately afraid. The cloud she'd felt around her for weeks had descended again, and she was too exhausted to fight it, too shut down to call for help.

Somehow the Christmas season passed. During the next month she made whatever excuses she had to to keep people from calling her or coming around. She didn't see her brother once, and quietly slipped from view around town. Linda, the one person close to her during all this time, was in the midst of an exciting period in her life and, though she saw her roommate was feeling bad, she never guessed that this was the worst of times for Katherine. Having never experienced a deep depression herself, she could not read its signs.

It became a trial to get through each day. Katherine would sleep late, after lying awake most of the night, and when she finally managed to push herself out of the bed she would hurl herself into frenzied activity—cleaning the house and recleaning it, washing and ironing everything in sight, and even picking flowers for the house from their garden. In trying to arrange the flowers artistically she would come to an impasse and start in on a ritual of self-loathing. She couldn't get anything right, not ever! Why bother to try! She was worthless! Then she'd begin to shake violently. Finally she'd fall on her bed and gaze at whatever was on television, unthinking, until she dozed off. She only ate by forcing herself to, late in the day, and then only food she'd eaten as a child. Milk on cereal. Each night when Linda returned, she would find her roommate sitting bleary-eyed in front of the TV and the house immaculate.

Katherine began to use the small bottle of prescription sleeping pills her physician had given her after the birth. She carefully doled out one each night. During the day, alone in the house, she cried at nothing in particular. She couldn't wait for Linda to leave the house, despite the terror being alone brought; at least then she wouldn't have to make the superhuman effort to speak. The weather was continually gray. On the few days the sun came out at all, Katherine would tell herself she had to get out. But she never did. She didn't think of Christopher much at all during that whole month. The only person she ever called, and that was rarely, was her friend Art. Some years older and always good-natured and low-key, never pressuring her about anything, Art was a comfort at those times when she'd force herself to phone him. Sometimes, after talking to him, her mood would suddenly shift and she would be temporarily elated.

Finally, feeling hopeless but unwilling to wait it out any longer, despairing that her life would ever mean anything again, she telephoned me and asked the name of the therapist I'd told her about many months before. I was surprised to find she had been at home all that time. Everyone had assumed she'd been away. I asked if there was anything I could do and encouraged her to phone the therapist. She didn't want to see me but promised she would call the woman I'd suggested, someone I had seen myself and trusted for her sensitivity when I was depressed.

When the time came for her appointment she dragged herself out of the house, propelled more by fear than hope. She was more afraid of not going than of meeting this stranger, afraid that what she was experiencing would never end. No one in her family had *ever* gone outside to ask for help, had *ever* admitted a professional into his personal emotional problems. But Katherine found herself able to talk with the therapist rather easily. She felt well enough after the visit to call her brother and make plans to go to the city for the evening. They went out the next day and had dinner at a restaurant and even went dancing. They didn't get home till the middle of the night. Tom went back to his house but Katherine couldn't sleep.

Late the next morning, as she numbly followed her daily ritual and struggled to arrange the flowers just right, suddenly she felt a large black hole open up just in front of where she stood. Terrified, she staggered to bed, feeling utterly alone. She told herself this was what it was to go mad. She couldn't cry and so, in desperation, she began talking out loud to herself as a mother would. Over and over she said, "It's okay, baby. It's okay." The past month had been bleak enough to bring her to the point of thinking about suicide. But at that moment the idea of death was even more frightening than the hell she was living in.

She thought of her friend Art and reached out to call him. She described in a few halting sentences the terror, and Art said he'd be right over. Katherine suddenly remembered she was expecting Claire's little girl for the evening. It was Friday and, as she'd been doing every Friday, except when she was in bed with pneumonia, she cared for her while Claire went to her job. She hadn't looked forward to those evenings for many weeks now, but the weekly visits brought her a certain renewed strength and confidence that she could maintain some semblance of normality in her life. So she asked Art not to come over until later, after she'd put the little girl to bed. While she was taking care of her she was able to forget herself and her problems, because the child needed all of her attention.

When he came she tried to explain what was happening inside her. He listened quietly and held her as if she were his child. She asked him please to stay with her and he did, holding her close throughout the long night. She was able to cry and in time the dread passed and she slept.

She took herself to the next visit with the therapist and found once more that she was able to talk. "The terrors," as she referred to them later, only returned three times that week. Another hour with the therapist, another week at home, and this time the black hole came only once. This time it felt almost like a cleansing when it ended.

Her weekly visits were now of real help, great islands in a great dead sea of depression. The therapist had been willing to defer payment until Katherine was back working and she clung to the hope of each visit, knowing that the kind of work she did there brought blessed relief. She no longer turned to the sleeping pills and was sleeping more regularly. Her moods now seesawed sharply between bleak terror, when she felt cut off from the world, and sunny elation, when she felt a sense of connection with all of life. Slowly she began to talk to Linda and Art about what she was going through. The feeling of helpless terror came less and less and stayed shorter times. Although she was still depressed, she realized one morning that she hadn't felt desperate in more than a week. Her therapist suggested she should not consider this the end of those feelings, because they came from deep within herself, not from somewhere outside, but that she might try, when she was feeling good, to call the dread feelings up and spend a brief period of time with them while she was feeling safe and secure. This way she might begin slowly to become acquainted with a part of herself she didn't know and would also be less panicked when the feelings caught her unaware in the future. Her experience with Christopher had opened her and made her acutely sensitive and vulnerable and it would be a long time before she could integrate the meaning of it all into her life.

And so, after six weeks, Katherine found herself climbing back out of the blackness she'd slipped into. She continued to see the therapist for several more visits until, with no prospect of being able to pay, she stopped. But she vowed she would seek more help in therapy when she could afford it and that she would never, never let herself feel so alone again.

The end of the first year found her back in close contact with her brother and her parents. After she wrote her father a long letter describing some of what it had been like for her being pregnant, giving birth the way she had and then giving up her baby, he called to say that he had lived in private agony all those months, knowing what she must be going through and yet also knowing there was no way he could protect her from it. He admitted that he too had had terrible depressions and had hid them from everyone and felt all the more alone for it! Their shared experience has given her and her father a new understanding and feeling for each other, and that has been a gift.

Katherine spent the first anniversary of Christopher's birth at the birth home with most of the friends who had been with her in labor. We held a surprise party in her honor and shared a meal out on the patio. Then Katherine went back to the room where she had given birth and lain with Christopher, and she spent a few private moments in memory. She had still heard nothing from Christopher's parents or the attorney and had not received a word about her son, and this continued to trouble her. Some of her friends encouraged her to contact the attorney once more and if necessary to get her own attorney, someone who would pursue her right to know how he was doing, according to the agreement the parents had signed with her. Unable to believe the couple and the attorney would willfully break a written commitment, she continued to wait, past the time when the second progress report and picture were due. Finally, at the end of August, she dialed the familiar number in New York City. The attorney was out of town, his secretary told her. Katherine left a strongly worded message that suggested she might have to take legal action; but she has never followed up on the threat and she never heard from the attorney again.

Does she regret her choice of parents or think of herself as Christopher's real mother? No. *"They* are his parents now," she can say. "They've really been his parents since the day I gave him to them." And, she admits, were she to examine her own two parents with the same strict criteria she has judged the adoptive parents of her son, her own parents could be found lacking too. The couple she chose have done their best, considering their fear of her. Today she feels that any woman who chooses the adoptive parents for her child has a responsibility not only to find a good and loving home for her child, but to find a solution that meets *her* needs as well. She really ought to make the decision on two different counts—finding people she trusts will give her child what she would have given him if she were able, and also finding people who will treat her fairly and with compassion. Katherine feels she made a wise choice about a couple who will love and care well for her son. As a woman attempting to do something extraordinary in the way of adoption and who had no models to follow to help her through the process, she did the best she could. And that is what she will have to live with.

Evelyn and Arnie with their two adopted sons:
Joss, age two, Diane's child; and Bowie, son of Lisa, age seven days

A Shared Beginning

It was a shock to Diane to realize that she might be pregnant. She was twenty-three and her life had no real direction yet. Her relationship with her boyfriend of several years had been on-again, off-again for some time. They no longer lived together. She knew what his response to pregnancy was likely to be. Yet no matter what, she would look forward to being a mother. She had always wanted children.

She knew other mothers who were single. Some had ended up that way in the middle of pregnancy or in the first few months after the baby came, when the baby's father decided he wanted out. Many of those mothers were bitter. But Diane also knew a few who had planned their pregnancies even though they knew they would probably be parenting alone. They were usually in their thirties, unmarried and with careers, women resigned to the prospect of no stable adult relationship but wanting to have children nevertheless. Thinking about what it would be like having no father sharing the parenting, she was aware that there were others, men and women friends, who would make good aunts and uncles. She was sharing a large house with some of these friends and felt she had a family there; that made it easier to contemplate raising a child. It never even entered her mind to have an abortion or give the baby up for adoption.

From the beginning Diane planned a home birth. She knew of two midwives, Mary and Debbie, who had attended many births together. As soon as she got the confirming test result she made an appointment to see them, and soon began to feel part of a close circle of women who were all planning home births.

The pregnancy went along smoothly. Except for the fact that her boyfriend reacted as she'd expected he might and mostly stayed away, Diane felt good and strong and glad to be alive. Seeing the midwives for prenatal care meant leisurely visits at their homes, having tea, talking with other pregnant women on the way in and out, taking classes together.

When she was in her fourth month of pregnancy the size of her abdomen increased considerably between two visits and one of the midwives mentioned to her that a reason for this could be that she was carrying twins. But twins didn't run in Diane's family or her boyfriend's and she laughed at the idea. At the next visit the other midwife examined her and thought for a moment she heard a faint second heartbeat. But it could have been her imagination; they'd wait a bit and see. In June, six months pregnant and very much larger, Diane visited the midwives again. At the door she nearly bumped into a woman who was just leaving. "She must be pregnant too," Diane thought, and scanned the other woman for signs. The two smiled at each other and Diane asked when she was due. Not for another five months, she was told. They laughed at how big Diane was already and then went their separate ways.

Mary told Diane about the woman she'd just met. Her name was Evelyn, and Mary was very worried about her. She had already lost two babies, one in a stillbirth, the other in a miscarriage. And it looked as if she might lose this one early in pregnancy. The baby didn't appear to be growing and Mary was sending her to a physician for a consultation.

As Mary listened carefully to her abdomen, Diane tried to imagine what it must be like to lose a baby while carrying it and felt blessed for having such an easy time. Then Mary looked up, worried. This time she was sure she heard two distinct heartbeats. They looked at each other for a long time in silence. There was nothing to say. Diane went to the phone to make an appointment with a physician for a scan to determine how many babies there really were.

The scan left no doubt. Diane went home to bed. At first there was no thinking, just a numbness over her whole body. Then there was one clear thought behind the numbness. "If I have twins," she whispered to herself, "I will only keep one. I'll give one up for adoption."

The midwives thought it best to give Diane a little time to absorb the news before they talked with her about what it meant. For one thing, everything about the birth would change. There could be no home birth now. But that was nothing compared to the problems facing Diane after the birth, raising two babies as a young single mother. Debbie and Mary would continue to see her through the pregnancy but they would not be her primary birth attendants. They had no hospital privileges and could only arrange to stay with Diane through labor if the physician agreed to it.

Diane did not want to get up the next morning, or any morning after that. It was as if someone had pulled a plug and all her strength and joy had drained out of her body. There was no caring, no emotion at all. Then came a sweeping wave of hopelessness and one thought turning over and over in her mind. "How will I make it alone with two babies?" From her conscious mind came the answer. "You'll have to give them both up." Then an immediate response from deep within. "I can't! I want to have a baby! I'll just keep one of them." And again her thoughts answered. "No. You can't do that. It's wrong to split up twins. You'll have to give them both up." When the internal dialogue ended, depression engulfed her. She could hardly get out of bed, much less sit up or call a friend. But she forced herself to sit in meditation every morning after her housemates had gone. Sometimes she was able to free her mind of all anxiety, all thought, for a brief moment. Just the practice helped. She asked God to show her the way through. No answer came. Her housemates were considerate and loving and sympathized with Diane's pain, but they had no answers either.

When Diane went for her next visit with Mary and Debbie, she was having a recurring image in her mind, a picture of herself healthy and with one baby. That is what she saw in dreams now and it was what came to her during meditation. She knew what it meant: finding parents for one of the babies. But an adoption was something very foreign to her. She couldn't imagine asking an agency to find parents. She would choose the parents for her child herself. She tried the idea out on a few people, of keeping one baby and giving the other up. Most of the responses were negative. "How could you even think of separating twins?" She never considered discussing it with her boyfriend. He would be no help. She had written her mother that she was pregnant when she first found out, and she knew that since her mother had already lost her only son to suicide, she was not going to risk her relationship with

Diane by criticizing anything Diane did. Yet Diane did not want to talk to her until she had come to her own decision.

It was to the midwives that she poured out her private anguish. "I'm going to give them both up." Mary and Debbie looked at each other. Debbie quietly asked Diane whether that was what she really wanted to do. "Oh, no," she blurted. "What I really want is just to have one baby!" "Well, then," Debbie said softly, "you've made your decision." "But what will other people think?" They had to remind her that the only person who could make this decision was the person who cared most and who had to live with the consequences, Diane herself. Suddenly Debbie had an idea. There was a couple she and Mary were seeing who wanted very much to adopt a baby. A son had been stillborn and only a week before the woman had miscarried for the second time. Diane knew immediately whom she must be talking about. Years later she would recall her reaction to Debbie's words. "It was as if my heart opened up and a big weight flew right out." She begged Debbie and Mary to call Evelyn right then and ask if she and her husband would be interested in meeting her; she left exhilarated and impatient. She didn't have to wait long. Evelyn, sounding very excited, phoned the same day to say yes, she and her husband, Arnie, were interested.

On a Monday afternoon Diane took the bus over to Evelyn's. Arnie was out of town on business. The women remembered each other from their brief encounter and there was no stiffness between them. They talked excitedly for four hours. Diane couldn't help noticing the lovely home, all the special belongings Evelyn and Arnie had collected in their twelve years together. She liked the way they lived and looked forward to feeling as good about Arnie as she did about Evelyn. They arranged to meet again when he could be there too.

From that day Diane's pregnancy had no cloud over it. She was as drawn to Arnie as she'd hoped she would be; and she and Evelyn began to see each other often, sometimes every week, and to talk on the phone in between. Sometimes they met at her house, sometimes at theirs. It was apparent to Diane from the first meeting that this couple was anxious about the adoption. They had been disappointed in childbearing so often. Their greatest fear, that Diane would change her mind and not give them a baby, was a possible reality, but Diane had a fear of her own—that they would decide not to go through with the adoption. "And what would I do then?"

206

Talking freely together helped. One of their friends suggested it might be good if they went for joint counseling and they did, learning to listen for the nuances of one another's feelings and to express their feelings openly. It had always been difficult for Diane to accept her anger. Allowing it to surface, having someone listen to her without judging, really helped. Sometimes she could even laugh afterward. And she was beginning to see that she did not have an obligation to tell everyone she knew about her plans. For her own protection she became more discriminating.

Evelyn and Arnie were cautious and self-protective too. They postponed setting up a nursery for the baby even though they had an empty room in their house just waiting to be decorated. They were thinking of Diane as well as of themselves. She could change her mind. They cared about her feelings and by the end of the pregnancy had begun calling her daily just to chat and see if there was anything they could do for her. Diane appreciated the attention and the two women found a sisterly love growing between them.

Diane's mother was at first shocked. But she soon realized that Diane was doing the very best she could, given her circumstances, and she became increasingly supportive. In planning the birth Diane again turned to Mary and Debbie; she was still feeling no inclination to involve her boyfriend, since she hardly saw him at all now. He was still asking for distance, and she felt obliged to give it to him. When now and then she did see him, she would tell him how things were progressing but shared little else. Mostly her time was taken up just living, cooking for herself, swimming, walking, regularly sitting in meditation, seeing or talking to Evelyn or Arnie and the midwives. She talked a lot to the babies, stroking her abdomen in the places where she could feel they lay alongside each other. For several months now she'd noticed how different they seemed. "I know you need extra love and care," she whispered to the one that lay on the right side. She found herself rubbing that side all the more, even as she apologized to the other for neglecting it a bit. "I'm sorry to be spending so much attention on your brother or sister," she'd say. "But I know he or she needs me right now." She told no one about these private conversations, but she always felt the babies were communicating with her and that she was giving the weaker one strength by focusing extra attention on it. Meanwhile she and Arnie and Evelyn began to meditate together and "talk" with the babies, telling them they would be going to separate homes, that they were loved and needn't worry.

By the last month of pregnancy Diane knew it was time to move. Although her housemates had been very supportive and were looking forward to helping with the baby, they all had their own busy schedules. And they were no longer on the same rhythm that she was. She was slowing down more and more, finding her size cumbersome and feeling increasingly introspective. She was getting ready for the birth, and she felt she needed to find a quiet place to settle. She began looking in the paper but housing had never been easy to find, especially if you were on welfare, as she now was. But news spread, and it wasn't long before a friend called to say she knew of someone about to move out of an upstairs apartment in a complex of cottages and apartments. Diane went to see it. There were neighbors all around. A few retired people, a few children. Even trees and grass. She felt safe there. The apartment was over a garage. It had one small bedroom, a tiny living room, bathroom and tiny kitchen. When the baby was big it could have the bedroom, but at first they would sleep together. The woman who had the apartment said Diane could move in as soon as she moved out, in two weeks. That was exactly when Diane was due.

Evelyn and Arnie had offered to pay all of the costs pertaining to the birth. They'd been to a lawyer together to make sure they were doing everything correctly. It didn't leave much for Diane to worry about; and Evelyn and Arnie seemed more comfortable now too. Knowing her as well as they did by now, they realized how unlikely it was that she would change her mind after the birth. Evelyn and Arnie were to be with her throughout labor. The doctor had agreed that Debbie and Mary could be there too and also Diane's good friend Jan, despite the hospital policy restricting the number of people a woman could have at her birthing. The prospect of labor did not frighten Diane and the physician continued to assure them that as long as everything continued to go smoothly she should be able to have an uncomplicated natural delivery. If the babies were of reasonable size, as they seemed to be, and started breathing well on their own, they would not have to go to the nursery at all.

The one part Diane had not attempted to plan for was the transfer. She'd felt for some time that she was carrying a boy and a girl and had offered Evelyn and Arnie her son if she had one. She trusted the right way to give them the baby would be apparent to all of them when the time came.

Evelyn and Arnie finally painted and decorated their spare room. Twice Diane went to their house and sat with them in the baby's room while they silently focused on this little person who would soon enter their home. Diane moved into her new home in one morning with the help of all her friends. She was too big to do much of anything herself. Though she'd become accustomed to working around the immense belly that stuck out everywhere and now prevented her from bending over, she couldn't wait to have her old body back again. After everyone else had left she set up the kitchen just the way she wanted it, put away all the baby's things in drawers and borrowed a neighbor's vacuum cleaner. As she was finishing the last rugs she felt her first contraction. It came without warning but she knew immediately what it was. That evening, meeting Evelyn and Arnie for one more co-counseling session, she told them she thought she was going into labor. At two in the morning they received the call. "This is it," Diane said. "Stay calm, but come right over!" They were with her at the apartment for an hour, counting contractions, calling the midwives, the doctor and Jan, and then they drove her to the hospital.

Labor went as smoothly as predicted. The twins lay in easy positions for being born without complication and they responded well to labor. Debbie, Mary, Jan were all at Diane's side throughout, and Evelyn and Arnie too. It was a normal first labor; but to Diane it felt very long and very difficult. Contractions often left her brimming with emotion and she would cry and then feel better afterward. When she was past the first stage and her body was ready to push she felt her first wave of fear. It expressed itself as fear of pushing. Looking back later she thought it was probably the fear of letting them enter the world, where she would then have to give one of them up.

Arnie kept leaving the room to stand in front of the window of the nursery and look at the other babies. Debbie and Mary tried to make sure Evelyn and Arnie didn't get lost in what was taking place; but the couple didn't want to take any attention away from Diane. For her it was a time of supreme closeness to her friends. An anesthesiologist was on call because there were twins and he came into the room once to explain to Diane what he had to offer her in the way of drugs. At the mention of medication Diane's first reaction was "I'll take anything!" But Mary and Debbie reminded her how well she was doing, how she'd wanted a natural birth, and how much better it would be for the babies if there were no drugs or anesthesia. It was not very long before her cervix was open and she began to feel the need to push. She no longer thought about pain relief. The entire group now moved down the hall into the delivery room. And not very long after, a little girl was born. Holding her in her arms Diane said quietly, "Thank you, God. I've got my little girl." Evelyn and Arnie knew that the second baby was to be theirs, whatever its sex. Twenty minutes later it was born and Diane turned to them and said, "You've got your little boy."

Each baby weighed six pounds. But Diane had been right in her intuition that one of them might not be as strong as the other. The little boy's placenta, the organ that provided all his nourishment as he grew inside Diane, was almost a pound and a half smaller than his sister's.

Diane has no recollection of being shown her son. She never asked to hold him. Her arms were full with the daughter she named Malia. Evelyn and Arnie had followed their son, whom they named Joss, which is Chinese for "luck," to the nursery for examination because he had swallowed some amniotic fluid with a bit of his own stool in it. They stayed with him through the night and then left with him in the morning.

Suddenly the delivery room was empty. It seemed to Diane she had only held her daughter for an instant before one of the nurses took her away to the nursery for an exam. A different nurse was preparing to move Diane to her maternity room. It all happened so quickly she did not think to refuse. But the separation from her baby was brief; Mary went over to the nursery to make sure that she was brought right back to her mother.

It was late. The midwives, the doctor and Jan finally left to go home. As soon as they were gone the nurse announced that the baby could not spend the night with Diane but would have to go to the nursery. She was now too exhausted to put up a fight. So she and Malia spent their first night apart. Diane felt lonely and isolated and hardly slept, and early the next morning, when they finally brought Malia back to her, she resolved not to let her be taken away again.

Two of the other beds in the room were occupied by women who had also just given birth. They did not seem to mind that their babies were not with them during the night and the next evening Diane alone refused to allow the nurse to take her baby away. Early the second morning, feeling fresh and getting her old energy back, Diane began to ask everyone who came to check on her when she and Malia could go home. When the physician made rounds later in the morning he signed the discharge papers. Diane gathered her few belongings, and began to dress Malia in the outfit she'd brought. She couldn't wait to leave. At last her friend Jan came to take her and Malia home. Before going out the door Diane insisted on having one look at her son. They stopped at the nursery window while she scanned the cots for a familiar face. He wasn't there. Evelyn and Arnie had taken him home the day before.

When they reached the apartment Diane didn't ask Jan in; she wanted to be alone with her daughter at last. On a piece of cardboard she wrote in big letters "Do Not Disturb" and stuck it to the outside of the door. Then she sat down on the bed next to her daughter and burst into tears. At first the tears brought the memory of being in the delivery room after the birth when everyone had gone and she felt suddenly alone and helpless. She recalled each of the small abuses she'd taken from the staff at the hospital. What had cut her most deeply was the brusqueness of the woman who had come unannounced into her room to fill out the birth certificate. When Diane couldn't grasp one of her questions the woman raised her voice in irritation. All at once Diane was crying over the real issue, the feeling of a gaping hole inside where something had been wrenched from her body. It was a few minutes before she realized that her tears were for the baby she had given up. It felt good to cry and it wasn't long before her body relaxed, cleansed and swept by new feelings, mostly relief and joy that she was home at last with the daughter she'd longed to have.

Malia became the center of Diane's life every minute of the day. Diane had often been a babysitter as a teenager; it was a kind of preparation for what she was now doing, but it was nothing like it. Though Malia was separate in body from her, she still felt they were physically connected, by an invisible cord. When Malia awoke, Diane awoke; when Malia cried, Diane could do nothing but attend to her immediately. There was little else for her to do but be with Malia, so the first days were peaceful, sleeping when Malia slept, getting up in between to eat the food friends continued to drop off, to bathe or to write in her diary. She hardly took notice of the time or of one day's ending and another's beginning.

Arnie began to make daily visits to the apartment almost as soon as Diane was home, bringing with him fresh fruit and bagels from the shop Evelyn and he owned and asking if there was anything else Diane needed. When she'd been home part of a week he hesitantly asked if Evelyn and Joss might come for a brief visit. Diane wanted to see her friend and wondered what it would feel like seeing Joss. The visit was very short, for no sooner did Diane ask to hold Joss then she began to cry, and Evelyn, not knowing what to do for Diane, took her son and left.

The intensity of what she had felt when she held Joss left Diane feeling shaken. She had fully expected to grieve for him but not to feel what she had the moment he was in her arms, an intense physical longing. She determined to wait a bit before asking to see Joss again.

A week after the birth Diane unexpectedly found herself resenting Evelyn. At first she couldn't admit it even to herself. This woman had become her dear friend, as close to her as a sister. How could she? She felt she was betraying Evelyn by these feelings yet they did not go away. When Mary came to do a home visit Diane confided to her and, having dared to voice what she'd labeled unthinkable, she realized her feelings weren't bad or abnormal. Mary reminded her that it was just a normal part of the process of separation. Knowing this, Diane was able then to talk to Evelyn and at the next co-counseling session she felt the wall she'd been building between them vanish. They talked on the phone several times after that and Diane felt her love for Evelyn return. An hour a week for the next two months, in the safety and impersonality of the protected environment of counseling, they were all able to talk about the various feelings they'd been having since the birth, and Diane was able to share the extent of the sadness she felt about Joss. Joss and Malia were at those sessions too and Diane found she was now able to say goodbye to Joss. The other goodbye, the one she'd said at the hospital, had been spoken too soon, when she was yet too raw from giving birth to him to be able to feel the impact of his leaving. This time saying goodbye left a small lightness inside her.

Evelyn and Arnie had their work to do as well and much to express about the emotions they'd felt at the birth, at getting Joss, at having him home with them, and knowing all the while what Diane must be going through yet not being able to make it any easier for her. Diane could still legally take back Joss for several more months, and during this time he was technically only "visiting" Evelyn and Arnie; but the closeness they felt with her made speaking about their fears easier.

At home Evelyn was breast-feeding their son. She had started preparing as soon as she was fairly certain she would have a baby to adopt, gently milking the colostrum still in her breasts from the last pregnancy. She hoped to be able to bring in her own milk to feed this baby but if not she would nurse anyway and use a Lactaid. Joss started at her breast from the first day and within a few days she was already producing some milk; but it didn't seem to Evelyn to be enough. She'd hoped to be able to avoid entirely giving him formula, so she went to Mary and Debbie for advice.

At first they thought they had a simple solution. While Evelyn continued to nurse Joss and bring in her own milk supply by his regular suckling, Diane could easily increase her milk by using a breast pump between feedings and setting some aside for Joss. Physically it was easy enough for her to do this and she wanted to do it, for Evelyn and for Joss. But emotionally it quickly proved too much. The connection with Joss was too close for comfort, at the very time when she needed to be able to let go of him. So Mary and Debbie, realizing they had asked too much of Diane, instead created a mothers' milk bank especially for Joss. Mary called her nursing mothers and nine of them agreed to express some milk each day and put it aside in a container in the refrigerator. Arnie became the milkman, each morning collecting a couple of ounces of fresh milk from each house and bringing it home to Evelyn, where she put it in the Lactaid pouch and supplemented her own breast milk. This way she never had to give Joss a bottle of formula. He didn't care that the milk he drank came partly from a tiny flexible tube alongside Evelyn's nipple. With the help of the milk bank Evelyn had the time to increase her own milk to the point where, after six weeks, the milk bank could be retired. Breast-feeding was a pleasurable way to deepen her bond with her son, at the same time giving him protection from infection and future allergies. She continued for a year and a half.

Malia and Joss's biological father visited Malia, but infrequently. Every couple of weeks he would offer to watch her for an hour so Diane could go off somewhere by herself; but he never talked about his feelings toward his daughter. Nor did he even inquire about his son. Diane didn't push him. She sensed he was wrestling with some internal demons and anyway she had neither the desire nor the energy to mother him. She needed support and energy from others and she turned to her friends, not him, for her needs. She also called on Evelyn and Arnie. The two women, once their post-birth lives had settled down, began to get together with the babies at least once a week. They even took an exercise class together, bringing the babies with them. Diane felt comfortable calling Evelyn for advice once in a while, and Evelyn did the same. They were better friends than ever.

Privately Diane sometimes found herself envying Evelyn her life. For one thing she and Arnie never seemed to lack for money and could do whatever they wanted. But more than that, they had each other. It was impossible not to contrast her life with theirs. Despite her large circle of friends, Diane was alone in parenting and doing almost everything by herself. Where she had during the pregnancy realized that Evelyn might feel some envy toward her for being able to bear children, Diane had not anticipated feeling as she now did toward Evelyn. Evelyn and Arnie had a decade's experiences over her and their life had the smell of stability where hers, no matter how hard she tried, did not. She was happy with how they cared for Joss. The only thing she would have done differently herself was not to circumcize him. As for her feelings of resentment, she would just have to accept them when they came and live with them.

The months passed. To the world outside the sight of the two women, one red-haired and full-figured, the other dark-haired and slender, sitting together on a park bench watching their babies crawling on the grass must have looked ordinary enough. But under the placid external surface these two women were doing something unique.

I learned about Diane in a letter from one of her midwives, who is a friend of mine, and I went to meet her when Joss and Malia were seven months old. Diane showed me the photo album she'd been keeping since

214

her pregnancy began. There was a snapshot of her standing in a garden, long red hair in thick braids, looking every bit as if she were about to deliver. That was taken when she was only six months pregnant, just after they discovered she was carrying twins. There were many other pictures, mostly of Diane amidst friends. And a few of the labor and birth. One showed Evelyn at the side of the bed holding Diane's hand in both of her own. Someone had taken pictures of Diane and Malia together during their first days at home; and there were several of Diane, Malia, Evelyn, Arnie and Joss all together. In another Malia was in the arms of a young man who was smiling out at the camera. Her father, Diane said. There was a visit from Grandma. But the one that made a lasting impression on me was the picture taken on a bright sunny day in the park, Evelyn and Diane sitting next to each other on a bench with the babies on their laps. Evelyn was holding Malia and Diane was holding Joss.

My visit to Diane coincided with a transition in her life. She was feeling a growing need to be apart from Evelyn, Arnie and Joss, not even to hear from them by phone. And for the first time in months she was a little afraid of her feelings. "I'm worried I might not be able to let go of Joss. A couple of times recently after seeing Joss, when I hadn't seen him for a week, I've found myself thinking it was him I should have kept. I know that's because he is now the novelty. For the most part I haven't felt Joss is my son in a long time. But recently I have, and I've been wanting him." Diane wasn't considering changing her decision when she said that; she had already signed the final papers. It was the emotional not the legal bond that was giving her pain. And it wasn't the feelings that puzzled her but the fact that they had developed so strongly so long after she had actually given him up.

Whereas Joss used to be content when Diane held him, he was now going through a period of wanting only his mother's or father's arms. This surprised Diane and it hurt. "He always used to calm down if I held him. But the last time we were together nothing I could do helped. I ended up feeling angry at him." And again, afterward, had come feelings of resentment toward Joss's mother. Evelyn and Arnie understood when she explained that she wanted a rest and some privacy. It was time to look back over the past year of her life and review the

Diane and her two-year-old daughter, Malia, outside their apartment on campus

choices she'd made. And, alone with her thoughts and feelings, Diane knew that she had done the very best she could.

Diane was grateful for every bit of emotional support she received; she gave her share too. When an acquaintance found herself alone just before she was due to give birth, Diane became her special support. She was beside her throughout the birth and afterward went to the woman's home, with Malia in tow, and cooked and cleaned house and did for the new mother what others had done for her.

When Malia was a year old, Diane began to go out with several of the men she knew, though dating seemed too childish a term after all she had been through. As long as she carried some hope that Malia and Joss's father would desire a relationship with her again, there had been no real room for any other man in her life, but it was by now apparent that her hope conflicted with reality. She began to find his irregular presence in their lives irritating. His infrequent statements about how he'd like to babysit for Malia more often or how he'd per-haps like to have her for a year, while Diane went back to school, began to grate on Diane's nerves. She began making herself less available for his visits. She decided it was time to move in with other people again and found a small house and two friends to share it. Then she applied to college, was accepted, and asked for and got a government loan so she could be a full-time student and get off welfare.

In her first semester back at school Diane earned A's. Malia played at a nearby infant center on campus four hours a day while Diane went to classes. Her play group was small and the teachers provided con-sistency, so Diane didn't feel Malia was at a disadvantage not being with her those hours. They gave up breast-feeding and Malia took easily to being around others. Diane gave her full attention to Malia when she was with her, leaving homework for after Malia went to bed. Malia has always reacted to any stress her mother feels, so at the end of each semester Diane has to ask for extra help from friends to get them both through exam time.

The second semester of school Diane and Malia moved into inex-pensive student housing on campus. I visited them there when Malia had just turned two years old. There was still pain in Diane's eyes at the mention of Joss and his family. She needed to move a little further with her own life before she could take the continual reminder of all the things a stable happily married older couple can give a child that she still cannot give Malia. That year Joss did not get to Malia's birthday party. Arnie had a bicycle accident and couldn't bring him; for Diane it was just as well.

There was much excitement in Joss's house when I went to visit. Not only was Arnie still recovering from his fall, which left him with a broken collarbone, and Joss, who had been on the back of the bike, miraculously unharmed; but there was another surprise. Joss had a new baby brother named Bowie. And Bowie's arrival was just as amazing as Joss's had been.

Evelyn's best friend, Nancy, was the number-one milk mom for Joss. A friend of Nancy's from out of town came to visit and happened to mention that the sixteen-year-old daughter of a mutual friend was pregnant and looking for parents to adopt the baby. She had a steady boyfriend her age but neither of them could imagine being high school parents; however, by the time the young woman had discovered she was pregnant she was already feeling the baby move. She'd gone for a pregnancy test when she'd missed two periods but the test had come back negative. That was how she happened to be five months along before she knew for sure. Evelyn's heart skipped at the news and she asked Nancy to pass along the word that she and Arnie would be very happy to meet the young woman if she was interested. The young woman's mother and father, though divorced and living in separate states, each said they would support whatever decision she made.

And so it happened that Evelyn and Arnie received visits not just from the young woman, whose name was Lisa, but from her boyfriend and both her parents as well. Lisa had visited the county adoption agency before she heard about direct adoption but was not interested by what they had to offer. Evelyn and Arnie felt like members of the family getting the once-over but it was worth it, and after Lisa's father came to see them he warmly thanked them for all they were doing for his daughter. After they had everyone's blessings and Lisa had told Evelyn she wanted them for her baby's parents, there was the process of birth to go through all over again. Once again it was a natural birth, with Evelyn and Arnie present, along with Lisa's boyfriend and Lisa's mother. Diane had given encouragement to the young woman over the phone before the birth. And afterward Lisa told Evelyn she felt certain she had done the right thing giving them her son. She had not felt he belonged to her, and when she visited Evelyn and him in the nursery the next day she said she knew for sure. As I was talking to Evelyn, Arnie received a phone call from Lisa. It was only seven days after the birth. She and her mother were coming for a visit the next day and Arnie was going to make breakfast for everyone.

Evelyn is sensitive to the feelings of Bowie's mother, just as she has always been sensitive to Diane's feelings and needs. She smiled broadly when I mentioned Diane and volunteered that she continues to think of Diane and Malia daily. "I have a bond with Diane that is different from anyone else I know. It's beyond sister. It's beyond . . ." She could find no word that fit. Neither she nor Arnie feels Diane's or Lisa's existence is an intrusion in their lives. As Arnie says, "Getting a family the way we have has helped us become as good parents as we could be. I think God always has a hand on a family; but he's had both hands on ours." Bowie's birth announcement reads: "Bowie Jacob happily announces the adoption of his new family—Evelyn, Arnie and Joss, October 2, 11:05 a.m."

In the future Joss and Bowie will know no void about their roots; it is likely that Lisa and Diane will be a continued presence in their lives. They will probably also be familiar with their biological fathers. Diane often speaks about Joss to her daughter, just as Evelyn and Arnie do about Malia. The children have pictures of each other on their bedroom walls, and they each have a scrapbook of photographs about their birth. They also have the times they've shared. Diane and Evelyn and Arnie have promised each other that, if only for the sake of the twins, they will continue to spend time together and will always stay in contact. Today the visits are less frequent. Their lives have naturally taken them in different directions. When they do get together Diane no longer feels the same physical connection to Joss. That cord was finally broken, even though the grief is not yet finished. And when Evelyn and Diane do get together for part of a day it is no different from the way it was in the beginning. They still talk about their lives and the children, sometimes share a few tears over something that has happened to one of them.

They are friends. Diane says her relationship with Evelyn is the closest connection she's had with any female except her daughter. She wishes she could have accepted the reality of Joss's not being with her more quickly than she did but she knows some things cannot be rushed. Any sense of being different that she once felt for the path she chose has nearly disappeared as she has been absorbed back into the mainstream of her life.

EPILOGUE

There will always be adoptions because there will always be some children whose parents cannot provide for them. Raising a child is not easy, and love and affection are never all that it takes. Parenting takes time, focused attention, continued interest, money and work, long hours and hard work. Many of us are not ready or able to give this, at least not for the time being. Pregnancy *can* be a mistake. If children are not to be made to suffer at our hands, then adoption *must* always be one option, just as contraception and abortion *must* always be options.

Pat, Katherine and Diane in these stories are women who simply would not settle for the kinds of adoption their society, their church, their family and friends could offer them. They had to search for a different, a better way. They had no models to guide them and so their imagination was limited by what they knew. Had each of them known even one other woman in similar circumstances, she might have gone further toward creating an ideal adoption. Yet they had a vision. Women like these are pioneers. They open our eyes to what yet might be.

There can be no perfect adoption because adoption involves more than one person, because people's needs and desires and styles are different. The emotions involved are too complex for anyone to speak of perfection. But adoption can literally save lives, give people a second chance and bring much joy into the world. We certainly ought to be able to have kinds of adoptions that everyone can live with without remorse. We must begin by recognizing that no other person, no institution, no system can ever satisfy our highest yearnings. What a social system and the people in it can do is provide a structure that offers support and guidance in the tricky and often painful business of finding our own way through seemingly impossible situations in life. And we can ask that a system of adoption enable the individuals involved to participate as fully as they possibly can in the design of their adoption, and that it foster creativity and flexibility.

There will always be those parents who will not be able to provide what an infant or child needs but will not choose adoption. But surely the better the system of adoption we have, the more those who need it will be encouraged to consider it. The key seems to lie in giving people the information and support they need to face their limits honestly, and in offering kinds of adoptions that allow dignity.

The children will always be the most vulnerable participants in adoption because they are dependent on adults for their very survival. Any model adoption system must give the children, too, support and encouragement, and place in their hands whatever information will help them shape their own futures. Little has been written about the children of adoption, except of their desire and need to search for their roots. Certainly they often have special needs. Many parents have felt pushed to their limits by the anxiousness, emotionality, hyperactivity of children they've adopted. That adopted children often show signs of inner turmoil is natural, given the special stresses they have lived with from the time within the womb until they were finally given a permanent home with new parents. It requires *more* to be a parent of a child who has begun life in such stress.

Adoptive parents often come with special needs, too. Many come to adoption feeling that they have "failed" because they were unable to have children. They feel vulnerable and even desperate, and this is not the best way to enter parenthood. Yet the time of searching and waiting to find a child can be a positive time for adoptive parents, a time, like the nine months of pregnancy, to slow down and get ready for the changes a child brings into our lives. But when that time of waiting and hoping stretches into years, it can be extremely difficult; and if a child at last comes, then that child may have to bear the weight of its new parents' anxiousness.

The biological fathers of children given for adoption also have needs. Many men take years to discover just how significant an unknown child they brought into the world might be to them. But it is primarily the biological mothers that we have focused on in these stories. Theirs is a most difficult path, for they must anticipate and honestly assess their own limits of self and circumstance, and do this in the midst of the heightened emotions and sensitivity of pregnancy. And they must choose to raise or relinquish their child before knowing for certain whether they might have been good enough parents. If we want to create kinds of adoption that will encourage women to consider adoption, then we must look at how our attitude toward these women helps or hinders them. For it is *they* to whom we have done perhaps the greatest disservice.

The standards of adoption we now take for granted arose from within a society different from today's. Adoption in a world where unmarried women who became pregnant were considered immoral and dangerous to society, and where the children of such unions were branded illegitimate, *had* to reflect those uncompassionate attitudes. It is no wonder that early maternity hospitals and homes for unwed mothers went to great lengths to keep the identities of the women hidden or that names were changed on birth certificates and files kept under lock and key. Women and children deserved to be protected from stigma. They had no economic or political power and it was nearly impossible for children born out of wedlock or their mothers to move freely in the world if their background was made known. The stigma still exists but is no longer so great; yet the secrecy of this tradition continues to be the rule.

Adoption breeds insecurity. A normally thoughtful and compassionate mother of an adopted daughter put it quite honestly when, hearing about Katherine's adoption and her difficulties with the adoptive parents, she said, "What does she expect! Why should she have any rights to this child? After all, she gave him up, didn't she? Well then, she has forfeited all her rights!" Unwittingly pointing out her own insecurity as a parent of an adopted child, she continued: "How can you be so insensitive to adoptive parents, asking us to open our lives and homes and expose our children to the very people who gave them up in the first place?" This same mother then spoke about the great disappointment she and her husband felt when they found they could not have another child and how adoption was a godsend for them, how grateful she was to the woman who had enabled them to become parents. She did not see any contradiction in her attitude nor understand the source of it.

We honor the mother as long as she remains in the closet, as long as she can be a cardboard figure with no needs of her own. But let her become a real person with real needs, let her want to have any control over the adoption or any contact with the child she has relinquished, then she turns into the wicked witch of our dark imaginings. As individuals and as a society we have yet to acknowledge our own darkest fears, especially about women. We project our fears onto others.

Are we not then punishing the woman for doing what she feels is best for her child? And for what crime? For having become pregnant at the wrong time? Sex for a woman, because it can *always* result in pregnancy (unless she is infertile), becomes *her* crime, and unwanted pregnancy woman's punishment. Parenting in such circumstances can become either a twenty-year sentence or a twenty-year act of repentance to atone for the guilt of giving a child up. *Either* way her society can make a woman suffer. If women are not to be made to feel guilty and wrong for considering giving up a child for adoption, then they *must* be able to design adoptions that meet *their* needs. Part of this means being free to participate in or at least be kept informed of and able to observe that child's growth and future. Is this really so revolutionary?

We do not attempt to punish the parent who for some reason chooses to leave the family home in divorce, preventing him or her from ever again participating in the children's lives. At the very least there are visiting privileges, and today, joint custody. Yet we are still doing this to the women, and men, who give up a child for adoption. We may believe our motives are good, that we don't want to complicate a child's life and cause it additional confusion and pain. But there is no proof that it would be an added burden to a child to know the parents who have given it up for adoption. The children of divorce and remarriage learn to live with the fact of having extra adults in their lives and quickly make their own distinctions between different mommies and daddies. So that is not the real issue. Then what is?

We have wanted to believe that only certain kinds of women would give a child up for adoption. But Pat, Katherine, Diane and Maria do not fit our stereotypes. In fact, many social work professionals agree that it takes maturity for a woman of any age to consider adoption, because it is so much easier to grab on to a baby as a lifesaver. To consider adoption for her child, a woman of any age must be able to separate the baby's needs from her own needs, especially her need for love.

The first step toward a more humane kind of adoption is to make *every* woman's pregnancy as positive a time as possible, both for the woman *and* for the life she carries. Next is to give every woman full information about all her options and make all choices available to her. After that we can create a labor and birth that are as gentle and unforced as possible and allow as much time as the woman needs to be with her baby and settle on her decision before the transfer is begun. Then we can create an exchange that is more than just a transfer, that offers privacy, support and time. When the transition is gentle, done with compassion for each of the individuals involved and with conscious attention paid to all the details, the child can move directly to the welcoming arms of its new family from an affectionate and trusting relationship with its first mother and the home within her body. Parting, letting go and grieving can all be made easier with extra support from people who will be around if needed in the months to come. Then and only then will adoption be something other than a cataclysmic rupture in our most primal relationship, shaking our earliest sense of security, signaling abandonment, and leaving deep wounds.

In a sense the new parents can and perhaps should emotionally adopt the mother, *and* the father if he is present, along with the child, and do so as *early* in pregnancy as possible. Why? Because a birth mother needs to feel safe before she can move fully into a life without the child. Because we must always begin the subject of adoption with the understanding that giving to the woman who carries the child within her is the surest way to give to the child. Never forget—to nurture a child we must nurture its mother. They are a symbiotic pair.

It is not difficult to imagine many instances where the presence of the birth parent or parents could be of help in the child's later life. With divorce and death only two examples of changes that often occur in an adopted child's second home, it is all too common for a child to find itself in difficult circumstances a second time. And the woman or man who was once not ready or able to be a mother or father can over months or years become a fine second parent to help a remaining adoptive parent care for a child they *both* love. Even a year's time can make a great difference in a person's maturity.

Not long ago a woman who had given a baby up for adoption when she was fifteen discovered by accident that this very daughter is now living in the same town only two blocks from her! Today that woman is thirty years old and the child she gave up is the same age she was when she became a mother. She has learned from mutual acquaintances that her daughter, who knows *nothing* of her existence, much less her whereabouts, is being raised by her adoptive mother alone and that this woman must work full-time just to provide food and shelter. They are having a difficult time of it. "Should I," the birth mother wonders, "let this woman know that I am here? I can help now and I'd like to help; she is *my* daughter too." She has seen her daughter pass by on the street and so far has refrained from reaching out her hand. But she is there—silent, knowing, caring. Another time, another place, and this woman would not have to doubt her instinct of what she ought to do.

In the adoptions we have just seen we are witnessing only the beginning, the first halting steps of a few pioneers toward a new and yet unformed vision of the future. Let us follow, knowing that the time is ripe for such change, and see where these steps might take us.

ADOPTION RESOURCE
ORGANIZATIONS

I am a writer. I am not skilled in answering individual questions about specific personal issues in adoption. Therefore, I have put together a resource list of those who are able to help or to put you in touch with others who can.

There is no central organization "in charge" of alternatives to traditional adoption practices. There is, however, a growing international network of people helping each other.

If you contact any of these groups, please keep in mind that they are run mostly by volunteers and usually staffed by female labor. Some are membership organizations with newsletters and a modest member's fee. All of them deserve a financial donation whenever you ask any service of them; please include a self-addressed, stamped envelope.

The following list, although incomplete, covers most areas of adoption and all participants in the adoption triangle: adoptees, adoptive parents and birth parents.

ADOPTEES BIRTHRIGHTS
COMMITTEE
P.O. Box 3932
Lafayette, LA 70502

CUB (Concerned United Birthparents)
595 Central Avenue
Dover, NH 03820
Primarily support/advocacy for birth mothers

ALMA—National Office
P.O. Box 154
Washington Bridge Station
New York, NY 10033
Primarily search, research, and advocacy of liberalizing laws

INTERNATIONAL SOUNDEX
REUNION REGISTRY
P.O. Box 2312
Carson City, NV 89701
A one-woman search group, run by Emma May Vilardi

MIDWEST ADOPTION TRIAD

P.O. Box 37262
Omaha, NE 68137
Primarily a search organization

ORPHAN VOYAGE

Cedaredge, CO 81413
A one-woman support and referral service primarily for adoptees, run by 30-year-old veteran Jean Paton

PACER (Post-Adoption Center for Education and Research)

860 Bryant Street
Palo Alto, CA 94301
Specializing in support and community education for all parties involved

RESOLVE—National Office

P.O. Box 474
Belmont, MA 02178
Primarily support and counseling for adopting parents

TRIADOPTION LIBRARY

P.O. Box 5218
Huntington Beach, CA 92646
Clearinghouse and reference library on all aspects of adoption, including international referral service

Canada

PARENTS FINDERS

1408 West 45th Avenue
Vancouver, British Columbia
Canada V6M 2H1
Primarily to help adoptees search for birth parents

Australia/New Zealand

JIGSAW INTERNATIONAL

39 Manifold Road
Blackett
Sydney, Australia
Primarily to help adoptees search for birth parents

ACKNOWLEDGMENTS

I would like to thank Penny Bauer, Judy Bowman, Janaia Donaldson, Dick Fisch, Bob Gordon, Patrice Harrison-Inglis, Sally Lillis, Emilio Mercado, Cathy Sever, and Eleanor Davis for their encouragement and assistance.

And I would like to give special thanks to my dear friend Sue Goodman, my teacher Ayse Whitney, my mate, Don, my daughter, Molly, and my editors Elizabeth Catenaccio, Caroline Little, and Charles Elliott, who have each contributed their support, guidance, perceptions and skills. Without them this book would certainly never have been finished. I am most grateful.

A NOTE ABOUT THE AUTHOR

Suzanne Arms is a photojournalist, film-maker and author whose primary interests lie in the field of childbirth, mothering and the family. She has lectured widely on these subjects, done community organizing and served as a consultant to numerous groups. Her previous books include a photographic essay on pregnancy, titled *A Season to Be Born,* and *Immaculate Deception: A New Look at Women and Childbirth.* Suzanne Arms lives with her daughter Molly and her husband John Wimberley in Palo Alto, California.

A NOTE ON THE TYPE

The text of this book was set on the Linotype in Intertype
Garamond No. 3, a modern rendering of the type first cut by
Claude Garamond (1510–1561).
Garamond was a pupil of Geoffroy Troy and is believed to
have based his letters on the Venetian models, although he
introduced a number of important differences, and it is to
him we owe the letter which we know as old style. He gave
to his letters a certain elegance and a feeling of movement
that won for their creator an immediate reputation and the
patronage of Francis I of France.

Composed by Maryland Linotype Composition Company,
Baltimore, Maryland
Printed and bound by The Haddon Craftsmen, Inc.,
Scranton, Pennsylvania

Designed by Sara Reynolds